CONSULTING

CONSULTING

A Practitioner's Perspective

MOHAN KANCHARLA

Notion Press

Old No. 38, New No. 6
McNichols Road, Chetpet
Chennai - 600 031

First Published by Notion Press 2016
Copyright © Mohan Kancharla 2016
All Rights Reserved.

ISBN

Hardcase: 978-1-946280-38-1
Paperback: 978-1-946280-39-8

This book has been published with all efforts taken to make the material error-free after the consent of the author. However, the author and the publisher do not assume and hereby disclaim any liability to any party for any loss, damage, or disruption caused by errors or omissions, whether such errors or omissions result from negligence, accident, or any other cause.

No part of this book may be used, reproduced in any manner whatsoever without written permission from the author, except in the case of brief quotations embodied in critical articles and reviews.

Dedicated to

To all the People who have shaped my Learning | My Parents & Relatives, Teachers & Professors, Managers & Mentors, Clients & Colleagues, Wife & Daughters.

Contents

Prologue   *ix*

Part One | Consulting Basics

1. Consulting Basics   3

Part Two | Consulting Spectrum

2. IT Strategy Consulting   33
3. IT Architecture Consulting   51
4. IT Portfolio Management   75
5. IT Process Consulting   93
6. IT Governance Consulting   117
7. IT Infrastructure Consulting   137
8. IT Outsourcing Consulting   155
9. IT Transformation Consulting   173

Part Three | Consulting Competencies

10. Consulting Competencies   191

Epilogue   *215*
Bibliography   *217*
Index   *219*

Prologue

Consulting' is the only profession that teaches you to **Think how to Think** and **Learn how to Learn** - profound words of a visionary. In many ways, the first time I heard these words of wisdom was a turning point in my professional career. After spending a decade on the delivery end of technology in various capacities across the systems life cycle, I moved to the sales end for about five years. I was beginning to feel that I had done it all when the world of consulting opened up as an option, where I could put my learning and experience to better use and move up the professional value chain - a journey I started a decade ago.

With the decision made, it was time to act and deliver; only then, did I understand the real challenges of consulting. I then focused my attention on researching published material and discovered that very few books were available on the subject. Among the few that were, most looked at consulting from a freelance perspective: how to set up a business, how to create a legal entity, how to invoice, etc., with little information on how to create consulting offerings, deliver consulting engagements, build consulting competencies and skills.

Exceptions are books like *Managing the Professional Service Firm* by David Maister, *The McKinsey Way* by Ethan Rasiel and *The Seven Cs of Consulting* by Mick Cope, which provide good insights on consulting from industry and company perspectives.

This book attempts to address a third perspective, that of the individual or the practitioner. While the sections on the basics of consulting and consulting competencies are applicable to the consulting space in general, the consulting spectrum covers only Information Technology (IT) Consulting.

Chapter 1	Consulting Basics introduces the reader to the basics of Consulting in terms of defining Consulting, Consulting Space, Consulting Cycle, Consulting Frameworks and Consulting Spectrum.
Chapter 2	IT Strategy Consulting primarily addresses Business IT Alignment with some elements of Organization Design, Enterprise Architecture and IT Infrastructure, all of which are key components of an IT Strategy Roadmap.
Chapter 3	IT Architecture Consulting explains the Enterprise Architecture dimensions, that is, Business, Application, Infrastructure and Data Architecture and the linkages from one to another.

Chapter 4	IT Portfolio Management highlights the importance of Profiling Applications to baseline functional richness, overcoming technical obsolescence, if any, to future-proof the application portfolio.
Chapter 5	IT Process Consulting covers Process management and Service management and related Maturity frameworks applied for continuous improvement.
Chapter 6	IT Governance Consulting focuses on Organization design, Decision-making styles, Definition of Roles and responsibilities.
Chapter 7	IT Infrastructure Consulting includes Systems management, Server management, Storage management, Network management, Data Centre management and Business Continuity Planning.
Chapter 8	IT Outsourcing Consulting outlines Sourcing strategies taking into account both Application functionalities and Resource requirements, Transition planning, Delivery models and Vendor management.
Chapter 9	IT Transformation Consulting is the synthesis of all the above, which individually or collectively drive Transformation, complimented by Change Management and Program Management.
Chapter 10	Consulting Competencies offers insights into the skills required for Sales, Proposals, Teams, Delivery, Presentations, Report, Measures, Career and Maturity.

Lastly, let me express my sincere gratitude to my parents, who have bestowed upon me the greatest asset - education, to all my teachers who shaped my learning, to all my managers who taught me to think on my feet, to all my mentors who encouraged me to think out of the box, to all my colleagues who challenged every hypothesis, to all my clients who constantly raised the bar of perfection, to my wife who is my greatest critic, to my daughters who are my inspiration and above all, to the Lord Almighty.

... IT IS NOT MY MERIT, BUT HIS GRACE.

PART ONE

CONSULTING BASICS

CHAPTER 1

CONSULTING BASICS

Consulting is an 'Art' and not a 'Science' because the uniqueness of every context necessitates utmost care and commitment, because the problem statement is not stated but needs to be built from a hypothesis, because the solution is not replicable but has to be custom-built from fact-based analysis, because the expectations are ambiguous, yet the outcomes must deliver value.

As an art, consulting is, therefore, a relational process, an expression of expertise and analytics, an act of independent and unbiased judgment. It is continuous and a change agent, morphing in motion and mandating a strong foundation of first principles to master the craft.

In addition to defining consulting, this chapter provides insights into Consulting Space - the industry in general and the players, Consulting Cycle - phases for executing consulting engagements, Consulting Frameworks - tools and techniques of consulting and Consulting Spectrum - consulting types in information technology.

CONSULTING DEFINED

Consulting refers to advisory services aimed at enabling change and creating value for customers in the context of their business environment. The word 'Consultant', stemming from the Latin *Consultus* meaning 'Legal expert', is a professional who provides advice in a particular domain or area of expertise. Fortunately, there is only one meaning, although definitions abound. Two viewpoints are elaborated in the following paragraphs.

MANAGEMENT CONSULTANCY - ASSOCIATIONS' DEFINITIONS

Management Consulting, as defined by the Institute of Management Consultants, USA: "Management consulting is the providing to management of objective advice and assistance relating to the strategy, structure, management, and operations of an organization in pursuit of its long-term purposes and objectives. Such assistance may include the identification of options with recommendations; the provision of an additional resource and/or the implementation of solutions." (Source: www.imcusa.org)

Management Consulting, as defined by Management Consultancies Association, UK: "Management consulting is the practice of creating value for organizations, through improved performance, achieved by providing objective advice and implementing business solutions. In other words, management consultants help take organizations further than they would go on their own." (Source: www.mca.org.uk)

MANAGEMENT CONSULTANCY - AUTHORS' VIEWPOINTS

In *High Performance Consulting Skills*[1], Mark Thomas is of the view that Consultants are employed when an organization's strategy, structure, processes or systems fail to deliver the necessary levels of performance. Their contribution might involve a total solution or the provision of some form of specialist technical support for an agreed period of time.

In *Business Consulting*[2], Gilbert Toppin and Fiona Czerniawska opine that the test of a good consultant is not whether he or she has generated a unique insight, but whether that insight can be applied to produce positive results. Consultants cannot just be smart; they have to be capable of delivering a business outcome.

In *The Seven Cs of Consulting*[3], Mike Cope articulates that the consultants who survive and prosper are those with a predator instinct. They constantly search and ride the waves of new business theories. The key to professional success is not just technical mastery of one's discipline (which is, of course, essential), but also the ability to earn clients' trust and confidence.

Like a three-legged stool, the consultancy process must always be in balance and the needs of the client, consultant and consumer (end user) must be understood and maintained. Invariably, a consultant's work also involves the management of change. Successful consultants empower customers.

CONSULTING SPACE

The core competency of the consulting industry is advisory services, which is agnostic to the domain, geography, size and shape of organizations. In such an open marketplace, the way firms define their boundaries is very fluid; an overlap of offerings is inevitable.

---

1 Thomas, M. (2004). *High performance consulting skills*. Thorogood.
2 Toppin, G. and Czerniawska, F. (2007) Business consulting. *The Economist*.
3 Cope, M. (2000). The seven 'C's of consulting. FT Prentice Hall.

CONSULTING SEGMENTS

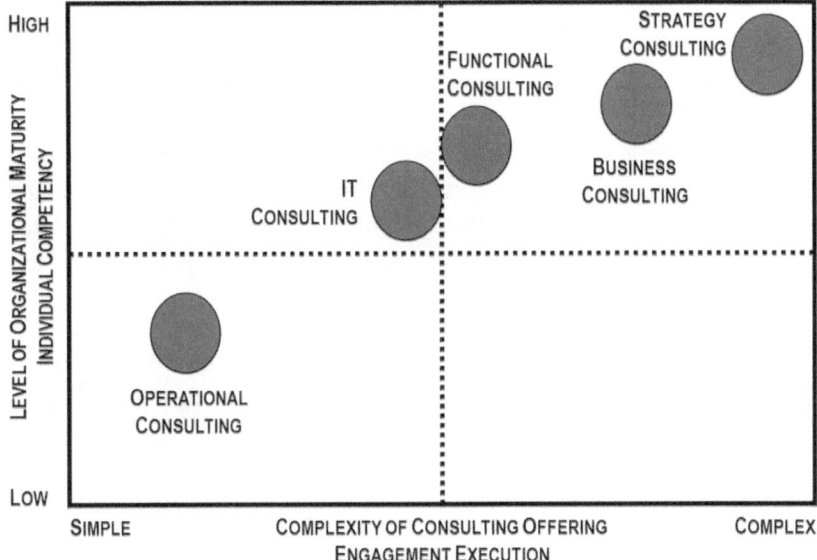

The graphic above uses the classic 2x2 matrix to represent various consulting segments, purely for the purpose of understanding. The axis considers the perspectives of both the practice and the practitioner, that is, the complexity of the consulting offering or engagement execution versus the level of organizational maturity or individual competency. The outliers are simple to complex and low to high, respectively.

1. **STRATEGY CONSULTING**

   Strategy consulting firms focus on direction setting and operate only at the Chief Executive Officer (CEO) or Board level, where advisory is by invitation. Firms and consultants in this space demonstrate high levels of maturity, positioning highly customized propositions with a high degree of complexity in execution.

   Typical engagements would be market-entry strategies, competitive positioning of products, mergers and acquisitions, etc. Turnaround time is limited but expectations are high, necessitating the involvement of experienced partners. The outcomes, a set of strategic directions requiring board approval, should, upon implementation, enhance value to the business and the shareholder.

2. **BUSINESS CONSULTING**

   Business consulting firms focus on business outcomes aligned with the defined corporate strategy. The offerings of such firms are strategy-focused and their consultants are capable of solving complex business problems. Customers are typically CEOs.

   Typical engagements are market growth strategies, studies to enhance customer service or improve time-to-market, etc. Timeframes are short to medium and require Subject Matter Experts (SMEs). The end deliverable is a business-strategy document that defines a set of priority initiatives required to achieve the desired business outcome, along with a business case.

3. **FUNCTIONAL CONSULTING**

   Functional consulting firms focus either on a particular function in organizations or an industry in general. Hence, they are also called domain-consulting firms. They operate in a niche space, so consultants have to be very strong in their industry domain. Buyers are respective C-Level Executives (CxOs).

   The best examples of functional consulting engagements are performance and pay policy definition, financial re-engineering in banks, regulatory compliance in insurance companies, etc. Timeframes are short to medium and would require functional experts. The end deliverable is an assessment report that establishes the current state and the initiatives required to reach the target state or course corrections required to achieve compliance.

4. **IT CONSULTING**

   The focus of IT consulting firms is on the technology of business and the business of technology. IT consulting firms operate in the region where IT intersects business. IT consultants are technology savvy and business oriented. Customers of their offerings are mostly Chief Information Officers (CIOs).

   IT Consulting engagements include strategy, governance, portfolio management, architecture and transformation consulting in the technology domain. Timeframes are medium to long and would require technology experts and SMEs. The end deliverable is a consulting report that outlines alignment with business strategy and/or a roadmap of technology initiatives that can deliver business value.

5. **OPERATIONAL CONSULTING**

   Operational consulting firms focus on operational efficiency in business operations. Their offerings are related to monitoring, measuring and managing operations. Consultants are seasoned managers, experienced in operations.

Consulting engagements in the purview of operational consulting are business process outsourcing, application/infrastructure outsourcing analysis, process optimization, program management, change management, etc. Timeframes are long and require hands-on managers with relevant experience. The end deliverables are dashboards demonstrating value that is realizable and sustainable.

CONSULTING FIRMS

A plethora of firms operate in each consulting segment. A dozen, selected from across the consulting space merely for representational purposes, are profiled here with information that is in the public domain.

```
STRATEGY                                                          STRATEGY
                                                                  CONSULTING
                    MCKINSEY
                            BOSTON CONSULTING GROUP
                    ..................................................

                             DELLOITTE          KPMG
                    PRICEWATERHOUSECOOPERS
                                                                  BUSINESS
                                         ERNST & YOUNG            CONSULTING
                                    IBM
                                              ACCENTURE
                    ........CAPGEMINI...............................
                    TATA CONSULTANCY SERVICES
                            COGNIZANT TECHNOLOGY SOLUTIONS        TECHNOLOGY
                                                                  CONSULTING
TECHNOLOGY                          INFOSYS
```

1. **ACCENTURE**

    Accenture is a one-of-its-kind global company providing management consulting, technology services and outsourcing company. It pioneered system integration and business integration and established itself as a leader in technology-enabled business services.

    The breadth and depth of its consulting capabilities differentiates Accenture from most other companies. Accenture is a leading global professional services company, providing a broad range of services and solutions in strategy, consulting, digital, technology and operations. (Source: www.accenture.com)

2. **BOSTON CONSULTING GROUP**

    Founded in 1963, the Boston Consulting Group (BCG) is a global business strategy solution provider with a leadership position since its inception. BCG's innovative growth-share matrix has been adopted globally by businesses.

BCG serves a variety of industries including retail, consumer products, telecommunications, transport, travel and tourism, process industries, insurance, media and entertainment, automotive, medical devices and technology, public sector, private equity, technology and software, healthcare payers and providers, engineered products and project business, energy and environment and bio-pharmaceuticals. BCG capabilities include strategy, operations, digital, change management, corporate development, mergers and acquisitions and technology services (Source: www.bcg.com)

3. **CAPGEMINI**

   Capgemini Group has been a leading global provider of technology, consulting and outsourcing services since 1967. It has a strong footprint in digital transformation.

   Capgemini's consulting services include digital transformation, strategy and transformation, supply-chain management, finance transformation, people and performance, marketing and sales and service. It operates across a dozen industries including aerospace and defense, automotive, banking, consumer products and retail, distribution and transportation, financial services, high tech, insurance, life sciences, manufacturing, oil and gas, public sector, telecom, media and entertainment and utilities. (Source: www.capgemini.com)

4. **COGNIZANT TECHNOLOGY SOLUTIONS**

   Cognizant Business Consulting is the business consulting arm of technology giant Cognizant Technology Solutions (CTS), an American multinational information technology, consulting and business process outsourcing company. Cognizant Business Consulting is positioned strongly in the technology-enabled business transformations space.

   Cognizant Business Consulting offers core consulting services including data and analytics, business-process services, organizational change management, customer-relationship management, supply chain, business IT strategy, infrastructure, merger and acquisitions and program management. It offers services in over 13 industries, including banking and financial services, communications, consumer goods, education, energy and utilities, healthcare, information services, insurance, life sciences, manufacturing, media and entertainment, retail, technology, transportation and logistics and travel and hospitality. (Source: www.cognizant.com)

5. **DELOITTE CONSULTING**

   Deloitte Consulting LLP is the consulting arm of Deloitte Touche Tohmatsu Limited, referred to as Deloitte, one of the 'Big Four' professional services firms.

Deloitte Consulting is organized into three service areas: human capital, strategy and operations and technology. The range of consulting services offered by Deloitte includes business process solutions, enterprise applications, human capital advisory services, strategy and operations and technology integration. Deloitte's consulting services span six major industries: consumer business, energy and resources, financial services, life sciences and healthcare, manufacturing and technology/media/telecommunications. (Source: www.deloitte.com)

6. **ERNST & YOUNG**

   Ernst & Young Consulting is the consulting arm of tax and accounting major Ernst & Young (E&Y) and is one of the 'Big Four' professional services firms.

   E&Y Consulting operates in over 12 major industries including automotive consumer products, financial services, government and public sector, life sciences, media and entertainment, mining and metals, oil and gas, power and utilities, private equity, real estate, technology and telecommunications. The firm advises on four core areas: performance improvement, risk, IT and financial services. (Source: www.ey.com)

7. **IBM**

   IBM's consulting group is part of its Global Business Services (GBS). Despite its century-old technology legacy, IBM has innovated its business model and moved away from the country-based business model to a global business services model. IBM has a strong footprint in providing end-to-end business covering all aspects, from business consulting to delivering business services leveraging its global workforce, technology leadership and in-depth domain knowledge.

   IBM GBS offerings include a strong portfolio of services in digital, analytics, cloud, mobility and innovation space. IBM offers its services in over 18 industries, including aerospace and defense, automotive, banking, chemicals and petroleum, consumer products, education, electronics, energy and utilities, financial markets, government, healthcare, insurance, life sciences, media and entertainment, retail, telecommunications and travel and transportation. (Source: www.ibm.com)

8. **INFOSYS**

   Infosys Consulting is the consulting arm of technology giant Infosys. It focuses on realizing business value through business process and IT transformation and builds upon the technology leadership of larger Infosys.

   Infosys Consulting provides seven core consulting services: strategy and architecture, business transformation, enterprise processes, enterprise applications, digital transformation, analytics and change. Infosys Consulting serves over 14 industries including automotive, consumer packaged goods, energy, financial services, healthcare, high-tech, manufacturing, insurance, life sciences, retail, resources, telecom, utility and others. (Source: www.infosys.com)

9. **KPMG**

    KPMG LLP consulting practice is the advisory wing of KPMG, one of the 'Big Four' and one of the largest professional services firms.

    KPMG advisory services have over fourteen service lines some of which have been recently added to reflect changing business priorities in the digital age. These service lines include analytics; business integration; business intelligence; business process management; change management; growth enablement; integrated business planning; organizational design; outsourcing; shared services; strategy and operations; talent management; technology enablement; and transformation (Source: www.kpmg.com)

10. **MCKINSEY & COMPANY**

    McKinsey & Company, founded in 1926, is a privately owned leading management consulting firm. It employs what it calls a 'one-firm' partnership model, with offices across the world sharing values and cultural norms. McKinsey has maintained its focus (according to the firm) of doing what is right for the client's business, not what is best for their bottom line.

    McKinsey offers client services in three broad categories - industry practices, functional practices and global themes. McKinsey's services to industries include business building, performance and structure management, organizational change, operations and customer management and merger and acquisition advisory services. McKinsey's functional practices are business technology, corporate finance, marketing and sales, operations, organization, risk strategy and sustainability and resource productivity. McKinsey's global themes include topics such as digital disruption, growth, leadership, long term capitalism urbanization, emerging markets and women matter (Source: www.mckinsey.com)

11. **PRICEWATERHOUSECOOPERS**

    PricewaterhouseCoopers (PwC) Consulting is the consulting arm of PricewaterhouseCoopers LLP, one of the 'Big Four' consulting houses.

    PwC Consulting commands a leadership position in deal advisory and business consulting. It offers a wide range of services on management, technology and risk consulting, operations, finance, organizational strategy and structure, process improvement, human resources effectiveness, customer impact, technology integration and implementation, big data and analytics, IT security, risk mitigation and crisis management. It also provides forensic services, including anti-corruption/fraud, forensic investigations, licensing management and cyber security, in addition to guidance on mergers and acquisitions - from strategy through integration - through their deals capabilities. (Source: www.pwc.com)

12. TATA CONSULTANCY SERVICES

Global Consulting Practice (GCP) is the consulting arm of Tata Consultancy Services (TCS), a global leader in technology services with four decades of expertise. GCP provides integrated, IT-enabled business transformation services, leveraging TCS' global delivery model, technological leadership, strategic partnerships with the world's leading technology vendors and ability to provide end-to-end business services including application, infrastructure and business process outsourcing.

GCP's services are categorized into two - business change and business technology optimization - in addition to a solutions group focusing on business transformation and a domain consulting group focusing on business advisory. Its services are offered in 13 different industries including banking and financial services, energy and utilities, government, healthcare, high-tech, insurance, life sciences, manufacturing, media and information services, metals and mining, retail and consumer products, telecom, travel, transportation and hospitality. (Source: www.tcs.com)

CONSULTING BODIES

1. INTERNATIONAL COUNCIL OF MANAGEMENT CONSULTING INSTITUTIONS (ICMCI)

ICMCI is the authoritative global organization for the development of world-class professional standards in management consulting. Founded in 1987, ICMCI has over the years established better working relationships between Member Institutes in over 44 nations, provided a common communication platform, instituted a code of ethics, and established a minimum standard for quality. At the core of ICMCI lies the Certified Management Consultant (CMC) designation that has now become an international benchmark. It is a measure of an individual management consultant's competence, objectivity, independence and professionalism. (Source: www.icmci.org)

2. INSTITUTE OF MANAGEMENT CONSULTANTS OF INDIA (IMCI)

IMCI is the premier body of management consulting professionals and the only registered institute of established management consultancy firms and practicing individuals in the country. IMCI was constituted in 1991 and was formerly known as Management Consultants Association of India (MCAI). The MCAI was founded in 1963. In 1989, IMCI became the first Asian organisation to be accepted for membership of ICMCI, the global apex body of Management Consulting Institutes. (Source: www.imcindia.co.in)

3. **ASSOCIATION OF MANAGEMENT CONSULTING FIRMS (AMCF)**

AMCF is the premier international association of firms engaged in the practice of management consulting. Founded in 1929 as AMCE, the Association of Management Consulting Engineers, AMCF today remains in the forefront of promoting excellence and integrity in the profession. The mission of AMCF is to promote an environment which fosters success of management consulting firms worldwide and the value they deliver to their clients. (Source: www.amcf.org)

4. **MANAGEMENT CONSULTANCIES ASSOCIATION (MCA)**

MCA is the representative body for management consultancy firms in the UK and has been at the heart of the UK Consulting Industry since 1956. The MCA's mission is to promote the value of management consultancy for the economy and society as a whole. MCA focuses on delivering value to members through three key objectives - being the voice of the industry, promoting a credible and professional industry and creating better engagement with and between members. (Source: www.mca.org.uk)

CONSULTING MARKET

The turn of the century saw significant demand for consulting on globalization initiatives such as ventures into emerging markets, outsourcing and overseas mergers and acquisitions.

Some pointers on the size and growth of the industry:

Various industry sources have sized the global consulting market from time to time. In general, the global consulting market is estimated to be in the range of USD 200 billion to USD 250 billion, the IT consulting market is estimated to be in the range of USD 40 billion to over USD 60 billion and the growth rate for consulting market is in the range of 4 – 8%.

Some pointers on the trends and direction of the industry:

Over the past decade, the consulting industry has gone through some major restructuring. While the 'Big Four' carved out their consulting arms as independent entities, all major consulting firms developed their footprint in the Far East. Emerging markets have shown promising growth for global consulting firms despite lower fees as compared to mature markets. The 'Big Four' have invested significantly to become full-service players, tapping into the complete value chain of clients' businesses.

Consulting Basics

In the current business environment, the ability of a consulting firm to deliver Return on Investment (RoI) has been a prime focus for buyers. As a result, consulting firms have transformed traditional consulting methods by introducing risk-sharing models, profit sharing and outcome-based pricing models. Globally, buyers of consulting services value strategy execution as much as strategy definition, leading major consulting firms to diversify their services and develop as global service providers.

With the boundaries between business and technology blurring, global consulting firms are expanding progressively into IT-led business consulting. All major consulting firms now have a technology arm that not only brings specialty into current technological trends but also provides a breeding ground for technology-enabled business solutions.

CONSULTING CYCLE

In consulting, the phases are not linear but cyclic; hence, the phrase 'consulting cycle'. This is because engagements can cover the full life cycle from understanding context to presenting recommendations or start in-between, covering one or more phases and end with presenting recommendations. For example, engagements can start by assessing current state, defining target state and presenting recommendations on feasibility to achieve.

Consulting phases-at times called consulting methodology-have fancy acronyms across firms, but in simple English, they are: a) Understand context, b) Assess current state, c) Define target state, d) Analyze gaps, e) Evaluate solution options and f) Recommendations and report. The six phases are valid from an engagement model perspective. However, in execution mode, analysis of gaps and evaluation of solution options are often merged together as the analysis and findings phase. Each of these five phases are explained below in terms of their objectives, activities and outcomes.

A quick note on the key players, to appreciate the activities better: At the client end, there is the engagement sponsor at an executive level and reporting to him is the engagement coordinator, working full-time with direct ownership for engagement execution. Mirroring the same, at the consultant end, are the engagement partner and the engagement manager, respectively.

Understand Context

Understanding the past in terms of context and drivers is the starting point. Most consulting engagements do not have a defined problem statement; what is available is, at best, a certain hypothesis. The first task, therefore, is to articulate this hypothesis and arrive at a problem statement.

The objective of this phase is to understand the client context and business drivers with an open mind, putting aside past experience to uncover specificities.

Key Activities of this Phase:

1. **Synchronize with the Sponsor**

    In a one-on-one interview with the engagement sponsor, the engagement partner should walk through the context to get a better perspective of not just the cause, but also the underlying symptoms. Determine the drivers that have necessitated the current course of action. Identify an engagement coordinator and prepare a list of stakeholders to be engaged, their profile and their span of control and responsibility. Get an understanding of the organizational culture and political dynamics.

    Explain the approach and methodology and assets and accelerators that would be leveraged for the engagement. Introduce the engagement manager and SMEs who will form a part of the engagement and provide the timelines/duration of their participation. Validate schedules and milestones and confirm deliverables, both intermediate and final. Ensure that the commercial terms and pricing schedule are clearly understood. Agree on a governance model and reporting structure.

2. **Engage with the Coordinator**

    The engagement coordinator is identified by the engagement sponsor to represent the organization for the duration of the engagement on a full-time basis. The engagement coordinator and the engagement manager from the consulting firm have complete ownership of the engagement and collective responsibility to deliver outcomes.

All the activities initiated with the engagement sponsor are detailed with the engagement coordinator. First, compile all documentation relevant to the engagement, including corporate profile, corporate strategy, business strategy, technology strategy, reports of prior studies, etc. Schedule meetings with stakeholders in a logical sequence, share questionnaires and request functional documentation through the coordinator. Similar planning is required for SMEs with regard to logistics, workspace requirements, meeting schedules, etc. Jointly finalize the engagement plan, milestones, presentations and report submission in sufficient detail.

3. **WORKSHOP WITH STAKEHOLDERS**

The engagement sponsor should call for an engagement kick-off workshop. This should be facilitated by the engagement coordinator and attended by all stakeholders. The engagement sponsor should brief all stakeholders on the background to this initiative, spell out scope, set expectations, request their active participation and introduce the engagement partner and engagement manager. The engagement coordinator should then elaborate on the engagement plan and seek confirmation on schedules, meetings and commitment to provide documentation and also review deliverables. The engagement manager then presents their understanding of scope, approach, methodology and execution model, stressing on the support and collaboration required to jointly realize the outcomes.

Sample agenda for the kick-off workshop:

Session 1	Introductions
	Chair: Engagement Sponsor
	Discussion Points:
	- Workshop objectives
Session 2	Engagement Context
	Chair: Engagement Sponsor
	Discussion Points:
	- Business drivers
	- Engagement scope
	- Expectations from stakeholders
	- Introduction of engagement coordinator at the client end, engagement partner and engagement manager

Session 3	Engagement Plan

Chair: Engagement Coordinator

Discussion Points:

- Engagement schedule
- Time and effort required
- Intermediate milestones
- Governance model

Session 4	Engagement Model

Chair: Engagement Manager

Discussion Points:

- Approach and methodology
- Assets and accelerators
- Analysis tools and techniques
- Documentation required
- Briefing on best practices, critical success factors and similar experiences

Session 5	Conclusion

Chair: Engagement Partner

Discussion Points:

- Facilitated Q&A to get everyone aligned

The outcome of this phase is a jointly developed and agreed-upon engagement plan, detailing the schedule, intermediate milestones, review and approval cycle, final presentation format and target audience, report structure and submission and governance model for the course of the engagement.

Assess Current State

Understanding the past (context) naturally leads to assessing the present (current state) in terms of functional capability, competence of resources and culture of organization. The objective of this phase is to baseline the organization and the functional areas that need to be covered by the engagement.

Key Activities of this Phase:

1. **Review Baseline Documentation**

   Baseline documents have a wealth of information and these must be revisited to extract insights for addressing current challenges. Baseline documents consist of organizational collateral, research material, consulting artifacts and internal reports.

   Organizational collateral includes corporate website, annual reports and sales and marketing collateral. Browsing the corporate website helps gain insights into the organization's history, vision and mission, growth model (organic or inorganic) and geographic spread. Annual reports provide information on the financial performance of the organization, other useful data-points are organizational structure and profiles of board members and management team; this might even help discover a past acquaintance or a well-wisher. Sales and marketing collateral help appreciate the breadth of the product mix or the depth of services offered.

   Research material refers to industry and analyst reports. Industry bodies, whether local, regional or global, exist for almost all industries. Reports from industry bodies articulate current performance of the industry, prevailing performance thresholds and future directions (economic and political). Analyst firms run periodic intra- and inter-industry studies, which are a great source for market trends and competitive positions.

   Consulting artifacts are presentations or reports consisting of findings and/or recommendations from previous engagements. These are client-consultant confidential documents and are made available only as abridged extracts, after non-disclosure agreements are signed, unless it is a mandatory pre-requisite to the current engagement. Organizations share these reports to ensure alignment with strategic directions or to validate throughput for implementation.

   As the name implies, internal reports are outputs of internal studies, functional documentation, business-process definitions, technology landscape and key performance indicators. Of all the sources mentioned, consulting artifacts and internal reports have the highest relevance to current-state assessment. The other two sources are background information and pre-requisite reading for a better connect with the customer.

2. **Interview Stakeholders**

   Organization specific information is gathered through interviews with individual stakeholders and validated through focused workshops at a function level.

   Individual interviews are facilitated discussions leveraging customized questionnaires to gain insights into the functioning of the organization in general, departments in particular and the challenges they face. Use this opportunity to hear out personal opinions and potential solutions. The modus operandi should not be a one-way survey but a two-way dialogue, demonstrating empathy and building trust. The questions should seek answers to the interviewee's role, responsibility, fact-file of their function, concerns/issues that are the cause for the current situation or drivers for the desired direction as perceived by them. Some interviews may require further detailing with some other colleagues, which must be followed-up. Minutes for all meetings are distributed to stakeholders with a copy to the engagement coordinator for review and approval. Approved minutes are to be shared with engagement sponsor for information.

Focused workshops are scheduled on a need basis to share a common viewpoint or to resolve matters of conflict, be it intra- or cross-functional. These workshops are facilitated by the consultants as neutral observers, presenting varied viewpoints, sharing similar experiences and best practices. The end objective is to create consensus.

3. Prepare Current State Report

Current-state assessment relies on information that is made available by the stakeholders, without any inference from external data-points or any reference to the desired end-state. Therefore, analysis at this stage is based on preliminary observations, plotted as heat maps or populated as a Strengths, Weaknesses, Opportunities, Threats (SWOT) analysis grid.

Heat maps are visual indicators of maturity level, illustrated red to indicate a negative value or alert, amber to imply a neutral state and green to infer a positive value or outcome. They are a basic assessment tool, easy to develop and simple to understand. Measurement levels can be, at granular data-point level or aggregated and measured at a functional level. All observations should have associated remarks giving reference to the information source and, where available, a note on the benchmark.

SWOT Analysis is the next level of assessment, leveraging information gathered and also the heat maps developed. Taking into account the maturity levels of functions, they are plotted onto one of the four quadrants. Cross-dimensional analysis can then be conducted on strengths versus weaknesses and opportunities versus threats to assess comparative positions and highlight co-relations that may exist.

The outcome of this phase is a report on the current state of the organization and relevant functional areas, depicting the baseline, benchmark (where applicable) and barriers to change in status quo.

Define Target State

Having understood the past (context) and assessed the present (current state), the next logical step is defining the future (target state) in terms of the required functionality of the target environment.

The objective of this phase is to visualize the required features of the target state and validate the gaps to be bridged.

Key Activities of this Phase:

1. **Big Picture Envisioning**

    The approach in current-state assessment is bottom-up: individual interview inputs aggregated at a functional level, validated through workshops and presented to the engagement sponsor. However, for target-state definition, the preferred approach is top-down: envisioning the big-picture with the engagement sponsor and presenting the same to the steering committee.

    In big-picture envisioning, for the first time, external data will be factored in, be it the consultant's past experiences, best practices, competitive insights, critical success factors or analyst reports. Big-picture envisioning is white-boarding the above insights in the context of the customer's situation and environment, taking into account the findings from current-state assessment. The key is being pragmatic and arriving at a set of strategic options. The envisioning exercise is chaired by the engagement sponsor and facilitated by the engagement partner with participation from functional heads.

    The strategic options are then presented to the steering committee, the approving authority for an in-principle agreement on the overall direction. Members of the steering committee are CxOs; the engagement sponsor and engagement partner participate.

2. **Scenario Planning**

    Big-picture envisioning pegs the endpoint; scenario planning is about exploring ways to reach this endpoint. The focus is on listing the options best suited for the current context.

    In scenario planning, external data is further leveraged to articulate realistic routes to reach the target state. Scenario planning is brainstorming in workshop mode on the above paths and short-listing scenarios that are realistic, taking into account the organization's culture, capability and aptitude to change. Scenario planning workshops are conducted per function by the engagement coordinator and facilitated by the engagement manager with participation from functional stakeholders.

Short-listed scenarios are then presented to the management committee, the approving authority for an in-principle agreement on the validity of the scenarios. Members of the management committee are function heads, with the engagement sponsor, engagement coordinator, engagement partner and engagement manager participating.

3. **TARGET STATE REPORT**

    Target state definition takes into account both the internal assessment findings and external data-points to build the big picture and list potential scenarios to realize the target state.

    The big picture highlights the strategic direction and how the organization as a whole would look, including different components describing functions and features. Potential scenarios are strategic options available to design and develop these functions, the building blocks for the new organization.

    The focus is on creating a sustainable end state, which is best achieved by incremental developments of functions, implemented in phases, resulting in an improved organization over a time horizon.

The outcome of this phase is a report on the target state for the organization and relevant functional areas, illustrating the desired end-state and scenario options that could potentially bridge the gap.

ANALYSIS AND FINDINGS

Analysis and findings phase is critical to the success of the engagement, as insights from findings help shape recommendations and the course of action for the organization to realize its objectives.

The objective of this phase is to analyze gaps, evaluate solution options and validate findings from analysis.

KEY ACTIVITIES OF THIS PHASE:

1. **ANALYZE GAPS**

    Gap analysis, as the name suggests, identifies the difference between the current state and the target state, the validity of the gap, its size and the difficulty in bridging it.

    Analysis of the validity of the gap actually re-validates the correctness of the current state and feasibility of the target state, necessitating a re-assessment, if needed, before evaluating solution options. Measuring the size of the gap helps in being realistic on recommendations. Assessing the difficulty in bridging the gap allows for an informed definition of the timelines to achieve the target state.

2. **EVALUATE SOLUTION OPTIONS**

   Solution options are evaluated for each of the feasible and prioritized gaps, in a two-step process - a standalone evaluation followed by a collective evaluation of one or more related gaps.

   In the standalone evaluation, each gap is evaluated in isolation, taking into consideration the effort/resources required and the time to bridge the individual gap. In collective evaluation, the standalone solution options are evaluated on a comparative basis in terms of potential cross-impact and possible synergies of alternative or aligned solutions. A business case is prepared for the optimal solution option.

3. **VALIDATE FINDINGS**

   Analysis findings are then presented to the management committee, the approving authority for an in-principle agreement on the validity of the findings, a pre-requisite to articulating recommendations. The presentation should cover context, current state assessment findings, target state definition, gap analysis and summary of findings with solution options. This forum is also used to discuss draft recommendations to gain general concurrence and internal buy-in.

The outcome of this phase is an interim presentation on the analysis, findings and evaluated solution alternatives to realize the target state.

RECOMMENDATIONS AND REPORT

The final phase of the consulting engagement, a culmination of all the hard work and an opportunity to gain credibility.

The objective of this phase is to present recommendations and prepare the consulting report.

KEY ACTIVITIES OF THIS PHASE:

1. **PRESENT RECOMMENDATIONS**

   Recommendations are run past the engagement sponsor first and then presented to the steering committee. All recommendations should have rationale from two perspectives, an internal situation that would benefit from this recommendation and a related external best practice that the organization could learn and leverage. All recommendations should be accompanied by a business case with a clear RoI.

2. PREPARE CONSULTING REPORT

The consulting report is the final deliverable, a summary of the complete engagement proceedings.

Sample contents for the consulting report:

Chapter 1	Introduction
	Engagement context, Engagement model, Engagement plan
Chapter 2	Current State Assessment
	Stakeholders interviewed, Summary of observations on the current state of the organization and its functions, heat maps and SWOT analysis
Chapter 3	Target State Definition
	Big picture vision and scenarios that would help meet organizational objectives, Definition and description of the target state
Chapter 4	Analysis and Findings
	Analysis of the gaps between current and target state, Findings with solution options to bridge the gap
Chapter 5	Recommendations on Way forward
	Recommendations with rationale and roadmap for implementation
Appendices	Additional information on methodologies, tools and techniques, consulting team profiles, etc.

CONSULTING FRAMEWORKS

Consulting frameworks help in executing the engagement in a systematic manner, accelerating analysis and articulating realizable recommendations. Each framework serves a certain purpose in a certain context only and should not be enforced where it does not apply. The better approach would be to choose alternative frameworks; it is acceptable to use multiple frameworks during the course of the engagement.

Overview of Select Frameworks

1. Balanced Scorecard

The Balanced Scorecard (BSc)[4], conceptualized by Robert Kaplan and Dave Norton, uses internal performance measurement to track and adjust business strategy. In addition to the usual financial perspective, it forces managers to incorporate the customer perspective, operations and the organization's innovation and learning ability.

- Financial Perspective: What is important for our shareholders?
- Customer Perspective: How do customers perceive us?
- Internal Process Perspective: Which internal processes can add value?
- Organizational Perspective: Are we innovative and ready for the future?

It provides a balanced view of performance, includes subjective measures and inputs of stakeholders. It brings attention to possibly conflicting dimensions, such as productivity versus employee satisfaction; high revenues versus high perceived value, as measured by customer satisfaction; and low maintenance costs versus minimal equipment downtime, as measured by operational efficiency. BSc can be built for the organization as a whole or for a specific business area (for example, IT Scorecard).

2. BCG Matrix

Created by BCG, this matrix is based on the product life cycle theory that can be used to determine what priorities should be assigned in the product portfolio of a business unit. To ensure long-term value creation, a company should have a portfolio of products that contains both high-growth products in need of cash inputs and low-growth products that generate a lot of cash. It has two dimensions: Market Share and Market Growth.

Cash cows are units with high market share in a slow-growing industry. They typically generate cash in excess of the amount needed to maintain the business.

Dogs, more charitably called pets, are units with low market share in a mature, slow-growing industry. These units typically break even, generating barely enough cash to maintain the business' market share.

Question marks (also known as problem child) grow rapidly and thus consume large amounts of cash, but with low market shares, they do not generate much cash.

Stars are units with a high market share in a fast-growing industry. The hope is that stars become the next cash cows.

---

4   ten Have, S. ten Have, W. and Stevens, F. (2003). *Key management models*. FT Prentice Hall.

3. BRAINSTORMING

Brainstorming can be effective in generating multiple ideas on a specific issue and then determining which idea or ideas offer the best solution. Brainstorming is most effective with groups of 8–12 and should be performed in a relaxed environment. It can be used whenever a large quantity of information is generated, before problem-solving, decision-making or planning.

Brainstorming starts with a diverging phase, a period of freethinking, which is used to articulate ideas. The facilitator introduces the topic and begins the discussion by asking specific open-ended questions. The answers or reactions are written down without any comments or further analysis. This is followed by a converging phase. Collected ideas are revisited, clustered and prioritized. The material is then taken as the basis for more analytical discussion.

Brainstorming helps reduce conflicts - all participants have equal status and equal opportunity to participate. Problems are defined better as questions arise - alternatives appear in a new or different perspective and novel approaches to an issue can arise during the process.

4. BUSINESS MODEL CANVAS

The Business Model Canvas, developed by Alexander Ostenwalder and Yves Pigneur, is a strategic management tool. It allows you to describe, design, challenge, invent and pivot the organization's business model.

The business model canvas is a visual chart with elements describing a firm's value proposition, infrastructure, customers and finances. It assists firms in aligning their activities by illustrating potential trade-offs. The framework captures nine key components of a business model: key partners, key activities, key resources, value propositions, customer relations, customer segments, channels, cost structure and revenue streams. A critical pre-requisite is to establish a common language among the stakeholders pertaining to the nine components and their relevance.

5. MCKINSEY 7S FRAMEWORK

The 7S Framework of McKinsey is a management model that describes seven factors to organize a company in a holistic and effective way. Together, these factors determine how a corporation operates. Managers should take into account all seven factors for successful implementation of a strategy. The 7S framework is a diagnostic tool for understanding ineffective organizations and driving organizational change.

The 3S's across the top of the model are described as 'Hard S's:

- Strategy: The direction and scope of the company over the long term
- Structure: The basic organization of the company, its departments, reporting lines, areas of expertise and responsibility
- Systems: Formal and informal procedures that govern everyday activity, covering everything from management information systems through to the systems at the point of contact with the customer

The 4S's across the bottom of the model are less tangible, more cultural in nature and termed 'Soft S's:

- Skills: The capabilities and competencies that exist within the company, what it does best
- Shared values: The values and beliefs of the company that guide employees towards valued behavior
- Staff: The company's people resources and how they are developed, trained, and motivated
- Style: The leadership approach of top management and the company's overall operating approach

6. PESTLE

A globally accepted framework to assess the target operating environment in a structured way based on a set of standard macro-environmental factors. It facilitates environmental scanning to identify key concerns and risks and plan aligned strategies and mitigation/contingency measures.

The framework helps assess business factors on the following dimensions:

Political, Economic, Social, Technical, Legal, Environmental (PESTLE) to analyze operating environment in a target market, country or region for entry, operation or target market analysis.

Variations based on context, chosen dimensions and aligned factors:

- PEST/STEP: Political, Economic, Social, Technological
- PESTLIED: Political, Economic, Social, Technological, Legal, International, Environmental, Demographic
- STEEPLE: Social/Demographic, Technological, Economic, Environmental, Political, Legal, Ethical
- SLEPT: Social, Legal, Economic, Political, Technological

The choice of dimensions and factors is limited by the context of the business situation, need for analysis, availability of information and end objective.

7. **POLICY OBJECTIVE MATRIX**

   The Policy Objective (P/O) Matrix, developed by Dr Ryuji Fukuda, is a tool for visualizing and translating top management's commitment to improvement and transformation into concrete activities, a technique to manage company-wide activities to achieve policies and objectives.

   A unique feature of the P/O Matrix is the depiction of Policies, Objectives, Targets, Principal/Supporting parties, Due dates/Milestones and Overall effects on a single page, with cross linkages.

   The P/O Matrix aims to provide a company with an enabling structure for achieving priority business plans and prevent it from falling into an undesirable state of affairs. It helps develop business plans by integrating the knowledge and experience of all employees and making this visible to anyone in the organization at any time. It periodically examines a company's performance in implementing priority improvement plans.

8. **PORTER'S FIVE FORCES**

   Michael Porter's five forces[5] is a framework for industry analysis. It draws upon industrial organization economics to derive five forces that determine the competitive intensity and, therefore, attractiveness of a market.

   - Supplier power: Strength of supplier bargaining power
   - Buyer power: Strength of customer bargaining power
   - Competitive rivalry: Comparative analysis of competition
   - Threat of substitution: Potential/ease of substitutions for products/services
   - Threat of new entry: Market attractiveness and ease of entry

   For each of the five forces, consider how well a company can compete:

   New entrants: Are there barriers to new contenders? For example, economies of scale, established brands, loyalty, risky capital requirements and difficult access to distribution channels.

   Substitutes: How easily can your product or service be substituted with another type of product or service?

   Buyers' bargaining power: To what extent can buyers bargain? For example, large volume purchases and low switching costs.

   Suppliers' command of industry: Competitive forces of suppliers mirror those of buyers.

---

[5] ten Have, S. ten Have, W. and Stevens, F. (2003). *Key management models*. FT Prentice Hall.

Existing competitors: Indicators of competitive threat from existing industry rivals are slow industrial growth, many and/or equally balanced competitors and products perceived as commodity.

9. SCENARIO PLANNING

Scenario planning[6] is built around the assumption that the business environment will change. Rather than trying to remove uncertainty, the challenge is to accept and try to understand it. The aim is not necessarily to 'get it right' but to illuminate the major forces driving the system, their inter-relationships and the critical uncertainties.

Scenario construction process:

- Identification and analysis of pre-determined elements: What events are taking place? Which trends are emerging that will have an impact on the business?
- Charting interrelationships: What is the likely combined effect on the operating environment?
- Development of scenarios depending on resulting uncertainties: Ideally, three scenarios, with four as an absolute maximum.
- Scenarios are most effective when combined with strategic vision and option planning.

10. SIX THINKING HATS

The Six Thinking Hats, developed by Edward de Bono, represent six thinking strategies. It is hypothesized that most people use only one or two approaches and develop thinking habits that limit them to those approaches. Six thinking hats is a structured system that can enhance the thinking process, encourage creative/parallel thinking, improve communication and speed up decision-making.

The key theoretical reasons to use the six thinking hats are to: encourage parallel thinking and full-spectrum thinking and separate ego from performance. Each of the six thinking hats represents a different type of thinking, which is identified by a color.

- White Hat Thinking: Data, facts and information known or needed
- Black Hat Thinking: Difficulties and potential problems (why something may not work)
- Red Hat Thinking: Feelings, hunches, gut instinct and intuition
- Green Hat Thinking: Creativity, possibilities, alternatives, solutions and new ideas

---

6 ten Have, S. ten Have, W. and Stevens, F. (2003). *Key management models*. FT Prentice Hall.

- Yellow Hat Thinking: Values and benefits (why something may work)
- Blue Hat Thinking: Manage the thinking process, focus, next steps and action plans

11. SWOT Analysis

SWOT analysis is a structured planning method used to evaluate the Strengths, Weaknesses, Opportunities and Threats in a project or business venture.

- Strengths: Characteristics of the business or project that give it an advantage over others
- Weaknesses: Characteristics that place the team at a disadvantage relative to others
- Opportunities: Elements that the project could exploit to its advantage
- Threats: Elements in the environment that could cause trouble for the business or project

Identifying SWOT facilitates planning of the key steps in achieving the objective. It can be used for an initial analysis before strategic planning or goal setting or competitive positioning.

Objectives should be set after the SWOT analysis. First, decision makers should consider whether the objective is attainable, given the SWOT. If it is not, a different objective must be selected and the process repeated.

12. Workshop Methods

Methods to facilitate structured interaction with clients/stakeholders at various levels and elicit outcomes based on the context. The choice of method is determined by purpose/intended outcome, participant profile, numbers and duration.

Workshops are conducted to enable an efficient and inclusive discussion. The facilitator plays an important part although everyone should share the responsibility for ensuring that the discussion is well-run, productive and participative. Participants are encouraged to think and act for the overall benefit of the group.

Facilitation tasks include helping the group decide on a structure and process for the meeting and limiting focus to one item at a time until decisions are made. The facilitator regulates the flow of discussion, drawing out quiet people or those with the most relevant expertise and limiting those who tend to dominate. The facilitator clarifies and summarizes points, checking for consensus and formalizing decisions, and ensures that a written record is made of any action points and decisions agreed at the meeting. Post-workshop outcomes need to be adequately summarized and published.

Consulting Spectrum

The consulting space is occupied by strategy consulting, business consulting, functional consulting, IT consulting and operations consulting offerings.

IT consulting is further segmented as IT **S**trategy Consulting, IT **A**rchitecture Consulting, IT **P**ortfolio Management, IT **P**rocess Consulting, IT **G**overnance Consulting, IT **I**nfrastructure Consulting, IT **O**utsourcing Consulting and IT **T**ransformation Consulting. Together, they form the consulting spectrum - the answer for a business problem when seen through an IT prism, abbreviated as SAPPGIO-T, akin to the VIBGYOR of a rainbow. The suffix T is the resultant Transformation, the pot of gold at the end of the rainbow for the business.

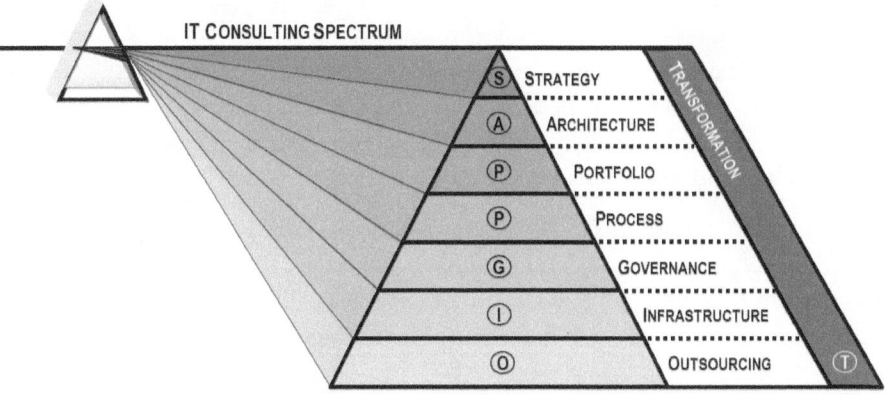

While there is distinct space in which each segment operates as core, there are also overlaps and dependencies with other segments, forming corollaries. Importantly, in IT consulting, the core and corollary are inter-changeable, depending on the client context.

In part II, each of the segments of the IT consulting spectrum are explained in detail, in separate chapters.

In each succeeding chapter, only the activities that are additionally required for the particular segment are explained in detail. For other activities, already covered but still needed, an overview is provided with the required degree of emphasis. Therefore, if the scope of the engagement spans across the spectrum, which is mostly the case, all the relevant segment chapters need to be studied to appreciate the big picture.

Furthermore, in each chapter, only the 'What' part of the specific consulting spectrum is explained and not the 'How', as the how part is very contextual and cannot be generalized. However, a good understanding of the what, along with the associated frameworks/enablers, will enable the consultant to accomplish the how; in the end, experience is the best teacher.

KEY LEARNINGS

Consulting is very contextual, every engagement is unique, so much so that each engagement requires the same rigor and commitment to execute, in spite of past experiences. Hence, in many ways it is an art.

Consulting segments in the consulting space are strategy consulting, business consulting, functional consulting, IT consulting and operations consulting from an industry perspective. A company perspective has three levels: technology consulting, business consulting and strategy consulting. From a market perspective, there is enough space for all to operate and grow and boundaries are blurring as all firms aspire to play at all three levels.

In a consulting cycle, key phases include understanding context, assessing current state, defining target state, analyzing gaps, evaluating solution options, presenting recommendations and preparing consulting reports. Consulting frameworks are tools and techniques to accelerate the analysis, validate findings and present recommendations in a coherent manner. The frameworks should be used judiciously, based on need and fit only.

When seen through an IT Prism, the answer to a business problem is SAPPGIO-T, the IT consulting spectrum. SAPPGIO-T encompasses IT **S**trategy Consulting, IT **A**rchitecture Consulting, IT **P**ortfolio Management, IT **P**rocess Consulting, IT **G**overnance Consulting, IT **I**nfrastructure Consulting, IT **O**utsourcing Consulting and IT **T**ransformation Consulting.

. Ω .

Part Two
Consulting Spectrum

Chapter 2

IT Strategy Consulting

IT has evolved as a strategic function that drives business. Strategic IT planning, therefore, becomes the CIO's critical obligation and depends on understanding new technologies and interpreting how they might be applied to benefit the business and provide value to the shareholder.

CIOs plan strategy by analyzing the present and re-imagining the future, gauging gaps and devising plans to bridge them and considering business needs, technology advancements, market forces and risk appetite. CIOs need to reach out to each business unit to understand their operational strategy, aggregate their requirements for IT and produce an IT strategy - a statement of the intended contribution of IT to the enterprise, expressed in business terms.

IT Strategy Consulting, the 'S' in SAPPGIO-T of the IT Consulting Spectrum, primarily deals with alignment of IT with Business and is invariably coupled with one or more of the following - IT Organization Design, Enterprise Architecture and/or IT Infrastructure.

In addition to a broad understanding of the IT Strategy Space, this chapter provides insights into IT Strategy Drivers, IT Strategy Framework and Approach for executing an IT Strategy engagement.

IT Strategy Space

Strategy is probably the business world's most used and abused word; there are strategies for everything.

Bruce Henderson offers a classical definition: "All competitors who persist over time must maintain a unique advantage by differentiation over all others. Managing that differentiation is the essence of long term business strategy."[7]

Henry Mintzberg, argues that strategy has five dimensions: 1) a plan or a course of action for the future; 2) a pattern or consistency in behavior over time; 3) a position, that is, particular products in particular markets; 4) a perspective or a fundamental

---

[7] Stern, C. W. and Deimler, M. S. (2006). *Boston Consulting Group on strategy*. John Wiley & Sons.

approach to doing things and 5) a ploy or a specific "maneuver" intended to outwit competition.[8]

Michael Porter defines strategy as "A company's position, trade-offs, and creating fit among company's activities. The success of a strategy depends on doing many things well and integration amongst them. If there is no fit among activities, there is no distinctive strategy and little sustainability. Management [then] reverts to simpler task of overseeing independent functions."[9]

The question, therefore, is how can management avoid such a trap? What should be done to achieve breakthrough results and performance? Robert S Kaplan and David P Norton observed that the ability to execute strategy was far more important than the strategy itself. Two keywords that executives of early adopters of BSc continually mention are alignment and focus. The study of successful Balanced Scorecard Companies further revealed a consistent pattern of achieving strategic focus and alignment. Although each organization approached the challenge in different ways, at different paces and in different sequences, five common principles were at work. These are referred to as the principles of a Strategy Focused Organization:

- Principle #1: Translate the strategy to operational terms
- Principle #2: Align the organization with the strategy
- Principle #3: Make strategy everyone's everyday job
- Principle #4: Make strategy a continual process
- Principle #5; Mobilize change through executive leadership

For good executives, there is no 'steady state'. The competitive landscape is constantly changing, so strategies must constantly evolve to reflect shifts in opportunities and threats. Strategy must be a continuous process.[10]

Strategy can exist at the three levels: Corporate, Business and Functional. Corporate strategy defines the overall vision and direction of an enterprise and the way various business units work together to achieve a vision. Business strategy articulates objectives for a business unit including the business it should be in, specific markets to operate in and specific products or services it should offer. Functional strategy articulates objectives for shared and common functions within an enterprise and accurate and cost-effective support for business units and larger enterprise to achieve objectives.

IT is one such common function, whose strategic goal is to create value, leveraging technology infrastructure and information capital applications. Robert S Kaplan

---

8   Mintzberg, H., Ahlstrand, B., and Lampel, J. (1998). *Strategy safari*. The Free Press.
9   Porter, M. (1996). *What is strategy?* Harvard Business Review.
10 Kaplan, R. S. and Norton, D. P. (2001). *The strategy-focused organization: How balanced scorecard companies thrive in the new business environment*. Harvard Business School Press.

and David P Norton define technology infrastructure as the shared technology and managing expertise required to enable effective delivery and use of information capital applications, which are broadly categorized as 1) Transaction processing applications or systems that automate basic repetitive transactions; 2) Analytic applications, that is, systems and networks that promote analysis, interpretation and knowledge-sharing and 3) Transformational applications, that is, systems and networks that change the enterprise's prevailing business model. Together, technology infrastructure and information capital applications make up the information capital portfolio.

The strategic readiness of information capital applications and infrastructure is the most meaningful measure of the value of an organization's information capital, that is, the degree of preparedness of the organization's information capital to support enterprise strategy, measured not by cost and reliability statistics but by strategic alignment.[11]

IT strategy should, therefore, be a well-thought out plan of action that provides adequate guidance on using technology resources across the enterprise and making decisions that help alignment with business and achieve corporate vision.

ELEMENTS OF IT STRATEGY

IT Vision	The stated vision of the IT function, outlining the purpose of its existence, the services provided and, most importantly, alignment with the enterprise vision. Underlying the IT vision is a set of guiding principles to translate vision into action.
IT Architecture	The design principles for understanding business from an IT perspective, primarily aimed at business process standardization and integration requirements of the organizations operating model.
IT Portfolio	The portfolio of the enterprise, prioritized programs and projects with associated plans to monitor progress and measure performance.
IT Services	The services that the IT department delivers to the business, the agreed-upon service levels covering both business and operations.
IT Infrastructure	The underlying network and communications infrastructure that serve as a backbone for the enterprise, configurations and capacity utilized/unutilized.

---

11 Kaplan, R. S. and Norton, D. P. (2004). *Strategy maps: Converting intangible assets into tangible outcomes.* Harvard Business School Press.

IT Governance	Governance arrangement, including governance mechanisms and processes, internally within the IT function and externally with interfacing functions.
IT Investments	IT spend on 'Run the Business' versus 'Change the Business'; comparisons with industry spend-distribution on transactional versus transformational application, application development versus application maintenance.
IT Business Case	A framework for decision-making, a tool to gain a sense of the funding required and the expected returns, both tangible and intangible.
IT Roadmap	The minimal expected outcome of a typical IT strategy consulting engagement; a synthesis of the analysis and findings from one or more of the above elements, resulting in a recommended direction to be realized incrementally.

IT STRATEGY DRIVERS

IT has become invasive in the current dynamic, and often turbulent, business environments, characterized by changing business needs and time-to-market demand for products and services, necessitating agility and adaptability.

FOUR MAJOR SCENARIOS THAT TRIGGER THE NEED FOR AN IT STRATEGY:

1. **INTERNAL BUSINESS CHANGE**

   Whenever there is a significant change within the enterprise as a whole or within some of its most prominent business units, IT strategy is reassessed to support this change. In other words, any change within the enterprise usually creates new information needs. If such needs can be fulfilled with the current IT set-up, then the change is 'business as usual' for IT. If such a change mandates IT to perform above and beyond its current capability, then IT strategy is redefined to facilitate the change.

2. **EXTERNAL BUSINESS CHANGE**

   Certain phenomena such as globalization, regulatory governance, taxation and legal and government enforcements cause businesses to rethink the way they organize, store and consume information within the enterprise. Such changes also lead to IT Strategy review and redefinition.

IT Strategy Consulting

3. **CHALLENGES OF OLD TECHNOLOGY**

   An outdated IT set-up could cause impediments to business growth. This is a very common situation that causes businesses to re-examine the IT strategy and empower it to be ahead of the game.

4. **OPPORTUNITIES FROM NEW TECHNOLOGIES, NEW BUSINESS MODELS**

   Trends like business and IT convergence and global IT outsourcing provide a compelling case for business to redesign their IT shops and, in turn, redefine the IT Strategy. Apart from benefits such as efficiency and scalability, such opportunities also provide significant cost advantages.

IT STRATEGY FRAMEWORK

The Business Motivation Model (BMM), developed by 'Business Rules Group', is a widely adopted industry standard for developing, communicating and managing strategic plans in an organized manner. The following is an adaptation for IT Strategy based on BMM V1.2, dated May 2014, published by Object Management Group (OMG).[12]

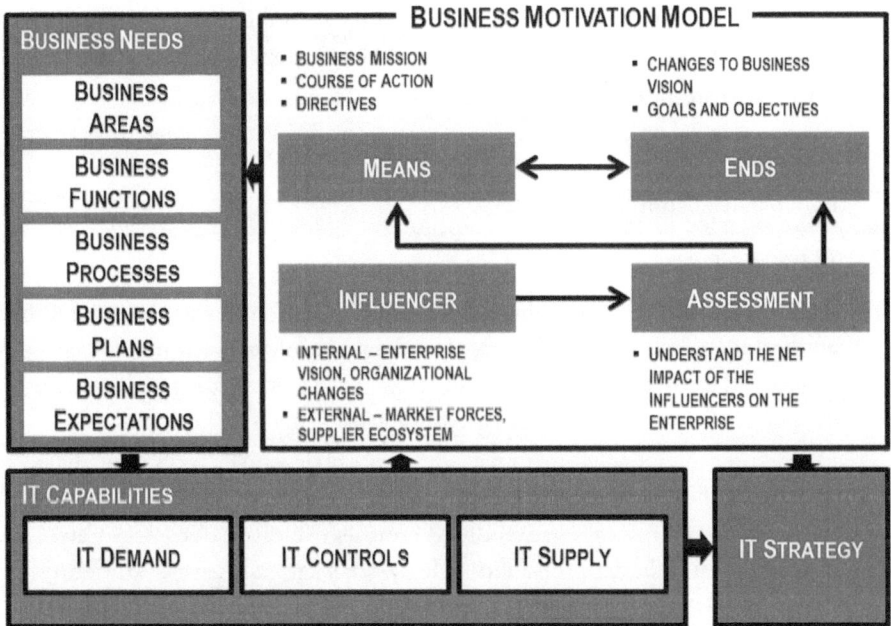

---

12 Adapted from 'Business Motivation Model V1.2' published by Object Management Group, 2014. BMG and OMG are either registered trademarks or trademarks of Object Management Group, Inc. in the United States and/or other countries.

Core Concepts of BMM

Fundamental to BMM is the notion of 'Motivation', which refers to the underlying intent behind an enterprise's choice of a particular approach, the results it is meant to achieve and how the results are measured. A cornerstone of BMM is: what an enterprise does is driven not by change but by how the enterprise reacts to a particular change. Therefore, recognition of change and its underlying drivers is a pre-cursor to BMM.

In principle, BMM speaks about four major concepts:

1. Influencers

Factors that have the potential to trigger a change within an enterprise. Influencers primarily fall into two broad categories:

External Influencers: These refer to factors originating outside the boundary of the enterprise being modeled. Some common external influences are regulation, competition, customer priorities, business environment, business partners, suppliers and technology.

Internal Influencers: These refer to factors that originate within the enterprise. Some common internal influencers are corporate values, enterprise heritage, enterprise culture, assets and resources and organizational changes.

These two categories are predominantly used as guidance; specific categories can be created based on particular business needs. The BMM also defines 'Influencing Organization', which refers to an external body that is a source of influencers, for example, regulators or competitors.

2. Assessment

An objective evaluation of some influencers with respect to their impact on the enterprise. Assessment expresses fact-based connection between the influencers, means and ends of the business. Although BMM does not mandate specific categories of assessment, it does support categories of a SWOT framework.

On the same lines, BMM also provides guidance on how to quantify or qualify the impact of influencers; this is referred to as 'Potential Impact'. Based on whether the impact is positive or negative, BMM provides two categories: Risk - Category of impact that indicates probability of loss or damage and Reward - Category of impact that indicates probability of gain.

BMM acknowledges that the same assessment can be interpreted differently by different stakeholders. It mandates tagging the stakeholder conducting the assessment, thereby facilitating audit trail and traceability.

3. **ENDS**

   What the business seeks to accomplish. In BMM terminology, an End is either a business vision or some desired outcome. A vision is usually articulated by a vision statement that clearly indicates the future state of an enterprise. Desired outcome is a state that the enterprise wants to maintain or sustain.

   BMM further classifies desired outcome as: Goal - It amplifies a vision, that is, it indicates what must be achieved on a continuous basis to attain the vision; and Objective - Enterprises set objectives to achieve their goals.

   One objective can address multiple goals. Similarly, multiple goals can address a vision or part of a vision. Therefore, BMM provides a mechanism to interlink objectives with goals and goals with vision in order to maintain backward traceability.

4. **MEANS**

   Refer to the course of action that the enterprise chooses in order to become what it wants to be. A Means can be some asset, capability, technique, restriction, partnership, core-competence or any other resource that may be leveraged to achieve the ends.

   In BMM terminology, means are organized into 1) Mission: Like its counterpart, vision, Mission is indicated by a mission statement which makes a vision operative, that is, it indicates ongoing activity that makes the vision a reality; 2) Course of Action: An approach or a plan that indicates the best ways to deploy enterprise resources and capabilities to achieve desired results; and 3) Directives: Courses of action are governed by directives. In other words, directives are measures used to direct the course of action for the right outcome.

LEVERAGING BMM FOR IT STRATEGY

The BMM concept can be applied to an enterprise as a whole or to a function in the enterprise, like IT, to define strategic plans at the functional level.

Information needs of the business stem from multiple layers across the enterprise, resulting from a change triggered in a business area or function or process or plan, each with its own set of business expectations.

IT is then expected to have or acquire the necessary capabilities to accomplish these business expectations. The strategic plan that IT would then require is a mechanism to manage demand, a set of controls to ensure compliance and a seamless supply of skills to service the business needs.

BMM is one such framework that can be leveraged meaningfully to align IT with business. Influencers are the underlying business needs, assessed against existing IT capabilities and defined strategic initiatives that are the means to achieve the ends, that is, the business expectations. Other frameworks that equally fit the purpose are Business Model Canvas and BSc.

IT Strategy Approach

The execution model of an IT strategy engagement would broadly traverse the following phases - Understand Context, Assess Current State, Define Target State, Analysis and Findings and Recommendations and Roadmap. The duration, depth or degree of detail may vary, but all these phases must be touched upon in any engagement.

Understand Context

The objective of this phase is to understand the context in terms of the drivers, business, technology, stakeholders, scope and outcomes. The target audience is the engagement sponsor and/or the engagement coordinator.

Key Activities of this Phase:

1. **Understand Drivers**

   A genuine understanding of real drivers is a pre-requisite for developing or designing an effective IT strategy. It provides insights on the real motive and importance of the initiative, on which awareness is not always uniform. One must go beyond the symptoms to unearth the cause. This requires trust, diplomacy, probing and experience sharing.

2. **Understand Business**

   A deep understanding of the company's past is essential to assess the present and shape the future. Study the journey from its inception, taking note of organizational dynamics like shareholder management, executive accountability, financial performance, mergers and/or acquisitions, products and services, customer satisfaction, growth in terms of size and geographical spread and work culture. A good source of information is the company's annual reports and website.

   Additionally, review industry reports to get a sense of industry trends, the client's relative position/standing in the industry and insights into competition.

3. **Understand Technology**

   A high-level understanding of the IT environment is essential even for an IT strategy engagement. The key is to understand IT alignment with the business, the various business functions supported by different IT applications, the underlying infrastructure platform and the structure and governance of the IT organization.

Business IT alignment is the most common reason for organizations revisiting their IT strategy. The weak link can be in any of the above dimensions.

4. **UNDERSTAND STAKEHOLDERS**

    Understanding people is the next logical step following understanding of business and technology. At this stage, the people study is restricted to key stakeholders to obtain their collective buy-in. This involves executive alignment with the sponsor, connecting with decision-makers, their perspective, their priorities and how much the planned outcomes mean to each of them. Knowing who your adversaries are is as important as who your evangelists are; both are bound to exist in any context.

5. **UNDERSTAND SCOPE AND OUTCOMES**

    Lastly, re-confirm the scope stated in the proposal and the statement of work with the engagement sponsor. Seldom are they exact; variations are likely because of a difference in understanding or interpretation. Be prepared to accommodate some modifications, assuming they do not majorly impact cost, time and/or effort.

    Equally important is a common understanding of the outcomes/end deliverables in terms of coverage and depth. This process is initiated in this phase and must be monitored in all phases, through creation, review and sign-off of interim deliverables.

    The outcome of this phase is a re-confirmed engagement scope, plan and agreed-upon list of deliverables.

ASSESS CURRENT STATE

The objective of this phase is to baseline all the in-scope elements on an as-is basis. The idea is to hear the voice of the customer in their own words. The target audience is the engagement coordinator, key business owners and technology leaders. Baseline can be performed by reviewing documents or interviewing key business owners.

KEY ACTIVITIES OF THIS PHASE:

1. **CURRENT BUSINESS FUNCTIONS**

    The starting point for current-state assessment is the client's business. Baseline the relevant business areas and business processes of the core functions and, if needed, all or some of the supporting functions. A good source of information is the business strategy document.

Most organizations have a corporate strategy document developed at a group level and authorized by the board. CEOs then develop their business strategies in alignment with this corporate strategy.

The study of business strategy is essential to understand the organization's vision, mission, values, strategic directions, revenue projections, growth targets, product/pricing strategies, market entry/exit strategies, customer-acquisition strategies, competitive landscape and measures for internal operational efficiencies covering people, process and technology.

The business strategy is translated into action through business plans. The strategic initiatives required to translate the vision into a reality are prioritized and detailed through a well-defined scope and structure, stakeholders, schedule and systems for management and monitoring.

The next step is to move from documentary evidence to a reality check. Interview business owners to get an overview of their function, goals, challenges, opportunities for improvement and, more importantly, their perspective on the current initiative, their requirements and expectations from IT. Capture all of this, even if this is not directly related in the current scope; it pays to have this information and offers a chance to over-deliver.

2. **CURRENT TECHNOLOGY ENVIRONMENT**

Technology environment is the platform on which IT services the business. It includes software applications, service delivery processes and supporting infrastructure.

A general picture of the business architecture would have emerged from the previous step. This step focuses on understanding how business architecture is translated into application architecture, showing the linkages between the business functions and IT applications. For each application, gather documentary evidence on application scope, business criticality, ownership (bespoke versus third party), functional coverage, technology readiness, process and procedures, expected service levels and production support history.

Interviews are conducted at a strategic level to get CIO insights on expectations from CEO/Chief Financial Officer (CFO)/Chief Operating Officer (COO), business alignment, business drivers for IT, IT budgets and spend patterns, IT goals and growth plans, IT scorecard, IT organization structure, IT leadership profiles, governance mechanisms and general IT challenges. At the operational level, interview individual application owners on current challenges, application-development plans, application maintenance support, degree of automation and standardization, service-delivery management, key performance indicators and dependencies with external agencies like regulatory bodies or vendor community.

3. CURRENT ORGANIZATION STRUCTURE

Organization structure baseline is required to understand the culture of the organization, decision-making styles, governance processes and work ethic of the employees, essentially the people dynamics.

It is preferable to first conduct interviews. In discussion with the CIO, understand the number of direct reports, distribution of business functions or IT portfolio, delineation of roles and responsibilities, span of control, scope of operations, governance mechanisms and monitoring functions like Office of CIO and Program Management Office. In confidence, also get some insights into the professional/personal profile of key stakeholders. Collectively, these inputs help classify stakeholders as influencers, decision-makers, for or against the current initiative or simply neutral and the organization's aptitude for change.

Documents to review are published organization charts - business and IT, job descriptions, skills, competencies and associated performance indicators.

The outcome this phase is the first interim deliverable, the current-state assessment report. Baseline data is assessed to arrive at high-level observations, based on which heat maps are generated. These demonstrate the health of the organization in terms of people, process and technology.

DEFINE TARGET STATE

The objective of this phase is to define the target state of all the in-scope elements on a to-be basis. The idea is to hear the customer's aspiration. A key difference from the previous phase is that here, one is expected to provide thought leadership and a reality check, having understood the current state. The executive sponsor, key business owners and technology leaders make up the target audience. Target state can be defined by: a) brainstorming in workshop mode with cross-functional teams and b) leveraging the expertise and experience of the consulting firm.

KEY ACTIVITIES OF THIS PHASE:

1. TARGET BUSINESS FUNCTIONS

This is the time to qualify strategic initiatives and quantify strategic directions. How can growth targets be achieved? What products can best deliver these results and at what price? What business functions are affected? How do we optimize the underlying business processes and build synergies? Such questions are best resolved in a cross-functional workshop, brainstorming with respective business heads and the executive sponsor to debate and decide on target definitions.

Illustrative themes for discussion include:

- Portfolio of policies, parameters for prioritization, impact on the enterprise;
- Objectives for identified improvement initiatives, measures and means to achieve targets;
- Products to launch in new markets, alliances that can help foray into new geographies;
- Operational efficiencies required in business processes, effective utilization of resources;
- Enterprise exposure to risk, management and mitigation;
- Automation of manual activities, need for an integrated and consistent service delivery;
- Adoption of non-traditional techniques of training delivery (for example, eLearning, Webinars);
- Facilitation of a culture of knowledge creation, consolidation and reuse;
- Accuracy and timeliness in reporting to internal and external stakeholders and
- Most importantly, identification of IT imperatives.

2. **Target Technology Environment**

The next round of debate is on identified IT imperatives. What is the scope of these imperatives? What is their span of control or impact? What are the business dependencies? What are the underlying technologies? Are they obsolete? What is their future-proof quotient? These questions require a healthy debate between the business and IT, chaired by the executive sponsor and moderated by the consultant. The expectation is to define the target technology platform.

Illustrative themes for discussion include:

- Linkages between IT imperatives and business imperatives;
- Contribution to new business strategies, prioritizing IT projects;
- Creating or improving strategic applications and reducing complexity;
- IT spend pattern, IT investment distribution, cost-benefit analysis and return on investment;
- Discovering and deploying innovative new technologies;
- Instituting a flexible enterprise architecture and design principles;
- Performance metrics and measures, best practices and benchmarks;

- IT infrastructure, configuration and capacity utilization, security and business continuity;
- Quality of information provided, improving decision making and
- Most importantly, leveraging technology to gain competitive advantage.

3. **TARGET ORGANIZATION STRUCTURE**

   The final dimension of target-state definition is the organization itself, in terms of structure, resources and capabilities. How should the organization be restructured to support the redefined business model, functions and/or processes? What should be the size of the resource pool? How should these resources be distributed? What skills and competencies should the resources master to service the enhanced technology platform? The target audience for brainstorming on these questions should be limited and left to the discretion of the executive sponsor. Ideally, a small forum of one or two business and IT representatives participating under the supervision of the sponsor should suffice. Some discussions may happen sans consultants because of organizational sensitivities.

   Illustrative themes for discussion include:

   - Nature of organizational structure, centralized versus de-centralized;
   - Decision-making styles, authoritative versus collaborative;
   - Matchmaking of executives to entities and span of control versus span of influence;
   - Roles and responsibilities, job descriptions and competency profiles and
   - Most importantly, organizational readiness to change.

   The outcome this phase is the second interim deliverable, the target-state definition report. Debates should yield a desired end-state that is feasible and sustainable with the buy-in of all stakeholders. Representation may vary from function to function, but at a minimum, the target state is defined in terms of the result of change, rationale for change, rewards for action and risk of inaction.

ANALYSIS AND FINDINGS

The objective of this phase is to analyze the gaps between the current state and the target state. Key business owners and technology leaders form the target audience. Analysis is carried out across business, technological and organizational dimensions, individually and collectively, leveraging suitable tools and techniques. A simple but powerful representation of the gaps is Spider Webs. Findings in one dimension are validated across dimensions to ensure that there are only positive synergies and no negative impacts. Most of the work in this phase is carried out by consultants, reaching out on a need basis to the respective stakeholders for validating the analysis and the executive sponsor to playback the findings.

KEY ACTIVITIES OF THIS PHASE:

1. **BUSINESS ANALYSIS**

    Business functions are analyzed in two stages: a) a static assessment of the business based on parameters like policy, product, price, projections and performance in terms of how they currently stack up and the degree of development required for achieving business objectives and b) finding associated IT imperatives to help the business realize target outcomes.

    In BMM terms, the core concepts that would apply to business analysis are the influencers, assessment and the ends, taken together as input and processed across business areas, functions and processes to arrive at outputs in the form of business expectations with defined business plans. This involves analyzing which influencers have an impact on the enterprise and how they can achieve the business vision.

    Similarly, in BSc terms, financial and customer perspectives would be applied to business analysis to examine revenue growth, IT investments, IT spend and markets, products and alliances. Analysis is at the perspective level and findings are the resultant linkages.

2. **TECHNOLOGY ANALYSIS**

    Technology is analyzed across multiple dimensions, depending on the scope of the engagement. Dimensions include enterprise architecture (EA), application portfolio, governance, process definitions, control mechanisms, service management, infrastructure and security. Technology analysis too is a two-stage process. The first stage is an extension of the business analysis to IT imperatives to validate established linkages.

    Findings from BMM, based on analysis of influencers, assessment and ends are now extended into means to determine the IT initiatives that can drive the business from current to target. Similarly, in BSc terms, the financial and customer perspectives are extended into internal process perspectives to determine enhancements required to architecture, applications and processes to enhance maturity, management and monitoring.

    In the second stage, dimension-specific frameworks are used to evaluate solution options and arrive at recommendations, for example, The Open Group Architecture Framework (TOGAF) for EA, MIT CISR Arrangement Matrix for governance and The Information Technology Infrastructure Library (ITIL) for process. Note: these frameworks are explained in further detail in relevant chapters.

3. **ORGANIZATION ANALYSIS**

   Organization analysis is pre-dominantly a people analysis: the profile of executives, the positions they hold and the culture of the organization as a whole. The findings from both business and technology analysis form the basis for organization analysis. Parameters considered are organization models, decision-making styles and responsibility versus accountability.

   The assessment concept of the BMM is again leveraged from a people perspective and the means and ends are revalidated. Using BSc, findings from financial, customer and operations perspectives are leveraged to analyze the business dependence on IT, business risks due to gaps in IT organizational structure and IT innovation capability. A simple representation of findings from such analysis is the Responsible, Accountable, Consult and Inform (RACI) Chart.

   The outcome of this phase is the third interim deliverable: a summary of analysis and inference, based on the findings. All findings are validated, prioritized and presented to the executive sponsor before developing recommendations. The presentation is a collection of outputs of the respective frameworks, with notes on inferences and dependencies.

RECOMMENDATIONS AND REPORT

The objective of this phase is to prioritize findings and develop recommendations. The target audience comprises the executive sponsor, key business owners and technology leaders. Each recommendation is evaluated individually to determine the importance/impact of implementation and the timing of implementation. Completion of this exercise results in the IT strategy roadmap, a logical grouping of recommendations sequenced in a time horizon, typically short-term, medium-term and long-term.

KEY ACTIVITIES OF THIS PHASE:

1. **DEVELOP BUSINESS CASE**

   A business case is a verbal or written proposal that defines a problem or opportunity, the solution, cost to implement and benefits that will be realized. It puts the investment decision into a strategic context and positions the business objectives and options that will affect both the decision and the investment itself. A business case provides the information necessary to make a decision on whether a project should proceed. It is the indispensable first activity in the life cycle of an investment.

A pre-requisite for developing an acceptable business case for any solution is an understanding of the assumptions necessary to estimate the costs and anticipate the benefits. These assumptions could be financial, business, market, commercial or organizational.

Steps to develop a business case: 1) Define cost model, 2) Define benefit assessment model, 3) Conduct Financial Analysis and 4) Conduct Sensitivity Analysis. Applicable techniques include Net Present Value, RoI, Total Cost of Ownership, Net Cash Flow and Payback Period.

The discipline of writing a business case forces us to make tacit assumptions explicit and document the reasons for pursuing a recommendation.

2. Prepare Roadmap

The roadmap provides possible ways of migrating towards the target state considering the business priorities, IT capabilities and organizational readiness to change. The roadmap is typically spread over three horizons:

- Horizon 1: Initiatives are very critical and impact current IT functioning and need to be initiated immediately in the short-term (within 6 months).
- Horizon 2: Initiatives need to be started in the medium-term (6–18 months) as they would enable early gains for the enterprise.
- Horizon 3: Initiatives are considered low priority but important for sustenance and would need to be re-examined on an ongoing basis. Timeframe for implementation is long-term (18–36 months).

The outcome this phase is the final deliverable, the IT Strategy Report. A detailed compilation of the organizational context, drivers, interim deliverables like the current-state assessment, target-state definition, analysis and findings and the business case and roadmap form this phase. The report is prepared by the consultants and submitted to the executive sponsor for sign-off.

Key Learnings

IT strategy is a statement expressed in business terms of the intended contribution of IT to the enterprise. In a generic sense, strategy is a plan, a pattern, a position, a perspective and a ploy.

Strategy can exist at three levels: Corporate, Business and Functional. IT is a function, whose strategic goal is to create value, leveraging technology infrastructure and information capital. Key elements of an IT strategy are vision, guiding principles, portfolio, services, infrastructure, governance, investments, business case and roadmap.

Scenarios that trigger an IT strategy are: internal business change, external business change, challenges of old technology and/or opportunities from new technology.

BMM developed by Business Rules Group is a widely adopted industry standard for developing strategic plans. In principle, BMM speaks about four major concepts - influencers, assessment, means and ends. The structure of BMM can be applied to an enterprise or to a function like IT. Mapping of business needs and expectations to IT capabilities, applying the concepts of BMM is one optimal way of defining an IT strategy.

IT strategy is developed based on a comprehensive and inter-connected study of business, technological and organizational dimensions of the enterprise and includes understanding drivers, assessing current-state, defining target-state, analyzing gaps, evaluating solution options and developing recommendations based on business case and an implementation roadmap that helps realize strategic objectives of IT and business.

. Ω .

CHAPTER 3

IT ARCHITECTURE CONSULTING

Architecture is foundational to any structure or system. It embodies the building blocks or business components and their relationships to each other and the environment.

In the IT world, EA provides a planning and design framework for executing IT strategy. EA is to an organization what a blueprint is to a city. Just like the roads, railways and buildings on the blueprint are the building blocks of a city, EA defines the building blocks for the business in terms of key IT elements like applications, information, technology and infrastructure.

IT Architecture Consulting, the 'A' in SAPPGIO-T of the IT Consulting Spectrum, primarily deals with EA definition and design. EA is an integration of business, application, information and technical architecture that helps IT become more agile to serve business requirements.

In addition to a broad understanding of the EA Domain, this chapter provides insights into EA Components, EA Framework and the Approach for executing an EA engagement.

ENTERPRISE ARCHITECTURE DOMAIN

Architecture is an ancient science; the Acropolis at Athens is a living example of the core architectural concepts of modularity and connectivity. An analogy from modern times are Lego blocks; each block is standard in structure, enabling easier coupling and de-coupling.

The dictionary defines architecture as the art or practice of designing and constructing buildings; the style in which a building is designed or constructed, for example, gothic architecture; or the complex structure of something like the chemical architecture of the human brain or the logical organization of a computer. EA is not defined in dictionaries but in IT/Architecture forums.

Mike Rollings of Burton Group defines EA as a planning, optimization and design discipline that is fundamentally based on dependency, implication and constraint analysis. It results in a set of artifacts that capture and communicate aspects of design.[13]

---

13   Rollings, M. (2008). *Enterprise architecture is more than engineering*. Burton Group.

MIT Centre for Information Systems Research (MIT CISR) defines EA as the organizing logic for business processes and IT infrastructure, reflecting the integration and standardization requirements of the company's operating model.

The Open Group defines 'enterprise' as any collection of organizations that have a common set of goals. The term 'enterprise' in the context of EA can be used to denote both an entire enterprise, encompassing all its information and technology services, processes and infrastructure or a specific domain within the enterprise. In both cases, the architecture crosses multiple systems and multiple functional groups within the enterprise.

EA thus provides a long-term view of a company's processes, systems and technologies so that individual projects can build capabilities and not just fulfill immediate needs. The timing of an initiative is important; understand the drivers to appreciate the imperative.

The drivers for EA are manifold. Business drivers arise when enterprises embark on business expansion, be it inorganic growth through mergers and acquisitions or organic growth through globalization or introduction of new products and services. Other business drivers are business improvement to offer superior services to customers or a change in leadership. Technically speaking, EA is mandated when enterprises are limited by legacy applications and are in need of a technology refresh or leverage of the latest technology and solutions available in the market. The external environment can also influence the need for EA; examples are regulatory compliance and industry benchmarking.

Jeanne Ross and Peter Weill of MIT CISR define EA as the organizing logic for business processes and IT infrastructure, reflecting the integration and standardization requirements of the firm's operating model. As long as a firm does not change its basic operating model, EA should guide development of business applications and infrastructure and support management efforts to identify new ways to leverage IT in the firm. In doing so, EA drives operational efficiency, customer-service responsiveness, product/service innovation and strategic agility.[14]

ENTERPRISE ARCHITECTURE PRINCIPLES

Principles are general rules and guidelines, intended to be enduring and seldom amended. Principles may be just one element in a structured set of ideas that collectively define and guide the organization, from values through principles to actions and results.

Depending on the organization, principles may be established at an enterprise level or a functional level. Enterprise principles provide a basis for decision-making

---

14 Ross, J. and Weill, P. (2002). Distinctive styles of IT architecture. *MIT CISR Briefing*, II(1A)

IT Architecture Consulting

throughout an enterprise and inform how the organization sets about fulfilling its mission. IT principles, on the other hand, provide guidance on the use and deployment of all IT resources and assets across the enterprise. They are developed to make the information environment as productive and cost-effective as possible.

Architecture principles are a subset of IT Principles that relate to architecture work. They reflect a level of consensus across the enterprise and embody the EA spirit and thinking. EA principles can be further divided into: a) principles that govern the architecture process, affecting the development/maintenance and use of EA and b) principles that govern the implementation of the architecture, establishing the first tenets and related guidance for designing and developing information systems. All principles should have an understandable, robust, complete, consistent and stable definition and a strong rationale and implication.

ILLUSTRATIVE PRINCIPLES

Leverage existing investments for economies of scale	EA enables product standardization which, in turn, drives reduction of costs on purchase, support and administration. Implementation will require a robust and scalable asset management solution.
Reduce IT complexity	EA reduces complexities of the IT environment and lowers total cost of ownership by centralizing information and eliminating redundant infrastructure components. Hardware, operating system, middleware and other platforms should be consolidated across a type of delivery architecture within an organization, to avoid complexity of environment.
Future-proof technology	EA brings the promise of reliability and on-time delivery, creating confidence in the IT organization's capability. Implementation of proven solutions decreases risk levels as underlying system architecture specifies re-use of proven industry standard solutions and infrastructure. Performance includes response time, throughput and optimal utilization of processing capacity and network bandwidth.
Manage IT as a portfolio	EA aims to avoid duplications in function and reduce redundant spending. Identify processes and procedures to ensure that portfolios are kept current with sufficient resources.

Develop applications based on standard and open architecture	EA enables support of key business requirements reliably as per agreed service levels and within business case parameters. Open architecture facilitates interoperability and reusability of components. Implement systems that are scalable and can support increasing volumes if proportional processing, storage and communication resources are made available.
Ensure integrity and availability of business data	EA helps overall availability of data by exploiting replication and redundancy solutions to support failure and unexpected scenarios. The implemented technical architecture should support 24x7 operations.
Ensure operational manageability	EA improves availability of applications through proactive monitoring and management and reduces dependency on application developers for routine operational support. Implement systems that enforce security in access of network, function and data. Security profiles should be role-based and should homogeneously address all levels of security, ideally through a single sign-on.

ENTERPRISE ARCHITECTURE COMPONENTS

Fundamental to the understanding of EA is the notion of a 'Business Component' that represents a real business concept that users can directly relate to. Business Components are of three types: a process component that implements a core business process, a data entity component or the data required for the business process and a utility component of functions useful for one or more business processes.

A business component implements a self-contained functionality, with high cohesion between services offered by the component and low coupling outside the component. Services provided by the business component are typically used by the same type of business users. Services are provided or requested through clearly defined interfaces. A business component should be amenable to replacement, to implement changed functionality that reflects changes in the business process, while keeping the component interfaces intact.

IT Architecture Consulting

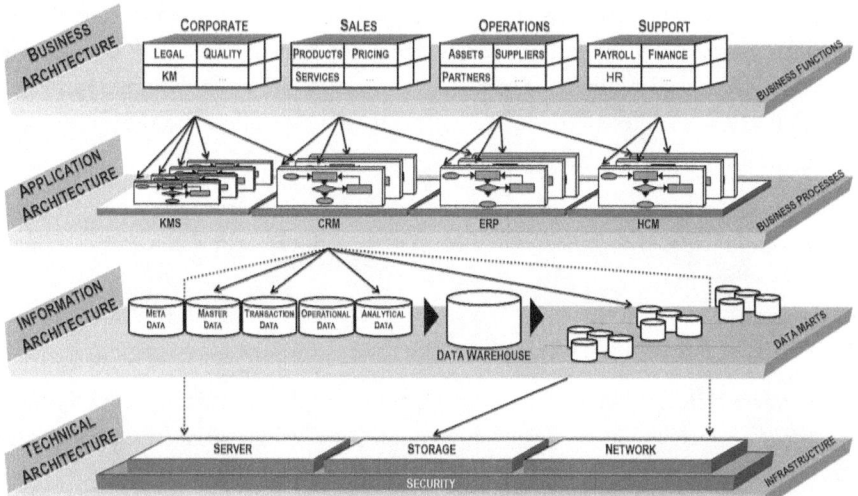

NOTE : KM – KNOWLEDGE MANAGEMENT, HR – HUMAN RESOURCES, KMS – KNOWLEDGE MANGEMENT SYSTEM, CRM – CUSTOMER RELATIONSHIP MANAGEMENT, ERP – ENTERPRISE RESOURCE PLANNING, HCM – HUMAN CAPITAL MANAGEMENT

A logical view of interactions between such business components forms the blueprint for business architecture, which, in turn, becomes the basis for application architecture, co-relating business functions to application portfolio. The underlying data that support applications, including its structure and storage, shapes information architecture. Technical architecture then is the topology of the configurations and communication protocols of all associated infrastructure elements. Individually, these architecture types are also referred to as architecture components or layers. Collectively, they form EA.

Business Architecture

Business architecture is the basis for describing and understanding a business. It represents the collective understanding of the business model, strategies, functions, current and future requirements, processes and information. Business architecture is the basis for understanding a business from an IT perspective. It describes 'how' business is done (what processes are followed now and are expected in the future), 'who' is involved and 'where' it is to be performed for key business drivers to be realized.

The architecture provides an expression of the dependencies, implications and constraints on the implementation of a future business capability as a result of that understanding. Reference models resulting from business architecture activities provide ways to describe the capability gaps inhibiting business performance and overall operational effectiveness.

The starting point for developing comprehensive business architecture should always be a clear understanding of the company's main source of competitive advantage. Other constituents of business architecture are essentially the output of the organization, manifested in the products and services it offers and the processes in the organization that realize this output.

Business Architecture is dynamic in nature. A variety of internal and external factors would impact business architecture at various points in time, causing continuous iterations.

APPLICATION ARCHITECTURE

Historically, enterprises were focused on delivering applications for specific business requirements. Each application, generally bundled the business process support along with the information required to enable that process, tightly.

Application architecture is derived from business architecture. As in the case of business architecture, application components are identified from business processes, encapsulating functionality that is related, logical and manifested in software. Note: one software application may comprise more than one application component.

Application architecture components are used in two ways: 1) To clearly define an enterprise-level framework of application functions, packages and solutions that will ensure the desired processes, information events and business structure previously defined are implemented effectively and 2) To tie the content of the application architecture back, initially to previously defined business architecture and finally, to desired business strategy, directions and capabilities. This dual usage ensures both forward integration and backward traceability.

The chosen set of one or more reference architecture will provide known, proven combinations of application architecture components to improve the productivity of future design activities.

INFORMATION ARCHITECTURE

An information strategy provides a holistic approach to managing information that is a) Important to an organization's business, b) Best supports its business goals and strategies, and c) Improves its confidence in information when making business decisions.

Information architecture builds on the structured design of information that serves as the means to describe, discover, access and exchange information for fixed or recurring transactional contexts and for workflows among the parties involved. The architecture presents a holistic view of information flows in an organization including the effects of related business processes.

Although information architecture efforts historically focused on structured data like databases and file systems, the scope should also include unstructured content such as documents and rich media. Information architecture must address content convergence to solve issues of information glut, especially on enterprise-wide initiatives such as compliance and relationship management.

TECHNICAL ARCHITECTURE

Technical architecture represents an independent framework to facilitate business operations across delivery channels, separation of business processes associated with data capture, processing, storage, retrieval and implementation of technical components that help leverage technology for business advantage.

Technical architecture comprises software and hardware capabilities required to support the deployment of business, application and information architecture. Capabilities include IT infrastructure, middleware, networks, communication, processing and standards.

Technical architecture is built on four layers. The presentation layer manages information presentation through different channels. Business logic layer consists of technical components that fulfill major business processes, functions, workflows and rules engines. Data layer looks at data storage and operational data-management requirements of the enterprise. Lastly, the platform layer describes the operating environment required for technical components to run.

ENTERPRISE ARCHITECTURE FRAMEWORK

TOGAF is an architecture framework, a tool to aid the acceptance, production, use and maintenance of architecture. It is based on an iterative process model supported by best practices and a reusable set of existing architectural assets.[15]

TOGAF is developed and maintained by The Open Group, a vendor-neutral and technology-neutral consortium. The Open Group works with customers, suppliers, consortia and other standards bodies. Its role is to capture, understand and address current and emerging requirements, establish policies and share best practices; to facilitate interoperability, develop consensus and evolve and integrate specifications and open-source technologies; to offer comprehensive services to enhance the operational efficiency of consortia; and to operate the industry's premier certification service.

The following is an adaptation from TOGAF Version 9 (Published by The Open Group, January 2009) with specific emphasis on Architecture Development Method (ADM).[16]

---

15 TOGAF® is a registered trademark of The Open Group.
16 ADM© is a copyright of The Open Group.

ARCHITECTURE DEVELOPMENT METHOD

The ADM, a result of contributions from many architects, forms the core of TOGAF. It is a method for deriving organization-specific EA and is specifically designed to address business requirements. The ADM describes: 1) a reliable, proven way of developing and using EA; 2) a method for developing architecture on different levels (business, application, data and technology) that enables the architect to ensure that a complex set of requirements are adequately addressed and 3) guidelines on tools for architecture development.

The ADM provides guidance for architects on numerous levels. It provides a number of architecture development phases (Business Architecture, Information Architecture, Technology Architecture) in a cycle, as an overall process template for architecture development. It provides a narrative for each phase, describing objectives, approach, inputs, steps, outputs and cross-phase summaries that cover requirement-management.

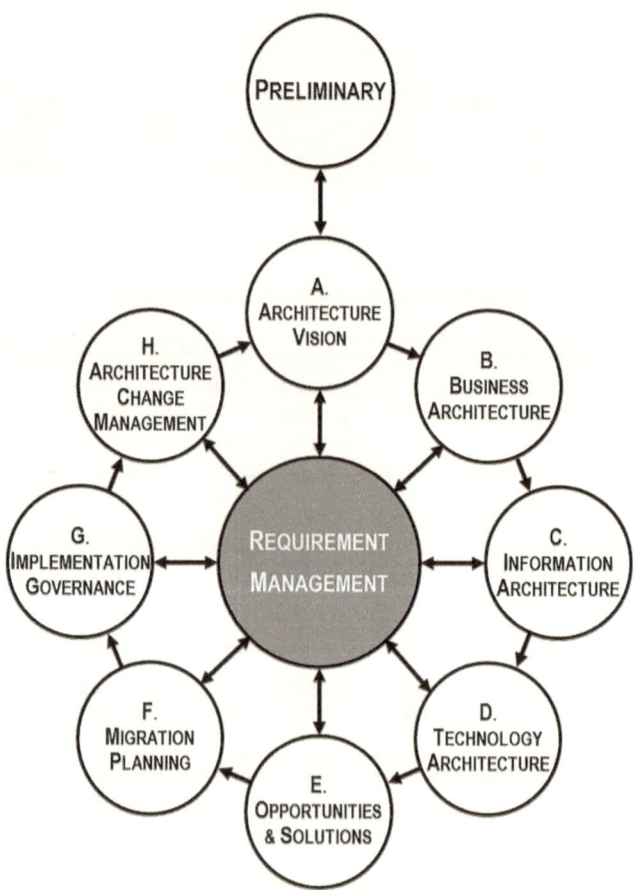

The ADM supports the concept of iteration at three levels:

Cycling around the ADM: The ADM is presented in a circular manner indicating that completion of one phase of architecture work directly feeds into subsequent phases.

Iterating between phases: TOGAF describes the concept of iterating across phases (for example, returning to Business Architecture on completion of Technology Architecture).

Cycling around a single phase: TOGAF supports repeated execution of the activities within a single ADM phase as a technique for elaborating architectural content.

The ADM is applied iteratively throughout the entire process, between phases and within them. Throughout the ADM cycle, results should be frequently validated against original requirements, both for the whole ADM cycle and for the particular phase. Such validation should reconsider scope, detail, schedules and milestones. Each phase should consider assets produced from previous iterations of the process and external assets from the marketplace, such as other frameworks or models.

An overview of each of the ADM phases is outlined below:

1. **PRELIMINARY PHASE**

    The preliminary phase prepares an organization to undertake successful EA projects. Its objective is to identify and scope the elements of the enterprise organizations affected and define the constraints/assumptions and the organization's architecture footprint, that is, the people responsible for performing the architecture work, where they are located and their responsibilities.

    Inputs for this phase are the organization's business goals, business drivers, IT strategy, organizational model for EA and other architecture-related artifacts. Key activities include scoping the enterprise organizations affected and establishing the EA team and organization. The output is a tailored architecture framework including architecture principles and request for architecture work.

2. **PHASE A: ARCHITECTURE VISION**

    Architecture vision is about project establishment. It is necessary to validate the business context and to create the approved 'Statement of Architecture Work'. The objective of this phase is to define and organize an architecture development cycle and articulate an architecture vision and value proposition to respond to requirements and constraints.

    The tailored architecture framework and all existing architecture documentation serve as inputs to the architecture vision. Key activities include identifying stakeholders' concerns and requirements and assessing the organization's readiness for business transformation based on which the architecture statement of work and plans are developed. The output is architecture vision documents that cover high-level stakeholder requirements, baseline view and target vision of the architecture domains.

3. **PHASE B: BUSINESS ARCHITECTURE**

    The business architecture phase describes the baseline business architecture and designs the target business architecture required to realize the agreed architecture vision. The objective of this phase is to select architecture viewpoints to demonstrate how stakeholder concerns are addressed in the business architecture and to select tools and techniques to validate these viewpoints.

    The primary input for business architecture is the agreed architecture vision and associated principles. Key activities include selecting the right reference models, developing baseline business architecture, designing target business architecture and evaluating architecture options based on gap analysis. The outputs from this phase are the architecture definition document, architecture requirements specifications and architecture roadmap document populated with the business architecture components.

4. **PHASE C: INFORMATION ARCHITECTURE**

    Information architecture is about documenting the fundamental organization of IT systems, embodied in the major types of information and the application systems that process them. It represents both data architecture and information architecture. The objective of this phase is to define the types and sources of data needed and the kind of application systems necessary to process the data and support the business.

    The primary input for information architecture is the agreed architecture vision and business architecture along with associated data and application principles. Key activities include selecting the right reference models, developing baseline information architecture, designing target information architecture and evaluating architecture options based on gap analysis. The output from this phase is the updated architecture definition document, architecture requirements specifications and architecture roadmap document populated with the information architecture components.

5. **PHASE D: TECHNOLOGY ARCHITECTURE**

    Technology architecture is about documenting the fundamental organization of IT systems, embodied in the hardware, software and communication technology. The objective of this phase is to develop a target technology architecture that will form the basis of the subsequent implementation and migration planning.

The primary input for technical architecture is the agreed architecture vision, business architecture and information architecture. Key activities include selecting the right reference models, developing baseline technology architecture, designing target technology architecture and evaluating architecture options based on gap analysis. The output from this phase is the updated architecture definition document, architecture requirements specifications and architecture roadmap document populated with the technology architecture components.

6. **PHASE E: OPPORTUNITIES AND SOLUTIONS**

    This phase describes the process of identifying delivery vehicles (projects, programs or portfolios) that deliver the target architecture identified in previous phases. The objective of the phase is to review the target business objectives and capabilities, consolidate the architecture gaps and to generate and gain consensus on an outline implementation and migration strategy.

    The primary inputs for identifying opportunities and solutions are the architecture vision, architecture repository (business, data, application and technology architecture documents) and change requests for existing programs and projects. Key activities include determining business constraints for implementation, consolidating interoperability requirements, validating dependencies and identifying transition architecture. The output from this phase is a high-level implementation and migration plan.

7. **PHASE F: MIGRATION PLANNING**

    Migration planning addresses how to move from the baseline to the target architecture by finalizing a detailed implementation and migration plan. The objective of this phase is to ensure that the implementation and migration plan is coordinated with the various management frameworks in use within the enterprise and to confirm the transition architecture defined in the opportunities and solutions phase.

    The primary input for migration planning is the strategic migration plan and impact analysis of various projects. Key activities include confirming management framework interactions for the implementation and migration plan, assigning a business value to each project and prioritizing migration projects based on cost/benefit assessment and risk validation. The output from this phase is a detailed implementation and migration plan and re-usable architecture building blocks.

8. **PHASE G: IMPLEMENTATION GOVERNANCE**

    Implementation governance defines how the architecture constrains implementation projects, monitors it while building it and produces a signed architecture contract. The objective of this phase is to govern and manage an architecture contract covering the overall implementation and deployment process and to ensure that the program of solutions is deployed successfully, as a planned program of work.

The primary inputs for implementation governance are the architecture roadmap, transition architecture, governance model and migration plan documents. Key activities are performing enterprise architecture compliance reviews, implementing business and IT operations and conducting post-implementation reviews. The outputs from this phase are compliance assessments, deployment of architecture-compliant solutions and recommendations on architecture compliance, service delivery and performance metrics.

9. Phase H: Architecture Change Management

Architecture change management ensures that the baseline architecture remains fit-for-purpose. The objective of this phase is to ensure that changes to the architecture are managed in a controlled manner and to establish an architecture change-management process for the new EA baseline that is achieved post-implementation.

The primary inputs for architecture change management are change requests due to business and technology changes and change requests from lessons learnt. Key activities include establishing value-realization process, analyzing architecture change management and developing change requirements to meet performance targets. The outputs from this phase are the changes to architecture framework and principles.

10. Requirement Management

This is a dynamic process applicable to all phases and addresses the identification of requirements for the enterprise. The ability to deal with changes in requirements is crucial to the ADM process, since architecture, by nature, deals with uncertainty and change, bridging the divide between the aspirations of stakeholders and a practical solution. The objective of this phase is to provide a process to manage architecture requirements throughout the phases of the ADM cycle and to identify requirements for the enterprise, store them and feed them in and out of the relevant ADM phases, which dispose of, address and prioritize requirements.

The inputs for the requirement management process are first, the high-level requirements produced as part of the architecture vision and then, the detailed requirements generated from each architecture domain. Key activities include identifying changed requirements, re-assessing priorities, resolving conflicts, generating requirements impact statements and updating the requirements repository. The outputs from this phase are the changed requirements and requirements impact assessment.

ENTERPRISE ARCHITECTURE APPROACH

The execution model of an IT architecture engagement would broadly traverse the following phases: Understand Context, Assess Current State, Define Target State, Analysis and Findings and Recommendations and Roadmap, touching upon each of the architecture components in every phase.

UNDERSTAND CONTEXT

The objective of this phase is to understand the context in terms of drivers, business, technology, stakeholders, scope and outcomes. The target audience is the engagement sponsor and/or the engagement coordinator.

KEY ACTIVITIES OF THIS PHASE:

1. **UNDERSTAND DRIVERS**

   EA engagements are triggered when there is strategic change in the business direction or when technology or innovation can be leveraged for better operational efficiency. In such situations, organizations see a potential need for improvisations on one or more of the architecture layers.

   Drivers that necessitate enhancements to the business architecture component are increasing enterprise system reliability, availability and scalability or establishing easier communications with external partners. Better integration across applications drives application architecture. For information architecture, the driver would be enabling better management of data. For reduction in redundancy of infrastructure services provided by different IT groups or heterogeneity of infrastructure components across lines of business, technical architecture needs to be revisited.

   On the other hand, if the mandate is to design architecture governance principles or compliance mechanisms or to deploy an efficient operating model, the impact would be across all architecture components, leading to redefinition of EA as a whole.

2. **UNDERSTAND BUSINESS**

   The architecture context need not be purely technical; understanding the need from a business perspective is equally important for defining EA. The key question to ask is: what is the business motivation to redesign EA - is it to aid higher levels of customer support or enable more effective cross-selling or establish a well-defined architecture process?

Business architecture is the starting point for EA. Responses to the above question will provide clarity on the business' expectations from IT and implications of the business architecture on application portfolio and technology platform.

3. **UNDERSTAND TECHNOLOGY**

    Once the business architecture is established, the focus then shifts to understanding technology to define the subsequent EA layers. In designing the application architecture, the need is to understand the complexity of application portfolio, correlating applications to the business functions they support. For information architecture, the need is to ensure integration of information and data, reducing redundancy. In case of infrastructure architecture, the emphasis is on the IT environment and the degree to which it is future-proof. Collectively, the objective is to improve the overall framework for IT management.

4. **UNDERSTAND STAKEHOLDERS**

    A sustainable architecture requires a coordinating structure for the development, deployment and governance of EA. The structure is multi-layered; the architecture review board is the apex body controlling all policy decisions supported by multi-disciplinary architects for each architecture component and a compliance team. Understand the communication protocols internally within IT and externally with business and vendors. Governance mechanisms should also ensure neutrality of the architecture teams. EA as a whole is accountable to the executive management.

5. **UNDERSTAND SCOPE AND OUTCOMES**

    The expected EA outcome is based on the business or technology need that is being assessed, the nature of impact on the architecture components, robustness of the reference architecture against which the gaps are analyzed and the quantum of correction required. Optionally, architecture governance, standards and compliance may be included.

The outcome of this phase is a re-confirmed architecture scope, architecture components to focus on and the agreed depth of coverage.

ASSESS CURRENT STATE

The objective of this phase is to baseline the architecture components and their inherent challenges and dependencies. The target audience is made up of the

IT Architecture Consulting

engagement coordinator, business leaders, application owners and chief architect of the IT organization.

KEY ACTIVITIES OF THIS PHASE:

1. **CURRENT BUSINESS ARCHITECTURE**

    While baselining existing business architecture, first identify the business components in the enterprise to localize the impact due to changes in the business environment and assist with decisions relating to the reuse of business components across units that have similar business processes.

    Once business components are identified, the next step is to group them into virtual layers based on operation domains to get a complete picture of the business architecture. This also enables a focus on business changes from an IT perspective.

    - Management and Control: Components that enable both management and control of the business (examples are risk management and finance)
    - Business Operations: Components that handle core business functions (examples are savings accounts in banks and merchandizing in retail)
    - Enabling Services: Components that have shared or common functionality, examples are Human Resources (HR), Quality Assurance and Knowledge Management.

2. **CURRENT APPLICATION ARCHITECTURE**

    Application architecture flows from the business processes identified in the business architecture phase. The current application architecture helps in a) understanding the relationship among applications and between applications and external agencies and b) defining the framework of information and technology architecture components that need to be implemented to support the identified application functions.

    Map the applications to the business components they support in a structure similar to the business architecture and document the characteristics in terms of business criticality, functional fit and flexibility to adapt to business change, platform diversity, future readiness, vendor interface, developmental plans, maintenance history and open issues.

3. **CURRENT INFORMATION ARCHITECTURE**

    Information architecture is a discipline for organizing and classifying information across enterprise, organization and application boundaries, so that the business can use it effectively. To do this, the architecture should demonstrate an adaptable infrastructure - designed to facilitate access - definition, management, security and integrity of data across the enterprise.

Map the information to the application components that support the business, in a structure similar to the application architecture, highlighting the directions of data flow and attributes of data shared between applications. Capture metadata attributes like format, semantics, structure, access, redundancy, accuracy and management of data.

4. **CURRENT TECHNICAL ARCHITECTURE**

The logical application architecture will be used as a framework for building infrastructure architecture. The architecture is a combination of system services, enabling functions provided by the operating systems, platform services, logical computer processing elements needed to support the execution of business application and network communication services and components that provide connectivity between computing environments.

Map the infrastructure to the application and information components required to support the business. Collect configuration details of servers and storage, network topologies, communication protocols and surround factors that influence IT infrastructure. It is equally important to understand existing systems management processes. Infrastructure utilization is measured in terms of availability, reliability, performance and infrastructure security measures like access, authentication, encryption and audit.

The outcome of this phase is an as-is business, application, information and technical architecture and observations based on an initial assessment of the existing architecture.

DEFINE TARGET STATE

The objective of this phase is to envision the target state of the architecture components individually and their integration to form EA collectively. Target audience is the engagement sponsor, business leaders, application owners and the chief architect of the IT organization.

KEY ACTIVITIES OF THIS PHASE:

1. **TARGET BUSINESS ARCHITECTURE**

   The business architecture needs to answer the following questions: How does the organization plan to accomplish its mission? What is the model for communicating the business to various stakeholders across the enterprise?

In defining the business architecture, revisit the business vision, objectives and strategies, the IT vision. Study existing architecture blueprints in conjunction with new and emerging technologies. Prioritize the strategic direction of the enterprise: is it cost reduction, operational efficiency or economies of scale to enhance profit realization. Accordingly, brainstorm on what resources must be shared and how, roles and responsibilities for these resources and required skills, cost-allocation mechanisms and corresponding compensation needs, centralized support for shared services and associated service-level agreements. The key is to accomplish this task through joint planning with all stakeholders for a collective buy-in and sustainability. Getting the business architecture right is extremely critical as the rest of the architecture components are derived from these first principles.

2. **TARGET APPLICATION ARCHITECTURE**

The application architecture needs to answer the following questions: To what extent are the application components aligned with the business components? What is the quality of services being provided to the business?

In defining the application architecture, the target business processes - as defined in the business architecture phase - are logically grouped into application components. However, certain components identified may not directly map to business processes. A typical example is the intranet portal itself. While there is no explicit business process associated with the intranet portal, it is a separate application component. Accordingly, brainstorm on the functional coverage of the current applications and their fit with new application components and potential synergies of re-development or re-alignment. Ensure participation from both business and IT in these sessions.

3. **TARGET INFORMATION ARCHITECTURE**

Information architecture needs to answer the following questions: What data components are required by the application components? How is the data to be structured? What is the level of integration required for optimal usage of information?

In defining the information architecture, revisit related principles that define guidelines for the use and deployment of all information resources and assets across the enterprise. Additionally, brainstorm and arrive at a consensus on the various information elements that would form the basis for making future IT decisions. These must be expressed in language that the business understands and uses. The key is to develop information blueprints necessary to maximize the value, use and security of information assets.

4. **TARGET TECHNICAL ARCHITECTURE**

   Technical architecture needs to answer the following questions: What infrastructure components are required by the application/information components? What is the required configuration for operational efficiency? How is the quality of service to be defined?

   In defining the technical architecture, focus on data centers, domain platforms, delivery channels, security gateways/firewalls and systems management. Additionally, brainstorm on centralized versus de-centralized infrastructure and what is best suited for each. The key is to make available a resilient and reliable infrastructure with minimal redundancy.

   The outcome of this phase is the to-be business, application, information and technical architecture that is aligned with strategic objectives of the enterprise, addressing both business and technology drivers.

ANALYSIS AND FINDINGS

The objective of this phase is to analyze the gaps between the as-is and to-be states of each of the architecture components and to identify strategies to bridge these gaps to design the desired EA. Target audience includes business leaders, application owners and the chief architect of the IT organization.

KEY ACTIVITIES OF THIS PHASE:

1. **BUSINESS ARCHITECTURE ANALYSIS**

   In analyzing the findings of business architecture gaps, focus on the following five dimensions of the business process:
   - What: activities required to accomplish the business process, frequency of usage, current level of maturity and changes required to support the enhanced business process
   - Who: participants required to accomplish the above activities who could be primary or secondary
   - Where: location of activities - client-site, near-site, off-site or offshore
   - When: timing of the activities and interval for the complete business process, including idle times between activities, if any
   - Which: data, including metadata of information requested for and displayed on the various presentation layers.

   Once the above activities are completed, the process flow can be developed, that is, the how dimension. This provides the sequence of activities performed, establishes the decisions that control branches in the process, specifies which stakeholder performs each element, indicates information that is used, where the work is done and when it is performed.

2. **APPLICATION ARCHITECTURE ANALYSIS**

   In analyzing the findings of the application architecture gaps, focus is primarily on the business/technology linkages and, to a lesser extent, on the linkages to relevant stakeholders.

   - In a simple 2x2 matrix format, analyze relationships between business components and business processes, business components and application components, business processes and application processes, business processes and stakeholders, and stakeholders and capabilities.
   - Analyze the strategic and operational characteristics of the IT organization. How does IT react to market changes? What is its competitive advantage? How are investments and new initiatives prioritized? What are the key performance indicators? How is business performance monitored?
   - Analyze availability and associated skills of required stakeholders. Have the roles of business architect, application architect, information architect and technical architect been identified and assigned to individuals with sufficient experience? Are they aware of their responsibilities in the primary architecture space? Do they have an understanding of other architecture components?

   The above activities are only a pre-requisite of a refresher of the organization's business, technology and people perspectives. With this understanding, study the new business architecture to develop the new application architecture.

3. **INFORMATION ARCHITECTURE ANALYSIS**

   In analyzing the findings of information architecture gaps, focus is on structure and semantics, storage and retrieval of information, with emphasis on data integrity.

   - Analyze the complexity and criticality of information to the business. What is the quantum of data required in real-time? What is the quality of data provided?
   - Analyze the nature and frequency of business intelligence requested by business and accordingly determine the need for data warehousing, define data marts and establish protocols for master data and metadata management.
   - Analyze the importance of data quality and criteria for data privacy, enforced either by internal rule engines or external regulatory bodies. This helps in specifications for data masking.

The goal of information architecture is to have the right information in the right place and accessed by the right person. Develop information architecture based on this principle and aligned with both the business and application architecture.

4. **TECHNICAL ARCHITECTURE ANALYSIS**

    In analyzing the findings of technical architecture gaps, focus on configuration and control mechanisms of the infrastructure components.
    - Analyze data center capabilities and applications, domain platforms for sites/networking/delivery channels, systems management and security policies.
    - Analyze the suitability of centralized or decentralized infrastructure for data centers and sites.
    - Analyze environments available for application development, testing and production.
    - Analyze security policies for business-to-business transactions and business-to-customer transactions.

    Infrastructure architecture, though the last architecture component, is like the last mile, critical to the quality of service. It should be aligned with all three architecture components and be flexible, available, reliable and scalable.

    The outcome of this phase is a set of findings, based on an integrated analysis of the gaps in the architecture components that can help shape architecture recommendations for the enterprise.

RECOMMENDATIONS AND REPORT

The objective of this phase is to synthesize the solution options and recommend strategic directions that are mutually exclusive to the specific architecture component and collectively exhaustive for EA definition. The target audience is the engagement sponsor, business leaders, application owners and the chief architect of the IT organization.

KEY ACTIVITIES OF THIS PHASE:

1. **DESIGN ARCHITECTURE BLUEPRINT**

    Architecture blueprint is a sequence of architecture diagrams starting with business architecture, linking to application architecture, which, in turn, links to information architecture, which is finally linked to technical architecture, all adhering to architecture principles and standards. The success of the blueprint lies in the strengths of the linkages.

The blueprint includes recommendations to bridge gaps, solution options with advantages and disadvantages for each, plans for realization and notes demonstrating forward integration and background traceability. Architecture governance, explained in detail in the following section, is equally important.

2. **DEFINE ARCHITECTURE GOVERNANCE**

The architecture governance model consists of structures and processes that enable an organization to optimally manage its investments in technology from all aspects, including enterprise IT architecture and technology vendor management, to assess emerging technologies and identify and groom technical competencies.

Architecture governance is the practice by which EA is managed and controlled at an enterprise-wide level. It includes the following:

- Implementing a system of controls over creating and monitoring all architectural components and activities to ensure the effective introduction, implementation and evolution of architecture within the organization;
- Establishing processes that support effective management of the model within agreed parameters;
- Developing practices that ensure accountability to a clearly identified stakeholder community, both inside and outside the organization;
- Using release management and user test of architecture standards;
- Establishing and using a formal reference architecture, architectural methodology and design patterns;
- Integrating standards conformance with project management methodology; and
- Helping to ensure that transition initiatives currently underway are the right ones to support the organization's new business strategy.

Establish formal charters for governance bodies, detailing roles, responsibilities, authority and linkages within the governance structure. Reassess the structure of these bodies to ensure adequate representation from business and IT. Establish communication protocols to institutionalize governance structure across the business units and IT organizations.

Structurally, at the executive level, is the IT Steering Committee. It provides strategy and planning inputs to architecture vision, validates and supports results of architecture process/outputs and resolves internal IT conflicts and trade-offs with the business.

Reporting into the steering committee is the Architecture Review Board. It is responsible for establishing the architecture charter, reviewing/validating architecture work products, socializing the architecture process and governing compliance.

Reporting into the architecture review board is the Chief Architect and a team of Enterprise Architects. They are responsible for realizing the EA vision. Enterprise architects are SMEs in at least one of the architecture components, with exposure to the others.

Reporting to the chief architect is a team of business architects, application architects, information architects and technical architects, who create conceptual architecture layers and oversee the architecture development process.

The golden rule for EA governance is to avoid the 'ivory tower' mentality in architecture teams and to motivate business and IT to adopt architecture governance as an integral part of their work discipline.

The outcome this phase is the final deliverable, the EA Report, which is a compilation of observations from current-state assessment, expectations from target state and findings from gap analysis, including the architecture blueprint and governance. The report is prepared by the consultants and submitted to the executive sponsor for sign-off.

Key Learnings

EA is the bridge between strategy and planning. Its primary purpose is to optimize across the enterprise the often-fragmented legacy of processes (both manual and automated) into an integrated environment that is responsive to change and supportive of the delivery of the business strategy.

Scenarios that trigger the need for EA are business expansion, legacy modernization, leveraging new technologies, operational efficiency, cost reduction and/or avoidance, reducing redundancy, improving time-to-market, industry benchmarking or regulatory compliance.

The components of EA are business architecture (provides an understanding of the business as a collection of business components catering to specific business processes), application architecture (alignment of the application portfolio with the business architecture), information architecture (metadata of the information required by the application components) and technical architecture (underlying infrastructure to support the business operations), collectively governed by a set of principles that are understandable, robust, complete, consistent and stable.

TOGAF, developed by The Open Group, is a vendor-neutral and technology-neutral consortium. It is a tool to aid the acceptance, production, use and maintenance of architecture. It is based on an iterative process model supported by best practices and a reusable set of existing architectural assets.

The architecture development method advocated by TOGAF is a 10-step cycle and supports the concept of iteration at three levels. The first iteration includes only the preliminary phase, leading to the second iteration that starts with architecture vision and moves onto business architecture, information architecture, technology architecture, opportunities and solutions, migration planning, implementation governance and architecture change management. The third iteration includes only requirement management and is positioned at the core of the second tier, a dynamic process that is applicable to all the phases of the second iteration.

Therefore, EA is a force-multiplier for organizations to achieve business strategy. A well-defined EA demonstrates consistency in business processes, supported by aligned applications that make available reliable and secure information over an efficient infrastructure network. Supplement this success mantra with a sound architecture governance model to make EA sustainable for longer.

. Ω .

Chapter 4

IT Portfolio Management

Portfolio Management is an essential discipline for any IT organization. It involves helping IT get the most out of its budgets, sensitizing business constituents to the prioritization challenges that must be surmounted to ensure that the right projects are implemented and achieving satisfactory alignment between technology spending, effort and business goals.

The challenge facing IT departments is how best to manage their application portfolio while still achieving business effectiveness and minimizing cost. Often when organizations have a complex, aging environment with multiple siloes of applications, the result is high maintenance costs. Typical problems include redundant applications, complex infrastructure and numerous point-to-point application interfaces. In today's environment, funds available for strategic IT investments are limited, since a large proportion of the budget is dedicated to maintenance and support of legacy applications. The result is inflexible systems, prolonged implementation timeframes and a frustrated business community.

IT Portfolio Management, the first 'P' in SAPPGIO-T of the IT Consulting Spectrum, primarily deals with alignment of the application portfolio to support the business, measured in terms of functional fit and future-proof technical maturity, collectively enabled through right distribution of IT investments for optimal returns.

In addition to a broad understanding of the IT Portfolio Management Space, this chapter provides insights into Portfolio Management Segments, Portfolio Management Framework[s] and Approach for executing a Portfolio Management engagement.

Portfolio Management Space

IT Portfolio is a collection of projects with common goals. Portfolio Management, therefore, refers to the processes, practices and specific activities for continuous and consistent evaluation, prioritization, budgeting and finally selection of investments that provide the greatest value and contribute to the strategic interest of the organization.

In terms of a definition, Portfolio Management can be seen as 1) A Process and a framework to plan, create, assess, balance and communicate the execution of the IT portfolio; 2) Tools that analyze information and data like value, costs, risks, benefits, architecture, requirements and alignment with strategic and business objectives; and 3) Common business taxonomy and governance that defines policies, principles, guidelines and accountability.

In *IT Portfolio Management Step-by-Step*, authors Bryan Maizlish and Robert Handler refer to IT Portfolio Management as a combination of people, process and corresponding information and technology that senses and responds to change by communicating effectively, creating and cataloging a detailed value-based risk assessment, eliminating redundancies, scheduling resources optimally and monitoring/managing project plans from deployment to post-implementation including disposal.[17]

PORTFOLIO MANAGEMENT TENETS

Tenets are guiding principles that drive the definition to action.

1. **CROSS-PERSPECTIVE INFORMATION COLLECTION**

   The viability of any investment must be assessed from all perspectives by speaking to a variety of stakeholders; they bring in different insights based on their area of expertise. Accurately capturing and synthesizing these insights, analyzing them independently and inter-dependently and converting them into a decision-support system is a key focus area for portfolio management.

2. **IDENTIFICATION OF IMPROVEMENT OPPORTUNITIES**

   Opportunities for business improvement exist at all levels of the organization, from management teams to functional departments, and even to the level of project teams/individuals. Recognition of such opportunities is a key focus area for portfolio management. To promote a culture of continuous improvement, portfolio management establishes a process that evaluates financial, operational, quality and risk aspects to proactively identify and qualify such opportunities across the organization.

3. **ELIMINATION OF REDUNDANCIES**

   Redundancies cost money, engage resources and impede growth. Therefore, eliminating redundancies becomes a key priority for portfolio management. As a precursor, redundancies are identified by comparatively assessing all current and future technology initiatives, investments, dependencies and associated risks. Post-identification, decisions on pre-empting or delaying or merging investments

---

17 Maizlish, B. and Handler, R. (2005). *IT portfolio management step by step*. John Wiley & Sons.

become clear, which, in itself, can be a phenomenal cost-saving opportunity. Portfolio management transcends identification and elimination to deploying measures to ensure that such redundancies do not recur.

4. **FLEXIBILITY TO ADAPT TO CHANGING BUSINESS ENVIRONMENT**

   Often, even the best-laid business plans are revisited because of external influences like market regulations and industry trends, forcing organizations to re-prioritize business goals, cost estimates and resource distribution. Portfolio management should, therefore, have adequate in-built mechanisms to proactively respond to such changes.

5. **INSTITUTIONALIZATION OF CONTINUOUS IMPROVEMENT**

   Over time, organizations learn the predictive accuracy of various metrics deployed to measure the effectiveness of portfolio management process. These metrics must be evaluated progressively against actual outcomes in order to fine-tune the decision-making process. New metrics must be considered to avoid overstating or understating costs and benefits. In addition, portfolio management process should be constantly evaluated to address inefficiencies and deliver better results with certainty.

PORTFOLIO MANAGEMENT SEGMENTS

The management of an IT portfolio involves simplification of business processes, rationalization of applications, consolidation and/or virtualization of infrastructure and management of IT investments. The first three segments are related and managed through rationalization of the IT portfolio. The fourth segment focusses on reallocating funding to support priority initiatives, allowing organizations to balance appropriate levels of IT portfolio risk.

BUSINESS PROCESS SIMPLIFICATION

Business applications are a set of software components that are visible to and recognizable by the business; they address a business need by implementing or enabling a business function.

To simplify business processes, firstly understand what the business requires in terms of computing capability to enable it to function. Establish a clear link between applications and the business capabilities they support. Use standard classification of business processes to effectively tag applications in the portfolio by the business capabilities they enable. Explicitly articulate the trade-off between standardization and customization - highlight the actual costs of deviation from standards to weigh the benefits of standardization against the uniqueness of business demands. Establish rigor around alignment conversations with business partners - map applications to business processes to facilitate productive discussion around alignment of application investments with business goals.

Business process changes are expected to have the greatest impact on total cost of ownership and maintenance spend reduction.

Application Rationalization

Rationalization needs to be considered across the entire enterprise, using a holistic approach because a change in processes or architecture in one place can impact other parts of the business.

Application rationalization involves consolidating and terminating various applications, servers and databases. It also considers integrating various business processes and products that are duplicated or unutilized on account of change in demand. Application rationalization provides a framework for fact-based decision-making on application life cycle: which applications to maintain, which to invest in, which to replace and which to retire.

Application rationalization is about actively managing assets as a business function, to analyze current structure and characteristics of enterprise portfolio and provide recommendations across dimensions of function, technology and physical consolidation.

Infrastructure Consolidation

Infrastructure consolidation is the optimization of the infrastructure components on which the applications that support the business run.

Infrastructure includes all hardware components like servers, databases, desktops and laptops, networks and communications. To optimize infrastructure, it is imperative to have a fair understanding of the component's configuration, existing and required numbers, warranty, annual maintenance support and most importantly, the degree of usage of each component, to facilitate efficient use of current assets and plan for future consumption. Advances in technology should also be leveraged to reduce cost, increase availability and improve performance.

Investment Management

Investment management is a maturing process to evaluate, recommend and implement investments across the organization.

IT investments are broadly classified into 'Run the Business' and 'Change the Business'. The former pertains to operational and transactional costs, while the latter refers to strategic costs and investments in innovation. A clear understanding of the initial distribution and ongoing performance of the same is critical to effective portfolio management; it provides the ability to redistribute for better returns.

Portfolio Optimization

Portfolio optimization is aligning business, applications, technology, infrastructure and associated investments.

Businesses struggle to keep up with technology changes due to a complex and convoluted application landscape, caused by rapid changes in technology improved inter-operability, flexibility and lower cost of ownership. Portfolio optimization identifies synergies from individual segments to help businesses derive greater value from investments, by making the application landscape future-proof. It builds business capability with a long-term view of business and defines architecture standards to cater to future demand. Alignment with these standards can significantly reduce application and infrastructure costs.

Portfolio Management Frameworks

Portfolio Analysis Framework

Given the absence of a recognized and acknowledged industry framework, most organizations build their own in-house framework for portfolio analysis, leveraging individual experiences. The framework presented here is based on a synthesis of best practices from the industry and insights from research bodies.

Illustrative Parameters for Rationalization

Strategic alignment captures how well the application is aligned with the organization's strategy and objectives, measured in terms of business strategy alignment, IT strategy alignment and EA alignment.

Business value captures how well the application supports the current and future business and its users in their regular activity and how the business values these applications. It measures the functional quality of an application in terms of business criticality, level of integration with business process, usage profile, breadth of use, business-owner satisfaction and end-user satisfaction.

Technical value captures the application's technical quality, measured by its agility, scalability, configurability, flexibility, quality of code and alignment with the target technology stack.

Operational health looks at the consistency of the applications in meeting service-level agreements, measured in terms of incident management, system responsiveness, resolution time and performance.

Cost refers to the amount spent on sustaining the application and includes costs for hardware, software licenses, communication, network and personnel, collectively measured as the total cost of ownership.

Complexity refers to the application's maintainability based on parameters like business rules, frequency of business changes, modularity of functions, dependency on other applications, quality of documentation and availability of skills.

Risk monitors application parameters that contribute to a potential negative outcome for the business and the organization. The considered set includes financial risk on account of system being down, inconsistent data and security breaches and technology risks like data integrity, vendor support and dependency of key resources.

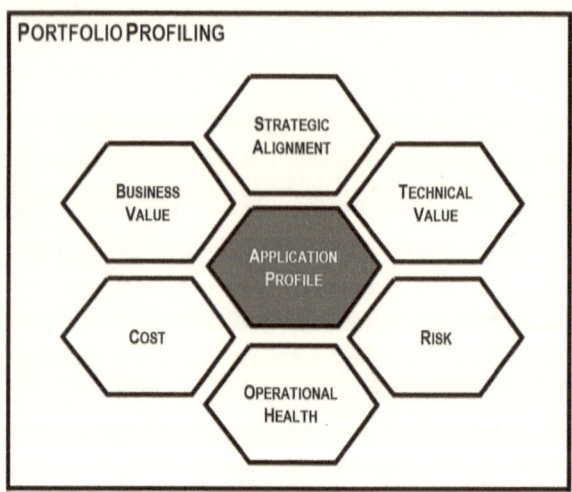

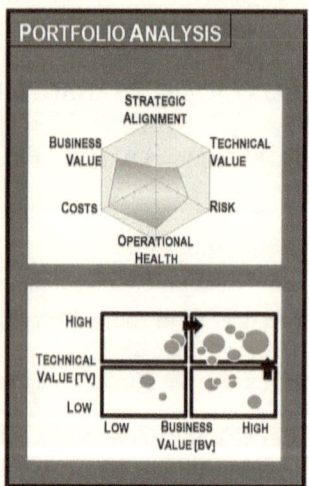

Generic Sequence for Rationalization

1. Profile each application in the portfolio. Basic data required are identification, application name and a brief description.
2. Analyze each of the seven components by rating their respective parameters on a scale of 1 to 5. In some cases, rating has to be applied at a sub-parameter level and aggregated to the parameter level.

3. Apply weightages to the parameters to arrive at the component score, graphically represented as a spider web. Apply weightages to each component, taking into consideration strategic directions and business drivers. The net score thus arrived is the application score.
4. Populate a series of 2x2 matrices on strategic value versus business value, business value versus technical value, technical value versus operational health, operational health versus complexity, complexity versus cost and cost versus risk.
5. Determine future direction for each application: should it be retired, re-engineered, renovated or retained.

INVESTMENT ANALYSIS FRAMEWORK

Investment Analysis helps an enterprise analyze IT assets and arrive at decisions on its portfolios, ensuring a balance between risk and return.

MIT CISR research found that firms invest in IT to achieve four management objectives:

1. Strategic: To gain a competitive advantage or position in the marketplace or for a major innovation (for example, time-to-market new product along with global launch)
2. Informational: To provide better information for any purpose, including to account, manage, control, report, communicate, collaborate or analyze (for example, sales analysis)
3. Transactional: To reduce cost of doing business or increase throughput for the same cost (for example, trade processing systems in a brokerage firm)
4. Infrastructural: To provide shared base IT capability in anticipation of future business needs (for example, Servers and Networks, Customer database)

MIT CISR Asset Class Framework, based on these findings, helps the enterprise distribute investments across strategy, information, transaction and infrastructure, analyzing performance and providing insights for re-distribution.[18]

ADOPTION FOR INVESTMENT MANAGEMENT

Investment mapping provides a picture of the present state of the enterprise portfolio. It sets a base to understand and define business goals and eases the decision-making process by classifying IT assets to establish where investments lie - the amounts at corporate and business unit levels and their purpose.

Investment analysis is benchmarking against industry standard to understand discrepancies in investment patterns and measuring investments against the

---

18 Weill, P. (2004). IT portfolio management and IT savvy - rethinking IT investments as a portfolio. *MIT CISR Research Article*

organization's business goals. These goals could be financial performance, operational performance, business value from application portfolio and firm-wide IT infrastructure.

Investment optimization is based on asset classification and analysis; IT investments are redistributed to meet the organization's objectives. Cost-focused organizations lean towards transactional and infrastructural investments, agile organizations focus on strategic ones and organizations seeking a balance focus on informational investments.[19]

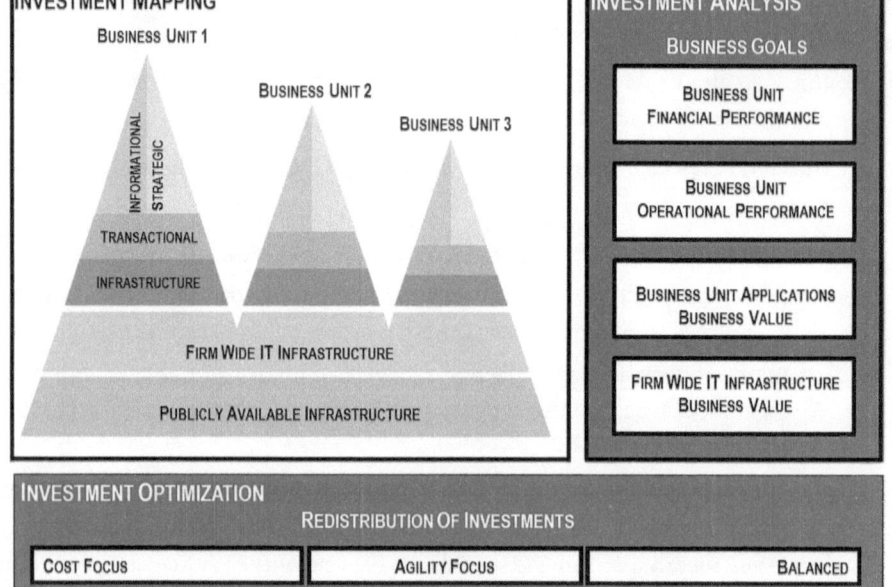

PORTFOLIO MANAGEMENT APPROACH

The execution model of an IT Portfolio Management engagement would broadly traverse the following phases: Understand Context, Assess Current State, Define Target State, Analysis and Findings and Recommendations and Roadmap, touching upon portfolio segments and portfolio analysis parameters as appropriate.

UNDERSTAND CONTEXT

The objective of this phase is to understand the context in terms of the drivers, business, technology, stakeholders, scope and outcomes. The engagement sponsor and/or the engagement coordinator form the target audience.

---

19 Weill, P. (2004). IT portfolio management and IT savvy - rethinking IT investments as a portfolio. *MIT CISR Research Article*

IT Portfolio Management

KEY ACTIVITIES OF THIS PHASE:

1. **UNDERSTAND DRIVERS**

   The drivers for portfolio management can be an external impetus like a merger or acquisition or internal initiatives like process simplification, product implementation, technology upgrade, architectural standardization, optimization of information interface, operational efficiency, infrastructure virtualization or cost reduction. Any of these drivers individually or collectively could trigger a portfolio management engagement with solutions such as process simplification, application rationalization, infrastructure consolidation or investment management.

2. **UNDERSTAND BUSINESS**

   Study the business to understand existing business capability and associated business components, functional coverage of applications and investment distribution between 'Run the Business' and 'Change the Business'. It is equally important to capture non-functional requirements like availability of mission-critical applications. In case of merger or acquisition, this must be replicated for each business entity, to understand standalone capability and synergies to remove functional overlaps.

3. **UNDERSTAND TECHNOLOGY**

   Study the technology environment to understand the technology stack in terms of platforms and products, database structures and dependencies, network and communication protocols. Pay special attention to age of applications, availability of support to gauge how future-proof the environment is and its sustainability. In case of merger or acquisition, this must be replicated for each business entity, to understand the environment in isolation and the enhanced potential for standardization and capacity utilization post-integration.

4. **UNDERSTAND STAKEHOLDERS**

   In portfolio management, the key stakeholders are business owners, external business partners and internal application owners. Often, conflicting objectives are debated: business need versus technical viability and technical requirement versus skill availability. One's position should be carefully presented so that others' positions are respected; the key is to arrive at a common understanding for collective benefit.

5. **UNDERSTAND SCOPE AND OUTCOMES**

   In portfolio management, unlike other consulting engagements, the outcome may not be known upfront, except when portfolio assessment is part of a larger initiative. In such cases, the expected outcomes should be aligned with the larger objective. The more common scenario is that improvement initiatives are determined after analysis of findings from current-state assessment, taking into consideration budget, effort, timeframe and benefit.

   The outcome of this phase is a re-confirmed portfolio management scope, portfolio management segments to focus on and their relative importance.

ASSESS CURRENT STATE

The objective of this phase is to baseline the technology environment in terms of strategic alignment, business value, technical value, costs, risks and operational health. The target audience includes the engagement coordinator, business partners, business owners and application owners.

KEY ACTIVITIES OF THIS PHASE:

1. **CURRENT BUSINESS FUNCTIONALITY**

   Parameters to be considered to baseline business functionality are strategic alignment, business value and risks.

   Strategic alignment is a combination of alignment with business strategy, IT strategy and EA. Indicative data-points to be captured are contribution to customer retention, service consistency, reduction in fulfillment-cycle times, self-containment in functional coverage, ease of introducing new functionality, modularity expressed as a percentage of functionality covered by one application and percentage of information covered by another.

   Business value is computed taking into account business criticality, breadth of use, usage profile, application life cycle and business-owner and end-user satisfaction. Indicative data-points to be captured are level of consistency, quality of support, number of business functions supported, number of users with access to the system, geographic spread of users and effort required for training.

   Risks to be catalogued and mitigated relate to business impact, support, service-level agreements, licensing, vendors and technology. Indicative data-points to be captured are degree of exposure to the organization if an application becomes unavailable, availability of resources with the right skills to support the application, commitment to comply with agreed service levels, adequacy of licenses in number and time to expire, financial and operational strength of vendors and application adherence to architecture standards.

IT Portfolio Management

2. **CURRENT TECHNOLOGY ENVIRONMENT**

   Parameters to be considered to baseline the technology environment are technical value and operational health.

   Technical value is a measure of agility and alignment, indicated in terms of technology stack and architecture, lifecycle of application, type and scalability of the application. Indicative data-points to be captured are ability to support a unified desktop; integrate with external database; support additional lines of business, business segments or products; application configuration and personalization; maintainability and quality of code.

   Operational health is a measure of performance, computed on complexity, incident management, system responsiveness and actual resolution time. Indicative data-points to be captured are frequency of business changes, volume of change requests, dependencies, maintainability, flexibility, configurability and documentation.

3. **CURRENT INVESTMENT DISTRIBUTION**

   Parameters to be considered to baseline investment distribution are portfolio costs. These are a combination of costs on hardware, software licenses, projects, personnel and infrastructure. Indicative data-points to be captured are the cost of each of these component on a year-on-year basis to optimize distribution of investments. Additionally, these costs must be aggregated to bucket them into an asset class in the MIT CISR framework and compare the distribution to industry benchmarks.

   The outcome of this phase is an as-is profiling of the portfolio of applications, along the above-mentioned parameters.

DEFINE TARGET STATE

The objective of this phase is to determine the most workable and sustainable technology environment that enhances the current strategic alignment, business value, technical value, costs, risks and operational health. The engagement sponsor, business partners, business owners and application owners are the target audience.

KEY ACTIVITIES OF THIS PHASE:

1. **TARGET BUSINESS FUNCTIONALITY**

   Determine the application's strategic and business value. This indicates how the applications are rated today and their future growth potential. The organization's appetite also needs to be adjusted accordingly.

In general, an application rated high value is important to the business today and tomorrow. It will most likely be a candidate in the target solution. An application rated low value, on the other hand, is of no or limited use to the business and should be considered for retirement as a priority. Medium-rated applications need to be further investigated and could be frozen temporarily.

2. **TARGET TECHNOLOGY ENVIRONMENT**

   Determine the application's technical value. This indicates the age of the application and helps identify the need for replacing/refreshing applications nearing the end of their life cycle. Operational health indicates the robustness of the application and adherence to service-level agreements.

   Application usage profile captures various aspects of its use by end users, in terms of number and category of users and geographic spread of usage. This provides a quick snapshot of an application's importance in the portfolio. Technology Stack refers to the underlying technology on which the applications have been built and maintained and comprises core development language, operating system, database and reporting tools.

3. **TARGET INVESTMENT DISTRIBUTION**

   Determine the investment distribution the organization needs to re-align to achieve its business objectives. Redraw the limits for 'Run the Business' and 'Change the Business' and the margins available to maneuver.

   An application's functional disposition will have an implication on its saving potential. For instance, savings potential for applications marked 'retire' would be the total cost of applications including cost of enhancement, maintenance, software, infrastructure, people and vendor or supplier. For applications marked 're-engineer' or 'renovate', the savings potential is either from maintenance costs or from enhancement costs or a combination of both. Savings in maintenance costs surface post recovery of enhancement costs incurred for re-engineering or renovation. Enhancement costs are time sensitive and tend to increase with time; hence, the sooner the application is re-engineered or renovated, the lesser the cost and higher the savings. This may have a ripple effect on maintenance costs. Finally, for obvious reasons the applications marked 'retain' would have no cost savings.

   The outcome of this phase is a description of the desired state of the portfolio of applications, along the above-mentioned parameters.

ANALYSIS AND FINDINGS

The objective of this phase is to analyze and benchmark findings from current-state assessment and target-state definitions.

Portfolio analysis is a very rigorous and iterative exercise, typically comprising variate and overlap analyses. Variate analysis is at the application level, a combination of uni-variate analysis (examining individual attributes) and bi-variate analysis (examining related attributes) and multi-variate analysis (examining a combination of one or more attribute). Overlap analysis, on the other hand, is between applications or combinations of applications, to relatively assess strategic value, business value and technical value to create the final application disposition: whether to retire, re-engineer, renovate or retain.

Target audience includes business owners and application owners.

KEY ACTIVITIES OF THIS PHASE:

1. **FUNCTIONALITY ANALYSIS**

    Functionality analysis includes uni-variate analysis of the strategic alignment, business value scores and bi-variate analysis of mapping between strategic alignment and business value, strategic alignment and risk, business criticality and risk.

    Insights to look for are the distribution of scores, the parameters that contribute to these low scores and impact of the same on business and functionality. For example, applications score low on strategic alignment mainly due to very low EA alignment. Business value scores are poor on breadth of use, business criticality and level of business-process integration.

2. **TECHNOLOGY ANALYSIS**

    Technology analysis includes uni-variate analysis of the technical value, operational health scores, bi-variate analysis of mapping between business value and technical value, business criticality and technical value, technical value and operational health and multi-variate analysis of strategic alignment, business value and technical value.

    Insights to look for are the distribution of scores, the parameters that contribute to these low scores and impact of the same on technology, process and operations. For example, applications score low on business value mainly due to the very low usage profile, limited breadth of use or decreasing life-cycle status and low scalability. Low operational health scores are primarily due to poor incident management and actual resolution time or due to business changes in these applications and lack of documentation.

Illustration of Multi-Variate Analysis:

- Functional quality versus technical quality for all applications with low business and strategic value: These are applications that are not important today and will not be important to the business tomorrow and are thus candidates for retirement.
- Functional quality versus technical quality for all applications with low business value and high strategic value: These are applications that are less important today but will be important to the business tomorrow and are thus candidates for re-engineering. Exceptions are applications with low functional and technical quality. It is preferable to replace these with more strategic applications.
- Functional quality versus technical quality for all applications with high business value and low strategic value: These are applications that are important for the business today and will be less important tomorrow and are thus candidates for renovation. Exceptions are applications with low functional and technical quality. It is preferable to replace these with more strategic applications. Other exceptions are applications with high functional and technical quality. It is preferable to retain these.
- Functional quality versus technical quality for all applications with high business and strategic value: These are applications most likely to be in the wanted portfolio and part of the target solution. Exceptions are applications with low functional and technical quality; it is preferable to replace these with more strategic applications.

3. **INVESTMENT ANALYSIS**

Investment analysis includes cost and investments analyses, that is, distribution as per asset classes including benchmark analysis, preferably with data for the past three years, and risk analysis.

Cost analysis is essential to understand savings potential and possible governance actions. Ideally, cost should be yearly actual values, if not year-to-date actual with projections for full year or as a last resort, full-year budget values. Costs to be considered are those for enhancement, maintenance, software, infrastructure, people and vendors or suppliers.

Investment analysis starts with classification of IT investments in the four asset classes to understand distribution pattern and their impact on the portfolio, the investment process/prioritization process followed and gap analysis against industry benchmarks over the past three years to understand deviations and in which asset classes. Note: deviations are not necessarily wrong; it is more important to know why they occur, because of short-term technology requirements or long-term strategic directions.

Risk analysis establishes the risk-return profiles of the IT portfolio. The risk is lowest in transactional investments, assuming a fairly stable environment. In informational and infrastructural investments, risk is moderate due to difficulty in acting on information to create business value and due to long life of most infrastructure and the uncertainty of business and technology. Predictably, risk is highest in strategic investments; the upside is huge potential, while the downside is 50% failure rate.

The outcome of this phase is an in-depth analysis of the application portfolio, current position and future disposition and analysis of IT investments, current distribution and deviations from industry benchmarks along with rationale for the difference.

RECOMMENDATIONS AND REPORT

The objective of this phase is to recommend the portfolio roadmap and directions for investment optimization. The target audience includes the engagement sponsor, business owners and application owners.

KEY ACTIVITIES OF THIS PHASE:

1. **PORTFOLIO MANAGEMENT ROADMAP**

    In building a portfolio management roadmap, the following guiding principles are adopted: cluster applications based on targeted dispositions and sourcing options and prioritize and sequence clusters with feasible and desired implementation time horizons (short-term, medium-term or long-term). These time horizons are directed by urgency to implement and potential cost savings.

    An essential element of the portfolio management roadmap is identifying and implementing quick wins, typically those that provide highest cost saving and risk reduction with minimum implementation effort. Quick wins could be consolidation opportunities associated with retirement, re-engineering or renovation; the exact nature and extent are derived from detailed analysis or consolidation through application stacking by removing high degrees of functional overlap or standard upgrade of common off-the-shelf products. On the infrastructure end, there could be quick wins in server consolidation.

    The most optimum option for an application is selected as the desired rationalization strategy and sourcing model for the application portfolio. Measures for success of the rationalization strategy are identified and included in the portfolio roadmap.

Illustrative measures of qualitative lead indicators are degree of confirmation in utilizing shared platforms and degree to which the funded initiatives directly assist in delivering the roadmap. Quantitative lead indicators are the target of net application inventory computed as base plus additions minus decommissioned inventory and target change in spend profile as a result of executing the roadmap.

Similarly, qualitative lag indicators are percentage of activities completed as per plan and percentage of enhancements that reflected the agreed roadmap. Quantitative lag indicators are percentage reduction in average number of applications by business function and by business process and percentage reduction in number of integration points for an application.

The portfolio management roadmap concludes with directions for portfolio optimization. These directions establish strong alignment of business strategy, business processes, application landscape, technology platform and infrastructure configurations to support future business and define architecture standards to future-proof technology. The last two would go a long way in managing and optimizing current and future IT investments.

4. **INVESTMENT MANAGEMENT AND OPTIMIZATION**

The investment management and optimization plan is based on the original investment plan, asset distribution, benchmarking results and current and future focus of the organization. Overlay findings from asset-class analysis and the recommended redistribution pattern. Include key process required to achieve target-class distribution and consolidate the impact of all the new initiatives on asset-class investments year-wise for three to five years.

Target distribution applies for the next three years. To arrive at an optimum distribution, take the existing distribution as the baseline and find out the forecasted investment distribution for year one. Compute the investment distribution in dollars by adding the overall expenditure on new initiatives for year one, distributed across asset classes, to the existing investment-distribution structure. Calculate distribution percentages and create the investment pyramid based on the forecasted investment distribution. Use this forecast for year one as the baseline for year two. Repeat these steps for every year. Compare this with the target distribution and repeat steps with different prioritizations to achieve the target distribution.

The outcome this phase is the final deliverable, the Portfolio Management Report. This is a compendium of application profiles, application analysis on core parameters, relative performance and dependencies and the recommended functional disposition, architectural standards and compliance mechanisms. Insights on investment spend and optimized distribution for sustainable growth are also provided. The report is prepared by the consultants and submitted to the executive sponsor for sign-off.

Key Learnings

Portfolio management is about helping IT get the most out of its budgets. It involves the processes, practices and specific activities to perform continuous and consistent evaluation, prioritization, budgeting and selection of investments that provide the greatest value and contribute to the organization's strategic objectives.

Portfolio management tenets that put the definition to action are: efficiently surface and qualify opportunities, eliminate redundancy, capture the right information from the right source, respond with agility to change and continuously improve the predictability of various metrics.

The management of IT portfolio involves simplification of business processes, application rationalization and consolidation or virtualization of infrastructure. Although on a different dimension, an equally critical component is the management of IT investments.

In the absence of an industry-defined framework for portfolio management, most organizations have resorted to organic methods that revolve around three simple steps - profiling applications' strategic alignment, business value, technical value, operational health, costs and risks; followed by uni-variate analysis of portfolio parameters, bi-variate analysis of related mappings and multi-variate analysis of cross-functional relations; and resulting in a functional disposition for each application: whether to retire, re-engineer, renovate or retain the application.

MIT CISR Asset Classes framework can be leveraged for investment analysis. The framework classifies investments as strategic, informational, transactional and infrastructural, analyzes the distribution in relation to industry benchmarks and helps in optimizing IT investments.

Finally, a unique feature to keep in mind in portfolio management engagements, unlike all other consulting engagements is that the target state is not defined upfront, but evolves as a result of the current state of the portfolio - where you are will determine how far you can or should go. This is what makes portfolio management, though assumed to be routine and simple, more complex, critical and challenging; most importantly, it needs to be continuous.

. Ω .

Chapter 5

IT Process Consulting

In the 'Technology Triad' of people, process and technology, process is more than just one of the three nodes; it is the glue that ties the triad together. Everyone realizes the importance of having a motivated, quality workforce, but even the finest people cannot perform at their best when the process is not understood or operating at its best.

Customers care about results, and results are created by processes, not by disconnected individual tasks. IT processes determine the operational capabilities of IT, help structure IT workflow and provide the ability to integrate activities, procedures, tools, technology, suppliers, people and responsibilities.

IT Process Consulting, the second 'P' in SAPPGIO-T of the IT Consulting Spectrum, primarily deals with definition, deployment, management, compliance and optimization of processes and services to improve productivity and deliver resilient IT services.

In addition to a broad understanding of the IT Process Consulting Space, this chapter provides insights into Process Consulting Dimensions, Process Consulting Frameworks and Approach for executing a Process Consulting engagement.

Process Consulting Space

Processes are a sequence of steps performed for a given purpose. Process improvement is a never-ending journey; it needs to be carefully planned, executed and sustained.

If processes are ad hoc or descriptions are not rigorously followed or enforced, or are highly dependent on current practitioners, they are termed immature and require firefighting, with no time to improve, just react. The added danger is the firefighters themselves could get burnt and may leave embers behind, which could be rekindled later.

At the other end of the spectrum are mature processes that help in fire prevention. These are defined and documented processes with descriptions consistent with the way work actually gets done and support from management. Process fidelity, if any, is evaluated and enforced; there is a constructive use of product and process measurement.

Organizations must ensure that such mature processes are institutionalized, by building an infrastructure that contains effective, usable and consistently applied processes. Organizational culture should convey the process and management should nurture this culture. Institutionalized processes endure; once proven, over time and across platforms, they are manifested as process models.

Process models provide a place to start improving, a framework for prioritizing actions, a common language and a shared vision, a way to define what improvement means for an organization. Process model is a structured collection of practices that describe the characteristics of effective processes and have an appraisal method to diagnose the state of an organization's current practices.

PROCESS IMPROVEMENT COMMANDMENTS

1. **LEADERSHIP COMMITMENT**

   The speed of the leader is the speed of the team. A continuous improvement approach requires commitment from top management. To successfully climb the maturity ladder, organizations must install and maintain impeccable improvement processes. To do this, organizations need a sustainable improvement mechanism that is adaptable to changing market circumstances. The organization's strategic goals drive process improvement. The key to success lies in the business implication, as this will bring improved employee morale and higher customer satisfaction.

2. **MANAGE CHANGE**

   Adopt an integrated approach so change involves people and is not imposed on them. Change management is designed to assist teams in telling the process-improvement story from initial actions to the improved state. It describes the goals, the motivation for improvement, the commitment required by various parties, the assumptions being made, the overall process to be applied in managing the initiative and the infrastructure required to manage and support it. Change management and communication are key components of the quality approach, encouraging organizations to continuously improve their methods, products and services.

3. **ORGANIZE AND PLAN**

   Planning is the catalyst for effective deployment and includes setting a strategic direction, determining the monitoring mechanism, making estimations, managing people, identifying tools and techniques and building trust and leadership in the organization. When applied at every phase, the Deming cycle of Plan-Do-Check-Act, keeps the project oiled and running.

4. **PEOPLE ARE THE ASSETS**

    People are the key to bring about any change. Generally, organizations that commit to process improvement rely heavily on their most valuable resources, their people. A good process-improvement framework along might not solve all the organization's problems; it must have process-oriented people to execute the process framework that has been laid down. Reward people and give positive reinforcement to drive success.

5. **ORGANIZATIONAL TRAINING**

    Training is an investment, not an overhead. Create a buy-in within the key leadership team for process training. Develop a training plan aligned with the organization's vision and business objectives. Time, money and resources need to be provided for learning capabilities and building knowledge.

6. **PROCESS IS THE BACKBONE**

    Process infrastructure is the foundation of sustenance. The framework chosen for process adoption should best suit and meet the organization's objectives. This will be an acid test for the executive management's thought leadership. Half the battle for process improvement is won if a right process framework is chosen by the organization. The framework should address the business, technology and people needs. Focus must shift away from crisis management and towards process management.

7. **METRICS BASED APPROACH**

    Track, monitor and manage performance. This is a performance-measurement system that improves the bottom line by reducing process cost and improving productivity. A performance-measurement system helps align strategic activities with an organization's strategic plan. The measurement system permits real deployment of strategy on a continuous basis; defines KPIs and metrics; captures status, progress and alerts and provides online real-time data to enable decision-making.

8. **ASSESS AND EVALUATE**

    Evaluate what you want because what gets measured gets produced. Any industry-recognized model is required to evaluate and assess current framework and processes followed in projects. Unless processes are evaluated, it is uncertain in what direction projects in the organization are headed. Also, this process gives leadership trust and confidence in the quality-assurance practices built into the products and applications being developed.

9. **IMPROVED COMMUNICATION**

   Communication is the central nervous system. It binds everything together, ensuring the right information reaches the right people at the right time. Communication is a vital link between all elements of an organization; it influences thoughts, feelings and actions in alignment with objectives and enables sharing of knowledge and information. The success of process and productivity improvement demands communication with and among all the organization members, suppliers and customers.

10. **FOCUS ON BENEFITS**

    Often, the organization's leadership team/sponsors are interested in knowing the outcomes of the process-improvement efforts and how solutions can be implemented. The methodology and approach used in projects are essential only if they arrive at the right conclusions and capture their attention in the beginning. The focus here is to translate project results into hard bottom-line savings and to mandate savings in improvement efforts across all business and technology platforms.

PROCESS CONSULTING DIMENSIONS

Process consulting broadly advises on two dimensions: process improvement and process optimization. The former relates to new development work and includes project planning, requirement definition, project execution, monitoring, supplier management and risk management. The latter is an extension of process improvement and involves optimizing processes and sustaining capability/maturity levels. Process consulting engagements rely heavily on industry best practice frameworks for baselining, benchmarking and benefit realization.

PROCESS IMPROVEMENT

Process improvement focuses on improved availability of business critical services through process standardization and stability, resulting in informed and timely decision-making. Nature of engagements include process benchmarking, model-based appraisals, cost of quality baselining and process transformation.

Investment in process-improvement initiatives should be treated like any other business investment, mandating a compelling business case aimed at reducing the cost of quality and thus enabling the delivery of greater functionality at a lower cost. Cost of quality shows how much the organization is currently spending on preventing, finding and fixing defects and allows comparison against industry benchmarks.

The most prevalent framework in process-improvement engagements is the Capability Maturity Model (CMM). This is a method for evaluating and measuring the maturity of the software-development process of organizations on a scale of 1 to 5. A revised version, the Capability Maturity Model Integration (CMMI), provides guidance for improving an organization's processes and managing the development, acquisition and maintenance of products or services.

Process Optimization

Building or sustaining efficient processes is beyond the realm of process-improvement or service-management initiatives. Optimization and continuous improvement, efficiency and effectiveness require lean thinking.

A lean organization understands customer value and focuses its key processes to meet those needs. It identifies and eliminate waste from key processes. This is about doing things quickly. The goals of lean thinking are to manage the business backwards, from the customer's definition of value, not forwards from the organization's structures and assets. The objective is to create lean processes or value streams to design and deliver value to customers with minimum wasted effort or time and to build a lean management system to manage and continuously improve these value streams.

Seven key steps to implement lean principles are: identify value-added activities and opportunities, implement value-stream maps, determine the order of the value-added activity, decrease the cycle time, eliminate non-value added activities, enhance value-added services to the customer and adopt improvements.

Process Consulting Frameworks

Capability Maturity Model Integration

The CMMI®[20], is a globally adopted capability improvement framework that guides organizations in high-performance operations. The CMMI-DEV model provides guidance for applying CMMI best practices in a development organization. Best practices in the model focus on activities for developing quality products and services to meet the needs of customers and end users.

The CMMI-DEV V1.3[21] model is a collection of development best practices from government and industry, generated from the CMMI V1.3 Architecture and

---

20 CMMI® is a registered trademark of Carnegie Mellon University.
21 CMMI® for Development, Version 1.3. CMU/SEI-2010-TR-033, Copyright 2010 by Carnegie Mellon University.

Framework. The CMMI Framework is the basic structure that organizes CMMI components and combines them into CMMI constellations and models. CMMI-DEV is based on the CMMI Model Foundation (model components common to all CMMI models and constellations) and incorporates work by development organizations to adapt CMMI for use in developing products and services. A constellation is a collection of CMMI components used to construct models, training materials and appraisal-related documents for an area of interest (for example, development, acquisition and services).

CMMI is based on the premise that, "The quality of a system is highly influenced by the quality of the process used to acquire, develop, and maintain it". CMMI provides a descriptive framework of the characteristics of mature processes in the areas it addresses. It facilitates enterprise-wide process improvement through a consistent and enduring approach that accommodates new initiatives.

CMMI is an excellent tool for taking an objective look at the as-is state of an organization and providing useful information on possible improvements, based on an understanding of business objectives and process needs. CMMI provides guidance on what needs to be done, but not how to do it. CMMI does not mandate the organization to target a particular maturity level or to undergo any formal, benchmarking appraisals; the organization does not have to use the whole model or focus on all the process areas. Organizations need to determine how to apply CMMI best practices to their processes for improvisation.

CMMI has evolved into a family of constellations addressing different aspects of software, systems and services development and acquisition. CMMI for development (CMMI-DEV) provides guidance for measuring, monitoring and managing development process. CMMI for services (CMMI-SVC) provides guidance for those providing services within organizations and to external customers. CMMI for acquisition (CMMI-ACQ) provides guidance to enable informed and decisive acquisition leadership. The constellations share 16 common processes and five to eight constellation-specific process areas.

CMMI Process Areas

Project Management	Process Areas - Project Planning - Project Monitoring and Control - Supplier Agreement Management - Integrated Project Management - Risk Management - Requirement Management - Quantitative Project Management
Process Management	Process Areas - Organizational Process Focus - Organizational Process Definition - Organizational Training - Organizational Process Performance - Organizational Performance Management
Support	Process Areas - Configuration Management - Process and Product Quality Assurance - Measurement and Analysis - Decision Analysis and Resolution - Causal Analysis and Resolution
Engineering	Process Areas - Requirements Development - Technical Solution - Product Integration - Verification - Validation

Services

Process Areas
- Incident Resolution and Prevention
- Strategic Service Management
- Service Continuity
- Service System Transition
- Service Delivery
- Service System Development
- Capacity and Availability Management

Acquisition

Process Areas
- Agreement Management
- Acquisition Validation
- Acquisition Verification
- Acquisition Technical Management
- Acquisition Requirements Development
- Solicitation and Supplier Agreement

CMMI process areas are further broken down into goals and practices. Goals are high-level statements of the outcome to be achieved by effective implementation of a group of practices. Goals could be specific, applicable to only one process area and could address the unique characteristics that describe what must be implemented to satisfy the purpose of that process. Goals could also be generic, applicable to all process areas; achievement of each of these goals in each process area signifies whether the implementation and institutionalization of each process area is effective, repeatable and lasting.

Practices on the other hand are descriptions of expected actions to be performed to achieve the goals of a process area. Similar to goals, practices are also specific or generic. Specific practices are considered important in achieving the specific goal that they are mapped to. Describe the activities expected to result in achievement of the specific goal of a process area. Generic practices provide the institutionalization features that will ensure that the process area will be effective, repeatable and lasting.

The CMMI assessment begins with a thorough appraisal of the process areas within the organization and comparison of the current state of the processes with the pre-defined industry best practices. Objectives could be to identify areas where improvement in processes can result in better organizational performance in terms of improved product quality, productivity, delivery reliability and predictability. Alternatively, objectives could be to prioritize and group areas for improvement to create a roadmap for process improvement. In each process area, the relevant practices are assessed on multiple parameters for adequacy and accordingly, the percentage of the goal achieved is tabulated, either in percentage terms or as heat maps. Results thus tabulated are then collectively analyzed to arrive at the overall maturity level.

CMMI Maturity Levels

Level 1 Initial

Processes are performed but often in an ad hoc/chaotic manner. Understanding of the current status of a project is limited; management practices may not be effective. Performance is difficult to predict and is dependent on competence of individuals. Immature processes result in fighting fires, with no time to improve.

Level 2 Managed

Organizational policies are established and followed. Processes are also established by projects but are still mostly reactive. Project management is disciplined, measurements and reviews occur at defined points with assigned responsibility and authority. Resources are made available to produce the work products.

Level 3 Defined

The organization is proactive and training needs are identified and provided. The organization has a standard process, which individual projects tailor to their needs. Processes are well-characterized, understood and effectively implemented.

Level 4 Quantitatively Managed

Statistical and other quantitative methods are used at the organization and project levels to understand past process performance, predict future process performance and future product and service quality. Processes are instrumented with well-defined and consistent measurements. Quantitative goals are set by the organization for products and processes. Therefore, process capability is quantifiable and predictable.

Level 5 Optimizing

Focus is on continuous improvement, based on statistical understanding of process performance. Measurements are used to select process improvements and innovations and estimate their cost and benefits. Analyses are concerned with addressing common causes of process variation to strengthen the process proactively and prevent occurrence of defects. Quantitative process improvement objectives for the organization are established and continually revised to reflect changing business objectives.

CMMI-DEV Process Areas Grouped by Maturity Levels

← SPECIFIC →	← GENERIC →					
ENGINEERING[1]	PROJECT MANAGEMENT[2]	PROCESS MANAGEMENT[3]	SUPPORT[4]			
		• OPM	• CAR			5 OPTIMIZING
	• QPM	• OPP			4 QUANTI-TATIVELY MANAGED	
• RD • VER • TS • VAL • PI	• IPM • RSKM	• OPF • OPD • OT	• DAR	3 DEFINED		
	• PP • REQM • PMC • SAM		• CM • MA • PPQA	2 MANAGED		
				1 INITIAL		

PROCESS AREAS
1. RD: Requirements Development
2. PP: Project Planning
3. OPF: Organizational Process Focus
4. CM: Configuration Management

TS: Technical Solution
PMC: Project Monitoring & Control
OPD: Organizational Process Definition
MA: Measurement & Analysis

PI: Production Integration
REQM: Requirement Management
OT: Organizational Training
PPQA: Process & Product Quality Assurance

VER: Verification
SAM: Supplier Agreement Management
OPP: Organizational Process Performance
DAR: Decision Analysis & Resolution

VAL: Validation
IPM: Integrated Project Management
OPM: Organizational Performance Management
CAR: Causal Analysis & Resolution

RSKM: Risk Management
QPM: Quantitative Project Management

Source: www.CMMIinstitute.com

Lean Principles

Lean principles have been developed and enhanced by Toyota Corporation, Japan, to create the Toyota Production System. Lean is a philosophy that shortens the timeline between the customer order and the shipment. By definition, lean is a team-based approach for identifying and eliminating waste, that is, all non-value adding activities, through continuous improvement by ensuring product flow at the pull of the customer, in pursuit of perfection.

Lean can be applied in any kind of IT/Business process or portfolio optimization scenario aimed at operational excellence. Lean promotes organizations to think proactively about continuously improving services/processes while improving effectiveness and efficiency in delivery.

Specify Value

Value is information or material in a form the customer is willing to pay for; value is defined by the customer and created by the producer.

IT Process Consulting

IDENTIFY VALUE STREAM

Value stream includes all actions, value-creating and non-value creating, required to bring a product from concept to launch and from order to delivery. These include actions to process information from the customer and actions to transform the product on its way to the customer.

Value-stream map is a simple diagram of every step involved in the material and information flows needed to bring a product from order to delivery. The process involves knowing the map, creating such maps for the current and future state and an action plan to implement changes to achieve the future state. Taking a value-stream perspective means working on the end-to-end process, not just individual processes and improving the whole, not just optimizing the parts.

ESTABLISH FLOW

What waste must be removed to create more value? Focus on elimination from value streams of waste, such as delays, defects and unnecessary complexity in processes, to improve value. Abbreviated as TIMWOOD, the seven types of wastes are Transportation, Inventory, Motion, Waiting, Overproduction, Over-processing and Defects. Non-value adding activities in these waste types are retrieving or storing files, commencement of development of modules that are not immediately required, searching for procedures or checklists,

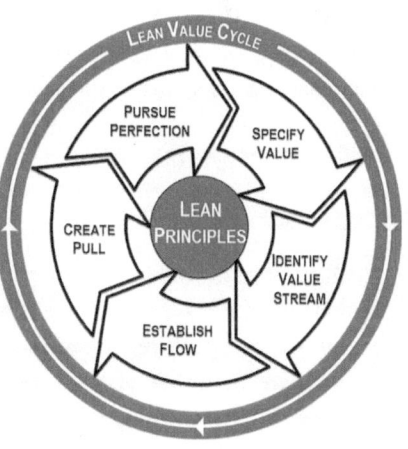

modules waiting for integration testing, requirements that assume customer appreciation, excessive reviews, non-conformance to specifications, etc. Tools like Just-In-Time and Kaizen can aid in identifying and removing waste.

CREATE PULL

What is the bare minimum production needed? Pull systems control flow of resources, people and information based on pre-established rules. They consist of processing based on actual consumption, well-planned work in process, management by sight and improved communication. They help in eliminating waste in handling, storage, speed, obsolescence, rework and excess paperwork. Tools like Kanban and Control charts can aid in controlling and balancing resource flow.

Pursue Perfection

What more can be improved? How can processes get leaner? Processes need constant improvement to keep up with competitors and satisfy customers. A truly lean organization has every employee striving to eliminate waste continuously on a daily basis.

Process Consulting Approach

The execution model of an IT Process Consulting engagement would broadly traverse the following phases: Understand Context, Assess Current State, Define Target State, Analysis and Findings and Recommendations and Roadmap, touching upon the two dimensions of process improvement and process optimization.

Understand Context

The objective of this phase is to understand the context in terms of the drivers, business, technology, stakeholders, scope and outcomes. The target audience is the engagement sponsor and/or the engagement coordinator.

Key Activities of this Phase:

1. **Understand Drivers**

    Organizations undertake process-consulting engagements primarily to enhance their operational efficiencies and/or benchmark their operational standards against industry best practice frameworks. Fewer operational thresholds or lower maturity levels are the result of low service quality, lack of agility and innovation and higher IT costs causing delayed time-to-market and poor customer satisfaction. Focus is on the customer, whether internal or external, understanding what they value, looking at end-to-end processes and delivering meaningful improvements through accelerated time-to-market, to enhance the overall customer experience.

    Process improvement drivers are 1) Operating efficiency for increasing productivity of skilled resources to respond to competitive pressures, market demands and changing demographics and gain access to new sources of specialized skills to raise the organization's responsiveness; 2) Operating flexibility to increase flexibility and speed of response to changes in market needs, to deliver competitive services and 3) Cost Reduction to reduce total costs, to maintain bottom-line competitiveness.

    Process optimization drivers are improving workforce productivity and quality of product and/or processes, reducing overall operating costs, delivering quicker results with business value and improving customer experience.

2. **UNDERSTAND BUSINESS**

   The aspiration of any business is to streamline its current state of operations for a world-class customer services operation. This can be achieved by improving service standardization, enhancing service quality and productivity and most importantly, reducing waste in processes. This requires a strong partnership between business, IT and suppliers. First, identify the organizational unit for which appraisal will be carried out; the resulting areas for improvement should enable cost effectiveness, operational efficiency and optimized organization design. Evaluate different operating models to roll out the proposed solutions and their potential savings.

3. **UNDERSTAND TECHNOLOGY**

   Identify the most important processes and activities where you can deliver the most impact and benefits. Understand processes related to application development, release management, configuration management and service management. Group processes into work streams to enable both atomic and aggregate analysis. Analyze current practices in the prioritized process areas, opportunity for improvement and potential for optimization. Establish a methodology for process definition, including a template in line with the process architecture. Leverage tools wherever appropriate and available or explore avenues for automation. Develop products and solutions that are fit for purpose. The goal is to streamline IT services to bring in efficiency and productivity, while reducing risk, complexity and cost of service delivery.

4. **UNDERSTAND STAKEHOLDERS**

   Resource needs are conflicting and competitive, leading to duplication of effort due to mushrooming and overlapping improvement areas; this lowers long-term sustainability of benefits. The answer to this dilemma rests in support from senior stakeholders, an input that is critical to generating momentum and delivering high-impact change. A senior executive should be designated as the process sponsor and empowered with a pool of process champions. The people who do the work know how to make it better. Use people friendly and pragmatic methods that create buy-in and momentum, so that change is implemented and solutions are fine-tuned as quickly as possible. Build a sustainable culture of continuous improvement by empowering and training people.

5. **UNDERSTAND SCOPE AND OUTCOMES**

   The dimension of the process consulting engagement determines outcomes. In process improvement, the scope lies in the targeted capability level or maturity level; in optimization, the scope is sustaining the improved state.

The outcome of this phase is a re-confirmed process-consulting scope, a process-consulting dimension to focus on and the target standard or framework to be used for improvement and for continuous improvement.

Assess Current State

The objective of this phase is to baseline current IT processes, availability of standards and compliance with the same, along with an understanding of the reasons for deviation, if any, and potential for optimization. The engagement coordinator, process sponsor, process champions, project managers and third-party suppliers form the target audience.

Key Activities of this Phase:

1. Process Improvement

    Process-improvement initiatives are primarily undertaken in the software-development or project-management life cycle and in most cases, the best-practice framework used for benchmarking is CMMI-DEV.

    In the identified organizational area for appraisal, select the process areas for which objective evidence needs to be collected for analysis. Study the organizational structure and gather project details in terms of scope, tools, technologies, deliverables and resources. Take care when selecting projects; pick mature or closed projects of different sizes and varying monetary value, using different life-cycle models executed in an onsite/offshore model and including external IT service providers. All these projects should have project managers who are diligent and are thought leaders.

    For assessing objective evidence, use direct artifacts like tangible outputs resulting directly from implementation of a practice (for example, work products) or indirect artifacts that are a side-effect or indicative of performing a practice (for example, meeting minutes) or affirmations (oral or written statements confirming or supporting implementation, such as questionnaires).

    Objective evidence is examined through document reviews and interviews. A document review is undertaken to understand practices in use in the organization. Tasks include mapping the organization's documents to the reference framework and confirming deployment and institutionalization of processes. For review, consider policy documents, standards and guidelines, project plans, estimation worksheets, process-improvement plans, process-deployment plans, training plans and trackers for deployment/compliance. A good practice is to follow a thread like the life cycle or an incident; leverage available expertise. Be aware of terminology differences when looking for specific information. Focus on identifying areas to be probed further during the interviews.

The purpose of interviews is to get information from the primary source and ensure that observations and findings are based on facts. Tasks include ascertaining firsthand how work is performed and managed and finding areas of strengths, weaknesses and organizational issues. Discover what people consider really critical issues, ensuring that multiple viewpoints are represented. Illustrative questions for project planning: How do you estimate the scope? How do you identify and document project risks? Illustrative questions for measurement and analysis: How are metrics of key activities in your organization defined? How are metrics collected, analyzed, stored, reported and maintained in your organization?

In going through both these methods, take notes and tag pertinent information, take care to avoid being judgmental or getting carried away by something that is interesting but is unnecessary for the assessment. Illustrative observations: incomplete and inconsistent processes and associated process governance, weak estimation process and ad hoc resource management. Articulate an intermediate state for these limitations prior to achieving the target state, like enhancing the quality team, building process elements for resource management and estimation.

2. Process Optimization

The best practice framework used mostly for process optimization is Lean. The starting point for current-state assessment is a series of lean workshops to understand the voice of the customer, business and process and to capture high-level value streams, pain points and lean metrics. Lean principles addressed are specifying value and identifying value stream.

Specify value by listing the services to be provided to the customer based on past data. Classify services into those that are critical and have a high impact, those that consume most effort and those that the respective service executives would like to have assessed.

Identifying value stream helps deliver process optimization; it is a visual representation of the sequential flow of process activities. It starts and ends with a customer, providing a systematic end-to-end view of the current environment, performance and potential for optimization.

In current-state value-stream mapping, the steps followed are drawing the external or internal customer and supplier, listing their requirements, drawing all process steps and listing all process attributes like name, individual tasks and processing time system used, number of operators, lean metrics and rework metrics. Next, list all inputs/outputs of the process steps and draw queue times between processes. Draw all communications that occur within the value stream, draw push or pull icons to identify the type of workflow and finally complete the map with any other data. Techniques like Supplier, Input, Process, Output,

Customer (SIPOC); Voice of Customer (VoC); Critical to Quality; Mississippi Charts and Fishbone Diagrams are used to build the Value-Stream Map (VSM).

SIPOC: Suppliers and Customers are entities, like a department, group or division. Inputs and Outputs are deliverables, the content or information to be used for further processing. Process step is an activity, typically should be between six and ten.

VoC helps to identify and interpret customer requirements and transform them into critical-to-quality metrics, which can, in turn, help measure VoC. Leverage customer list from SIPOC, associate it with a process and ask: What is wanted of this process? What is the most important characteristic of this process? Responses are captured as VoC and need to be rephrased as measurable critical-to-quality metrics.

Other techniques: Mississippi Chart is a tool used to identify the distribution of demand across the value stream. It helps identify high-demand areas and bottleneck areas for focus. Fishbone Diagrams are cause-and-effect analysis tools. Once the major categories have been identified, the team asks 'Why?' until the root cause of the effect has been identified.

Symbols used in a VSM are Start, End, Activity, Decision, Rework (flow depicted in reverse direction), Sub processes and Connectors (forward and backward).

Every VSM should have a Start and an End, taken from SIPOC. The first activity should be connected to Start and the last should be connected to End. Intermediate activities or interfaces with other processes leading towards the end should be connected to End. Activity descriptions should contain inputs received, processing required and output to be delivered. Every activity should have a role. Where applicable, multiple activities are depicted as branches. Identify rework loops. Capture effort, interval and pain points from a customer perspective along with estimated level of impact.

The outcome of this phase is an as-is profiling of existing processes and services provided to business by IT, along the parameters of the chosen best-practice industry framework in case of process of improvement and a current state VSM in case of process optimization.

DEFINE TARGET STATE

The objective of this phase is to determine the most realistic and sustainable maturity level for the selected process areas. The target audience is the engagement sponsor, process sponsor and process champions.

IT Process Consulting

KEY ACTIVITIES OF THIS PHASE:

1. **PROCESS IMPROVEMENT**

    The uniqueness of process improvement engagements is that the target state is pre-determined as part of the objectives; in fact, the current state is assessed against these goals, leading directly to gap analysis.

    In process-improvement initiatives, the target state could be defined by 1) Using CMMI as the improvement framework to appraise the process maturity of selected process areas against a certain capability level or to appraise the process maturity of the organization against a certain maturity level. 2) Using the findings of the appraisal to develop an action plan for bridging the gaps and improving internal processes.

2. **PROCESS OPTIMIZATION**

    In process-optimization initiatives, the target state could be defined by creating a single standard process using best practice from existing processes, applying lean principles, focusing on select value streams to be workable as on the target date and achieving efficiency gains to support the targeted capacity reduction.

    In future-state value-stream mapping, the steps followed are identifying the value add, non-value add and operational value and adding process steps in the current VSM. The customer would pay for value additions, even if the payment is theoretical; the principle here is that the customer would see the activity as adding value to the output. The customer would not pay for non-value additions as these do not add value to the unit from their perspective. Operational value additions are activities the customer would not pay for, but are essential to ensure the process or the business can run smoothly; they are also referred to as enabling value additions.

    Subsequent steps are designing future-state activity blocks, estimated performance and benefits and developing future-state value streams for select processes. Future-state activity blocks are action items that need to be implemented to reach the desired future state of a value stream. It forces end-to-end thinking, breaking the system into manageable but related loops for implementation and quantifying improvement potential.

    The outcome of this phase is a defined target capability and/or maturity using parameters of the chosen best-practice industry framework in case of process of improvement and a target-state VSM in case of process optimization.

ANALYSIS AND FINDINGS

The objective of this phase is to analyze and benchmark findings from current-state assessment. The target audience comprises the process sponsor, process champions, project managers and third-party suppliers.

KEY ACTIVITIES OF THIS PHASE:

1. **PROCESS IMPROVEMENT**

    Process-improvement analysis is twofold - one, a measurement of generic practices against generic goals applicable to the targeted maturity level and two, a measurement of specific practices against corresponding specific goals of the selected generic and/or specific process areas.

    The generic goal for CMMI Maturity Level 3 would be 'Institutionalize a Defined Process'. The defined process is a managed one tailored from the organization's set of standard processes as per the organization's guidelines; has a maintained process description; and contributes work products, measures, and other process-improvement information to the organizational process assets. The associated generic practices are 'Establish a Defined Process' and 'Collect Process-Related Experience'.

    Similarly, the specific goal for a selected generic process area like Requirement Management would be 'Manage Requirements'. The scope includes technical and non-technical requirements, received and generated requirements of the project and organization- and industry-specific requirements. Associated specific practices are 'Understand Requirements', 'Obtain Commitment to Requirements', 'Manage Requirement Changes', 'Maintain Bi-directional Traceability of Requirements' and 'Ensure Alignment between Project Work and Requirements'.

    Every practice in the assessment scope is characterized on a three-point scale. Red is high risk, implying that the model practice is judged to be absent or poorly addressed in the set of implemented practices. Yellow is medium risk, implying the model practice is judged to be partially addressed. Green is low risk, implying the model practice is judged to be adequately addressed. The optional purple indicates the model practice is not rated or judged due to lack of evidence of relevant practices.

    These practice-level findings are then aggregated at an organizational unit level. Risk is deemed high if at least 25% of practice-level instances are characterized as red; medium if less than 25% of instances are characterized red and less than 75% of instances are characterized as green; and low if at least 75% of instances are characterized as green and none are characterized as red.

The combined findings are further analyzed on impact versus control in order to draw up a list of initiatives to bridge gaps. Impact is measured in terms of quality of deliverables, resource required, effort, schedule and customer satisfaction. Control refers to whether the teams addressing the impact will be internal or external. Parameters considered for prioritization are contribution to business goal, cost to implement, time to implement, ease of implementation, urgency on the ground and return on investment.

2. Process Optimization

In process improvement, the emphasis for analysis is on process adherence or ways to measure the extent to which the process is being followed. In process optimization, the emphasis is on process effectiveness or ways to measure how effectively the process meets it objectives, process efficiency, ways to measure productivity and costs around process activities. Lean principles addressed are establishing flow and creating pull.

Value-added activities are those that change information to produce the output required by the end customer. Such activities should be retained for the future-state design; the objective is to improve them further.

In analyzing non-value added activities bear in mind that some of them are essential; they are performed to comply with regulatory or legal requirements or to minimize risk. Absolute non-value added activities are those that consume cost, time and resources but create no value in the eyes of the end user. The objective is to minimize essential non-value added activities and eliminate absolute non-value added activities.

Value-enabling activities are those that the business must perform to operate. Look for value-enabling activities, so they can be completed more efficiently.

In defining the target, the questions to ask are: What does the customer really need? Which steps and activities create value and which are waste? How can we make work flow with fewer interruptions? How do we control work between interruptions? How does the target-state design affect the value tree? Analyze the type of waste (TIMWOOD) in each non-value added activity and brainstorm on ways to minimize or eliminate them.

Illustrative strategies to reduce waste: Grouping operations along requirements and input flow can help make transportation easier and faster. Inventory-related waste can be eliminated by minimizing work items developed ahead of schedule and only undertaking work that is on the schedule. Improved design that clears workstations and puts everything close at hand can reduce waste in motion, thus minimizing cycle time. Waiting time is addressed through improved work planning, increased team flexibility, availability of resources and improved communications. Do work that is on the schedule only and once it is completed, perform continuous improvement activities rather than new work products, avoiding over production. Similarly, to eliminate over-processing, define a standard operation and train the team. Find root cause and eliminate waste using problem-solving techniques. Improve housekeeping and prevent possibility of missing information; essentially, improve the process capability to reduce waste in defects.

The outcome of this phase is an in-depth analysis of the practice areas of selected generic and specific process areas, the current capability levels, maturity levels and a prioritized set of initiatives to bridge the gap and achieve the defined target state in case of process improvement and a strategy to reduce waste in case of process optimization.

Recommendations and Report

The objective of this phase is to articulate recommendations and translate them into a roadmap for process improvement or optimization. The engagement sponsor, process sponsor and process champions make up the target audience.

Key Activities of this Phase:

1. **Process Improvement**

    This roadmap consists of process-improvement goals, focus areas or scope, deployment strategy and a collection of plans for communication, training and risk management.

    Process-improvement goals are expressed in terms of processes prioritized for improvement, the importance of enhancing these processes and their classification as short-, medium- or long-term. Clearly defined and expressed goals provide a foundation for formulating milestones, managing risks, keeping the initiative on track and ensuring its success.

    Process-improvement scope helps establish the boundaries of the initiative by defining the business areas, technology systems, high-level requirements for data, functions, processes and resources within the scope of the initiative, and those known to be out of its scope.

    Deployment strategy includes transition big-bang versus phased approach, guidelines for in-flight projects and new projects, critical success factors and measures and goals for a successful deployment. Goals may be quantitative or qualitative; measures include both operational and outcome-related.

Communication plan includes both formal and informal communications required for success, stating the purpose, frequency, target audience, method and message. The training plan is on similar lines. The risk-management plan identifies risks that could result from proceeding with this initiative and the issues that must be resolved for it to succeed. It is equally important to understand the risk of not proceeding with the initiative.

2. **PROCESS OPTIMIZATION**

The lean principle addressed is pursuing perfection. Three core components of the process-optimization strategy report are 1) Learnings from the current-state assessment in terms of existing capability/maturity levels, gaps in relation to the target, performance-related issues and sources of waste; 2) Design for future state based on lean principles and visual-management techniques where applicable, which includes impact of proposed organization, directional capacity planning and roles and responsibilities or resource pool to align with and support future-state design; and 3) Implementation plan with performance measures baseline and targets, deployment plan and requirements for pilot readiness, plus requirements for continuous improvement implementation and institutionalization.

Implementation sequence of recommendations are categorized according to priority to optimize the whole - quick do's, must do's, should do's and could do's.

Quick do's are recommendations/action items that can be addressed in a short span of time with minimum cost and effort and will help realize a reasonable amount of benefits; for example, define standard operating procedures and obtain buy-in from all relevant stakeholders.

Must do's are recommendations/action items that must be addressed to get benefits critical for the team. Although substantial effort and cost may be required to address these recommendations, they should be considered mandatory; for example, automate test-execution processes.

Should do's are recommendations/action items that should be addressed to realize some of the required benefits. Management can analyze these recommendations further. While there is some space for re-thinking, ideally these recommendations should be addressed at some point; for example, limit the scope of user-acceptance testing and accordingly define the scope of exit criteria.

Could do's are recommendations/action items that are nice if addressed. The expected benefit realized will make the team happy and motivated, but these can be put under lower priority; for example, automate the workflow notification to avoid manual uploading and mail communication.

Lean institutionalization can be either a big-bang approach (successful in organizations that have a top-down, hierarchical culture) or pilot-based approach (suitable for consensus-driven organizations where successful pilots initially build credibility on lean).

The outcome this phase is the final deliverable, the Process Consulting Report. It is a description of the current state of the practices in select process areas in relation to the targeted capability/maturity level, an in-depth analysis of the organization's standing with respect to practice goals at an individual process area level and organizational unit level, followed by recommendations to bridge the gaps and a process-improvement roadmap[s] or a process optimization strategy. The report is prepared by the consultants and submitted to the process sponsor for sign-off with a copy to the executive sponsor.

KEY LEARNINGS

People do not make mistakes because they want to; mistakes are made when the process allows them! Ensuring that things go right requires processes where things cannot go wrong.

Processes should be planned and executed in accordance with policy, employing adequate resources with the right skills to produce controlled outputs that are monitored, controlled and reviewed by relevant stakeholders. Processes need to be defined and documented and their descriptions must be consistent with the way the work actually gets done and must be supported by management. Organizations need to ensure that such mature processes are institutionalized.

Process consulting broadly advises on two dimensions, process improvement and process optimization. Process improvement relates to new development work and includes project planning, requirements definition, project execution, monitoring, supplier management and risk management.

The industry best-practice framework used here is CMMI. It provides guidance for improving an organization's processes and managing the development, acquisition and maintenance of products or services. CMMI assesses maturity of capabilities and/or process on a scale of 1 to 5, Initial to Managed, Defined, Quantitatively Managed and Optimized.

CMMI has evolved into a family of constellations addressing different aspects of software, systems and services development and acquisition. CMMI-DEV provides guidance for measuring, monitoring and managing development process. CMMI-SVC provides guidance for those providing services within organizations and to external customers. CMMI-ACQ provides guidance to enable informed and decisive acquisition leadership.

The constellations share 17 common processes and five to eight constellation-specific process areas. Each process area has specifically stated goals that have to be met to achieve the right maturity or capability in that process area. In addition, there are generic or global goals common to all process areas. Emphasis is on improvement.

Process optimization focuses on sustenance of capability/maturity levels achieved through process improvement. The focus is on eliminating waste by applying the principles of Lean. Abbreviated as TIMWOOD, the seven types of waste are Transportation, Inventory, Motion, Waiting, Overproduction, Over-processing and Defects.

The lean value cycle involves specifying value, identifying value, establishing value, creating pull and pursuing perfection. A key technique in this process is Value-Stream Mapping. It is a high-level process-analysis tool that helps understand the physical flow of material and information as a product/service makes its way through the value stream. VSMs help visualize the service-delivery flow, tie the entire process and demonstrate interaction between information and material flow. Remember, all value streams are different; always start with your customer.

In optimization, the emphasis is on effectiveness and efficiency. In order to enhance these, analyze and segregate them as value added and non-value added. Some activities could be essential and are referred to as enabling activities. The objective is to retain value-added activities, minimize enabling activities and eliminate non-value added activities.

In process consulting, improvement and optimization initiatives are continuous exercises; organizations should consider a progress appraisal once every year or two, to measure the degree of improvement, success of implementation and impact of institutionalization.

. Ω .

CHAPTER 6

IT GOVERNANCE CONSULTING

The intent of IT as an organization is to ensure that it meets the business objectives and the interests of all stakeholders, the need is an institution founded on constructive leadership and collaborative structures. The ingredients to achieve compliance are processes based on a common language and a shared commitment to address challenges. The term that best encapsulates this inter-play is Governance.

Governance broadly comprises of a structure defining responsibility and accountability, processes defining the sequence of actions to be followed, control mechanisms defining decision-making, metrics to measure and monitor the performance of the organization and a framework to facilitate orchestration of these elements.

IT Governance Consulting, the 'G' in SAPPGIO-T of the IT Consulting Spectrum, primarily deals with the entity, the IT organization. Elements critical to the successful functioning of the entity are the design of the governance structure and the definition and deployment of governance processes.

In addition to a broad understanding of the IT Governance Consulting Space, this chapter provides insights into Governance Consulting Focus Areas, Governance Consulting Frameworks and an Approach to executing Governance Consulting engagements.

GOVERNANCE CONSULTING SPACE

In order to understand the governance consulting space, pause for a moment and reflect on the importance of decision-making. It is essential to respond to changing business needs and marketplace dynamics. Uncertainty during decision-making increases risks. Sound monitoring and control of the outcomes of major decisions is essential to improve effectiveness and efficiencies. Governance is about defining the permissible degree of empowerment and/or control.

Governance is concerned with 1) Directing: Who determines the direction and how it is set? Is this clearly defined and communicated? 2) Controlling: Who owns the processes and services? Who defines the who, what, where, when and how of IT processes and services? Who improves them? What level of authority do they have in the organization? 3) Executing: Who participates in the day-to-day execution of the processes and services? and 4) Communicating: Who needs to know what and when? Is it only vertical or horizontal or a combination?

MIT CISR defines governance as "Specifying the decision rights and accountability framework to encourage desirable behavior in using IT." IT governance reflects the broader corporate governance principles while focusing on the management and use of IT to achieve corporate performance goals.[22]

Governance is fundamental to sustain the taken-for-granted business operations at a minimum and additionally to expand and innovate the business. Enterprise value today has transitioned from tangible assets like products, inventory, facilities, etc. to intangible assets like services, information, knowledge and patents, enabled by IT in a globalized environment.

PRINCIPLES OF IT GOVERNANCE

Peter Weill and Jeanne Ross of MIT CISR, after studying and working with hundreds of enterprises have distilled lessons from many outstanding leaders into 10 principles of IT governance. These provide a succinct summary to use as a primer, refresher or checklist to refine IT governance.

1. **ACTIVELY DESIGN GOVERNANCE**

    Many enterprises have created disparate IT-governance mechanisms. These uncoordinated mechanisms result from governance by default, introducing mechanisms one at a time to address a particular need (for example, architecture problems or overspending or duplication). Patching up problems as they arise is a defensive tactic that limits opportunities for strategic impact from IT. Instead, management should actively design IT governance around the enterprise's objectives and performance goals.

2. **KNOW WHEN TO REDESIGN**

    Rethinking the entire governance structure requires individuals to learn new roles and relationships. Learning takes time; therefore, governance redesign should be infrequent. More importantly, a change in governance requires a change in desirable behavior.

3. **INVOLVE SENIOR MANAGERS**

    Firms with effective IT governance have greater senior management involvement, largely in strategic decisions and to some extent in exception processes. Exceptions

---

22 Weill, P. and Ross, J. (2004). Don't just lead: Govern - how top performing firms govern IT. *MIT CISR Research Article*.

also require adequate attention as some may have strategic implications. CIOs must be effectively involved in IT governance for success; other senior managers must participate in committees, approval processes and performance reviews.

4. **MAKE CHOICES**

   Good governance, like good strategy, requires choices. It is not possible for IT governance to meet every goal, but governance can and should highlight conflicting goals for debate. As the number of trade-offs increases, governance becomes more complex. Top-performing enterprises handle goal conflicts with a few clear business principles.

5. **CLARIFY THE EXCEPTION HANDLING PROCESS**

   Exceptions are how enterprises learn. In IT terms, exceptions challenge the status quo, particularly the IT architecture and infrastructure. Some requests for exceptions are frivolous, but most come from a true desire to meet business needs. If the exception proposed by a business unit has value, a change to the IT architecture could benefit the entire enterprise. Formally approved exceptions offer a second benefit in addition to formalizing organizational learning about technology and architecture: they serve as a release valve, relieving the enterprise of built-up pressure.

6. **PROVIDE THE RIGHT INCENTIVES**

   A common problem encountered in studying IT governance was that incentive and reward systems were not aligned with organizational goals; this makes IT governance less effective. If IT governance is designed to encourage business unit synergy, autonomy or some combination of both, incentives for executives must also be aligned.

7. **ASSIGN OWNERSHIP AND ACCOUNTABILITY FOR IT GOVERNANCE**

   Like any major organizational initiative, IT governance must have an owner and accountability. Ultimately, the board is responsible for all governance, but the board will expect or delegate an individual (probably the CEO or CIO) or group to be accountable for IT governance design, implementation and performance. In most sizable firms, CIOs own IT governance. They then create a group of senior business and IT managers to help design and implement IT governance.

8. **DESIGN GOVERNANCE AT MULTIPLE ORGANIZATIONAL LEVELS**

   In large enterprises with multiple business units, IT governance must be considered at several levels. The starting point is enterprise-wide IT governance driven by a few enterprise-wide strategies and goals. Enterprises with separate

IT functions in divisions, business units or geographies require a separate but connected layer of IT governance. The lower levels of governance are influenced by mechanisms designed for higher levels.

9. **PROVIDE TRANSPARENCY AND EDUCATION**

   Transparency and education often go together; the greater the education the greater the transparency in governance processes and consequently, the greater the confidence in governance. In contrast, lesser confidence in governance translates into lesser willingness to play by the designed rules, setting off a downward spiral in governance effectiveness.

10. **IMPLEMENT COMMON MECHANISMS ACROSS THE SIX KEY ASSETS**

    Just having good customer loyalty (Relationship assets) without the products to sell (IP assets) will drain value. Not having well-trained people (Human assets) to work with customers or lacking the support of good data and technology (IT assets) will drain value. Not having the right buildings and shopfronts to work from or in which to make the goods (Physical assets) will drain value. Finally, not coordinating the investments needed (Financial assets) will also drain value. Many enterprises successfully coordinate their six assets within a project but not across the enterprise. In designing IT governance, review the mechanisms used to govern these key assets and consider broadening their charter (perhaps with a subcommittee) to IT rather than creating a new, independent IT mechanism.

    Alignment with these principles, coupled with leadership from the CIO, will lead to greater value from IT.[23]

GOVERNANCE CONSULTING FOCUS AREAS

Governance consulting focusses on structures, the right arrangement of IT functions and its integration points with business, processes highlighting the participation of business in IT matters, mechanisms to enhance business/IT alignment and measurements to monitor performance.

GOVERNANCE STRUCTURES

Governance structures are arrangements of IT functions entailing processes for decision-making, including the people who will make those decisions, to align an IT organization and enable implementation of business strategies and goals.

Given different strategies and organization forms, different enterprises will encourage different behaviors and hence different governance arrangements. An

---

[23] Weill, P. and Ross, J. (2004). Don't just lead: Govern - how top performing firms govern IT. *MIT CISR Research Article*.

effective IT governance structure consists of the CIO reporting to the CEO. This ensures that IT is part of the executive team where most strategy discussions begin and end. Without this seat at the table, IT will almost always be limited to a support organization as opposed to an enabling organization. Formation of virtual committees with business and IT participation should be encouraged for strategic direction on IT investments and alignment of business with centralized monitoring.

Governance Mechanisms

Governance mechanisms are roles, processes, decision-making bodies and communication approaches that ensure effective business and IT relationships by coordinating and aligning IT to higher-level business strategies.

Governance mechanisms are classified as business-linkage mechanisms (linking projects to company-level and business-level strategies), architecture-linkage mechanisms (linking projects to enterprise and business unit architecture) and alignment-linkage mechanisms (linking IT with rest of the business, particularly at the business unit level).

Governance Processes

Governance processes are a series of activities with defined responsibility and accountability and key performance indicators that specify what the business requires to achieve its objectives and how they are fulfilled by effective partnership between business and IT.

Governance processes are selected on the basis of organizational drivers, policies and objectives. For better manageability of processes, each enterprise-level process should be categorized into key processes and some key processes should be divided into sub-processes. All these should be enabled by a set of templates/tools for ease of use. Each activity in the process flow should have a person responsible and accountable for it. Emphasize continuous improvement of governance processes through regular review of key performance indicators and automation, for better control and faster adoption.

Governance Measurements

Governance measurements are predefined measures encompassing lag and lead indicators linked to an IT scorecard that ensures achievement of effective process performance.

Performance metrics should be used as a basis for the formation of IT scorecards across financial, customer, process and learning parameters. Process-performance metrics should be linked to IT goals and metrics that define what the business expects from IT. Formalize baseline and continuous benchmarking of performance for optimized functioning of IT.

Governance Layers

1. **Strategic Layer**

   The strategic layer provides direction to the functioning of IT and includes strategy and planning, investment management, demand management, EA, research and innovation and performance management. Focus is on reducing IT costs through overall process efficiency, providing a platform for scalability and flexibility, building an interface with external and internal partners and exploring innovative IT use to achieve business breakthroughs.

2. **Tactical Layer**

   The tactical layer is instrumental in providing necessary support for the smooth running of IT and includes application development, project management, assurance management, risk management, resource management, procurement management, vendor management and security management. Focus is on managing relationships between IT and business groups, addressing business needs in IT projects and managing cross-functional initiatives.

3. **Operational Layer**

   The operational layer pertains to the day-to-day functioning of IT and includes operations management, infrastructure management, application maintenance, service management and data management. Focus is on identifying options for reducing redundancy and segregating functions based on their applicability.

Governance Consulting Frameworks

MIT CISR Governance Arrangement Matrix

The Arrangement Matrix was created by MIT CISR as part of the MIT Sloan School of Management. CISR has a strong track record of practice-based research on how firms manage and generate business value from IT. Based on their study of 250 enterprises in 23 countries, Peter Weill and Jeanne Ross argue that IT business value results directly from effective IT governance.

The Arrangement Matrix is used to describe, analyze and communicate an organization's IT governance, based on a framework that uses a set of political governance archetypes for five principle decision domains. The matrix also identifies the mechanisms used to implement the governance arrangements.

It addresses what decisions must be made in the governance domain and who should make these and discusses governance archetype. Each governance domain area has an 'Input' field and a 'Decision' field to show who provides input for different governance decisions and who makes different governance decisions. The required information for the Arrangements Matrix should be filled by IT governance stakeholders.[24]

DOMAIN → ARCHETYPES ↓	IT PRINCIPLES		IT INFRASTRUCTURE STRATEGIES		IT ARCHITECTURE		BUSINESS APPLICATION NEEDS		IT INVESTMENT PRIORITIZATION	
	INPUT	DECISION	INPUT	DECISION	INPUT	DECISION	INPUT	DECISION	INPUT	DECISION
BUSINESS MONARCHY		EXEC. COMM.						EXEC. COMM.		EXEC. COMM.
IT MONARCHY				IT COUNCIL		IT COUNCIL				
FEUDAL										
FEDERAL										
DUOPOLY										
ANARCHY										

(MORE CENTRALIZED ↑ / LESS ↓)

☐ INPUT RIGHTS   ■ DECISION RIGHTS

GOVERNANCE MECHANISMS

EXECUTIVE COMMITTEE	CEO, CIO & BUSINESS UNIT HEADS
IT COUNCIL	CIO & IT UNIT HEADS
LEADERSHIP COMMITTEE	BUSINESS UNIT HEADS & IT UNIT HEADS

1. IT Domains

IT domains are areas where decisions at the intersection of business and IT need to be made. Five decisions of the IT domain are:

- IT Principles: High-level statements on IT use in the business.
- IT Architecture: Integrated technical choices to guide the organization in satisfying business needs or policies and rules for IT use.
- IT Infrastructure: Strategies for the foundation of IT capability (technical and human) shared throughout the firm and centrally coordinated.
- Business Application Needs: Specifying the business need for purchased or internally developed applications.
- IT Investment and Prioritization: Decisions around how much and where to invest in IT, including project approvals and justification techniques.

---

24 Weill, P. and Ross, J. (2004). Don't just lead: Govern - how top performing firms govern IT. *MIT CISR Research Article*.

2. **IT GOVERNANCE STYLES**

   Governance styles specify who provides input for decisions and who makes the decisions. The six archetypal governance styles involve different combinations of business and IT executives at different organizational levels:
   - Business Monarchy: Business executives (CxO); may include CIO
   - IT Monarchy: Individual groups of IT executives
   - Federal: Shared business executives and business unit leaders
   - IT Duopoly: IT executive and one other business unit leader
   - Feudal: Business unit leads and their key process owners

3. **IT GOVERNANCE MECHANISMS**

   Mechanisms used to make and enact decisions. Effective governance deploys three different types of mechanisms:
   - Decision-Making Structures: Organizational units and roles responsible for making IT decisions, such as committees, executive teams and business/IT relationship managers.
   - Alignment Processes: Formal processes for ensuring that daily behaviors are consistent with IT policies and provide input back to decisions. These include IT investment proposal and evaluation processes, architecture exception processes, service-level agreements, chargeback and metrics.
   - Communication Approaches: Announcements, advocacy, channels and education effects that disseminate IT governance principles and policies and outcomes of IT decision-making processes.

   Finally, IT governance is assessed on five important factors: enterprise setting, governance arrangement, governance awareness, governance performance and financial performance. Enterprise setting captures the industry, size, number of business units and the relationship between the business units, that is, level of synergy desired between business units. Governance arrangements describe which archetypes are used for each IT decision and which mechanisms are used for implementation. Governance awareness establishes how well everyone across the firm understands governance and identifies communication approaches to engaging management. Governance performance assesses the effectiveness of IT governance in delivering four objectives - cost-effective use of IT, effective use of IT for asset utilization, effective use of IT for growth and effective use of IT for business flexibility - weighted by their relative importance in the enterprise. Financial performance is measured in terms of profit, asset utilization and growth.[25]

---

25 Source: Copyright 2012 ISACA. All rights reserved. Used with permission.

Control Objectives for Information and related Technologies (COBIT)

COBIT 5 provides the next generation of guidance from Information Systems Audit and Control Association (ISACA) on enterprise governance and IT management. It builds on more than 15 years of practical use and application of COBIT by many enterprises and users from business, IT, risk, security and assurance communities. COBIT 5 is based on five key principles for governance and management of enterprise IT.

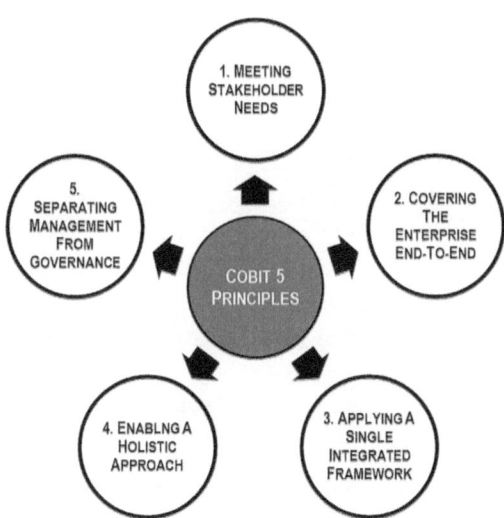

Principle 1: Meeting Stakeholder Needs

Enterprises exist to create value for their stakeholders by maintaining a balance between realizing benefits and optimizing risk and use of resources. COBIT 5 provides all required processes and other enablers to support business value creation through the use of IT. Enterprises can customize COBIT 5 to suit their own context through goals cascade, translating high-level enterprise goals into manageable, specific, IT-related goals and mapping these to specific processes and practices.

Stakeholder needs are influenced by numerous drivers, for example, strategy changes, changing business and regulatory environment and new technologies. Value creation for stakeholders means realizing benefits at an optimal resource cost while optimizing risk. Stakeholder needs can be related to a set of generic enterprise goals. These have been developed using the BSc dimensions and represent a list of commonly used goals across the enterprise. Enterprise goals cascade into IT-related goals, structured along the dimensions of IT BSc. Achieving IT-related goals requires the successful application and use of a number of enablers such as processes, organizational structures and information. A set of specific relevant goals can be defined for each enabler.

Principle 2: Covering the Enterprise End-to-End

COBIT 5 integrates governance of enterprise IT into enterprise governance; it covers all functions and processes within the enterprise. COBIT 5 does not focus only on the 'IT function', but treats information and related technologies as assets that need to be dealt with just like any other, by everyone in the enterprise.

Governance enablers are organizational resources for governance, such as frameworks, principles, structures, processes and practices, through or towards which action is directed and objectives can be attained. Enablers also include the enterprise's resources like service capabilities (IT infrastructure and applications), people and information. A lack of resources or enablers may affect the ability of the enterprise to create value. Governance can be applied to the entire enterprise, an entity and a tangible or intangible asset. It is possible to define different views of the enterprise to which governance is applied, and it is essential to define this scope of the governance system well. The last element is governance roles, activities and relationships. It defines who is involved in governance and how, what they do and how they interact.

PRINCIPLE 3: APPLYING A SINGLE, INTEGRATED FRAMEWORK

COBIT 5 aligns with other relevant standards and frameworks at a high level and can thus serve as the overarching framework for governance and management of enterprise IT.

COBIT 5 is a single, integrated framework that aligns with other latest relevant standards and frameworks. Thus, the enterprise can use COBIT 5 as the overarching governance and management framework integrator. It is complete in enterprise coverage, providing a basis to integrate effectively with other frameworks, standards and practices. COBIT 5 provides a simple architecture for structuring guidance materials and producing a consistent product set and it integrates all knowledge previously dispersed over different ISACA frameworks.

PRINCIPLE 4: ENABLING A HOLISTIC APPROACH

Efficient and effective governance and management of enterprise IT requires a holistic approach, taking into account several interacting components. COBIT 5 defines a set of enablers to support the implementation of a comprehensive governance and management system for enterprise IT. Enablers are broadly defined as anything that can help achieve the objectives of the enterprise.

COBIT 5 defines seven categories of enablers: principle policies and frameworks; processes; organizational structures; culture, ethics and behavior; information; service infrastructure and applications; and people skills and competencies.

The four common dimensions for enablers: 1) Stakeholders are parties who play an active role and/or have an interest in the enabler; they can be internal or external to the enterprise, having their own, sometimes conflicting, interests and needs; 2) Each enabler has a number of goals and by achieving these, enablers provide value.

Goals can be defined in terms of expected outcomes of the enabler and application or operation of the enabler itself; 3) Each enabler has a life cycle, from inception through an operational/useful life until disposal and 4) Good practices support the achievement of the enabler goals, provide examples or suggestions on how best to implement the enabler and what work products or inputs and outputs are required. Enterprises expect positive outcomes from the application and use of enablers.

PRINCIPLE 5: SEPARATING GOVERNANCE FROM MANAGEMENT

COBIT 5 makes a clear distinction between governance and management. These two disciplines encompass different types of activities, require different organizational structures and serve different purposes. Governance ensures that stakeholder needs, conditions and options are evaluated to determine balanced, agreed-on enterprise objectives to be achieved, setting direction through prioritization and decision-making, and monitoring performance and compliance against agreed-on direction and objectives. Management, on the other hand, plans, builds, runs and monitors activities in alignment with the direction set by the governance body to achieve the enterprise objectives.

Governance contains five processes: ensure governance setting and maintenance, ensure benefits delivery, ensure risk optimization, ensure resource optimization and ensure stakeholder transparency. Within each process, Evaluate, Direct and Monitor practices are defined. Management contains four domains, in line with the responsibility areas of Plan, Build, Run and Monitor. The names of the domains are chosen in line with these main area designations, but contain more verbs to describe them - Align, Plan and Organize; Build, Acquire and Implement; Deliver, Service and Support and Monitor, Evaluate and Assess.[26]

GOVERNANCE CONSULTING APPROACH

The execution model of an IT Governance Consulting engagement would broadly traverse the following phases: Understand Context, Assess Current State, Define Target State, Analysis and Findings and Recommendations and Roadmap, incrementally building upon governance structures, mechanisms, processes and measurements.

UNDERSTAND CONTEXT

The objective of this phase is to understand the context in terms of the drivers, business, technology, stakeholders, scope and outcomes. The engagement sponsor and/or the engagement coordinator make up the target audience.

---

26 Source: Copyright 2012 ISACA. All rights reserved. Used with permission.

KEY ACTIVITIES OF THIS PHASE:

1. **UNDERSTAND DRIVERS**

    IT governance initiatives are driven by an increasing pressure to run IT like business - requiring IT strategies to complement business strategies - or an increasing need for accountability on IT investments or an increasing pressure on threat management and regulatory compliance, this is the external perspective.

    Alternatively, enterprises undertake IT governance initiatives to: think and act like one organization; achieve global integration with local differentiation by building enterprise-wide capabilities; simplify the span of IT control at leadership levels and rationalize the IT organization structure for clearer direction and better management of IT through delineation of roles and responsibilities; increase collaboration/partnership and strengthen the organization's innovation capacity; improve quality of services delivered to business and enable growth; simplify the current environment and reduce business/operational risks; streamline operations and standardize processes; or enable definition of skills and competencies as per industry standards for the target operating model, this is the internal perspective.

2. **UNDERSTAND BUSINESS**

    Leverage business drivers to understand the enterprise's strategic directions. Is the goal of the enterprise to be profit-oriented, growth-oriented or a combination of both profit and growth? If it is the first, the focus is on profitability via enterprise-wide coordination and core competencies. In case it is the second, focus is on business-unit innovation with only a few mandated processes. In case of a combination, the focus is on asset utilization, that is, efficient operation by maximizing IT sharing and reuse. This orientation will help determine suitable governance mechanisms and metrics for measurement, ultimately leading to governance arrangements for the enterprise - to be centralized, decentralized or blended.

3. **UNDERSTAND TECHNOLOGY**

    Evaluate business needs to determine the guiding principles for IT. Ability to scale will mandate emphasis on transaction processing, information storage and connectivity. It will also ensure that applications are not dependent on underlying platform and scalability of infrastructure. Agility for business scenarios like mergers, acquisitions, market captures, globalization, etc. will require applications integration to be flexible and inter-operable with the right level of centralization for each component and flexibility for multiple formats.

4. UNDERSTAND STAKEHOLDERS

Understanding stakeholders is the most critical and difficult activity, with a direct impact on the end outcome. The stakeholder set is very varied and extends beyond IT to business, executive leadership and occasionally, the board. Stakeholder management in the context of governance consulting is extremely sensitive and must be handled delicately, with diplomacy, without succumbing to influence or prejudice. The idea is to hear a first-person account of the individual's roles and responsibilities (which is taken at face value) and insights on other interactions (which requires further analysis). The role of the executive sponsor is paramount; a good practice is to have a dedicated HR representative assist in interviews - to state the objectives of the initiative, introduce the consultant, explain the purpose for which the information is being requested and its importance and ensure protection and confidentiality of all information shared.

5. UNDERSTAND SCOPE AND OUTCOMES

In governance consulting, the scope of the engagement is a function of the focus areas to be addressed. It could be structure or processes in a standalone mode or structure and mechanisms or processes and measurements in combination or all four focus areas together. The expected outcome is ensuring the right structure with corresponding roles and responsibilities, defining authority direction and support for key governance activities, linkage of business and IT plans, establishing right processes along with key controls, understanding the enterprise's appetite for risk and compliance requirements and implementing effective change-management practices.

The outcome of this phase is a re-confirmed governance consulting scope, focus areas to consider structures and mechanisms or processes and measurements plus the required coverage in each focus area in terms of breadth and depth.

ASSESS CURRENT STATE

The objective of this phase is to baseline the current organizational structure, roles, responsibilities, accountabilities, span of control, sphere of influence and understand the prevalent governance arrangements, mechanisms, processes and measurements. The target audience is the engagement sponsor, the engagement coordinator, business leadership, IT leadership and chair of strategy, planning and governance committees.

KEY ACTIVITIES OF THIS PHASE:

1. CURRENT GOVERNANCE STRUCTURES

In assessing current governance structure, emphasis is on the current IT organization. Interview all key stakeholders to understand their individual roles, responsibilities, reporting lines (at least one level above and one level below), goals, objectives, personal motivations and key success criteria. Assess existing committees to ascertain who the chair is, what their charter is, what is the composition and the frequency of their cadence. Obtain individual insights on how they perceive the target organization, in light of the drivers being addressed.

2. **CURRENT GOVERNANCE MECHANISMS**

Assess how decisions are taken, that is, the closest archetype with regard to IT principles, IT architecture, IT infrastructure, business application needs and IT investments. With regard to investments, drill-down further on the distribution to infrastructural, transactional, informational and strategic asset classes. Understand how the operating model works and the approach to generating business value (by being an efficient operator, solution integrator or innovation enabler); cross-check this position with the preference for centralization and the effectiveness of IT governance in this model.

3. **CURRENT GOVERNANCE PROCESSES**

Start assessment with enterprise-level governance processes. These are a combination of key and enabling processes. Next, asses function-level processes across governance layers. It is critical to observe conformance and cross-linkages. Assess maturity of governance processes on factors like awareness and communication, policy standards and procedures, tools and automation, skills and expertise, responsibility/accountability and goal setting and measurement. Classify the maturity of each process as non-existent, initial, repeatable, defined, managed or optimized.

4. **CURRENT GOVERNANCE MEASUREMENTS**

Similar to processes, measures are also cascaded from business to IT to process and activity goals. Current-state assessment of governance measurements involves assessing the alignment of goals bottom-up and the defined metrics to measure achievement. Key metrics are cost-effective use of IT, effective use of IT for growth, effective use of IT for asset utilization and effective use of IT for business flexibility.

The outcome of this phase is an assessment of the IT organization from a governance perspective. Governance being a subjective assessment, the yield is on qualitative observations that help understand the organization's work ethic and culture.

DEFINE TARGET STATE

The objective of this phase is to define the target organization structure, roles, responsibilities, accountabilities, span of control, sphere of influence and the prevalent

IT Governance Consulting 131

governance arrangements, mechanisms, processes and measurements. The engagement sponsor, the engagement coordinator, business leadership, IT leadership and chair of strategy, planning and governance committees make up the target audience.

KEY ACTIVITIES OF THIS PHASE:

1. TARGET GOVERNANCE STRUCTURES

   In workshop mode, with business leadership and IT leadership, brainstorm on the business drivers to baseline the implication to and expectation from governance. Organizational structures are affected primarily by the business imperatives that define the strategic performance of a firm. IT functions are designed to reinforce these business imperatives, which are, in turn, derived from end-customer needs. Lay out the complete cycle and contemplate on what role[s] facilitate the movement from one stage to another; soon, the role of a Business Relationship Manager will emerge as key. The relationship manager acts as an interface between business and IT, helps business units by identifying solutions and helps IT by becoming an advocate of technology in business. Additional factors to consider are market dynamics, industry trends, customer needs, competitor moves, organizational culture, internal strategic directions like organizational growth and geographic spread.

2. TARGET GOVERNANCE MECHANISMS

   Define the orientation best suited to achieve business goals, taking into account the capabilities and challenges of the current IT organization. The orientation will have a bearing on governance mechanisms and arrangement. In profit-oriented firms, the governance mechanism should focus on seamless management incorporation of IT, tracking of business value by measuring and monitoring IT investments and allocation of IT costs to business units. In growth-oriented firms, governance mechanism should focus on selective decentralization, centralized corporate systems and infrastructure, decentralized business unit-specific application development and emphasis on resource management and integration. In general, the more strategic and business unit-focused the IT mandate, the closer IT resources must be to the business. IT organizations that are not aligned structurally with the IT mandate will have difficulty delivering on their value proposition to the business.

3. TARGET GOVERNANCE PROCESSES

   IT organizations are best designed around processes that deliver services to the business. In workshop mode, with IT leadership, shape the target governance processes; more importantly, get consensus and buy-in. For each IT function, across governance layers, identify the business touch points and study the business process to effectively define the necessary governance processes. Examples are project prioritization, project management, project development, quality assurance and implementation processes; for each such process, define an owner and the targeted maturity level. As the governance processes mature, IT becomes a better team-based organization, ready to assemble and deploy resources wherever and whenever business mandates.

4. **TARGET GOVERNANCE MEASUREMENTS**

Target governance measurements, the Key Goal Indicators (KGIs) and Key Performance Indicators (KPIs), are defined after defining the governance structure, mechanisms and processes. BSc is a fit-for-purpose framework. KGIs indicate whether a goal has been achieved or not, after the fact; the focus is on BSc's customer and financial dimensions which are lag indicators. KPIs are a measure of how well the process is performing, to predict the probability of success or failure; the focus is on the BSc's process and learning dimensions which are lead indicators.

The outcome of this phase is the design and definition of the target IT organizational structure, required roles at a functional level and committees at a group level and associated responsibilities and accountabilities. Implicitly included are the governance mechanisms, processes and measurements.

ANALYSIS AND FINDINGS

The objective of this phase is to analyze the gaps between the current state and the defined target state for each governance focus area and articulate findings to help shape recommendations. The target audience comprises the engagement sponsor, the engagement coordinator, business leadership and IT leadership.

KEY ACTIVITIES OF THIS PHASE:

1. **ANALYSIS OF GOVERNANCE STRUCTURES**

   Analyze attributes of the defined target state to test gaps in structural, alignment and functional options, and business risks arising from gaps in governance structure and operational risks in governance mechanisms. Recognized current realities and envisioned end-state, as identified by the CIO, will help shape the model best suited for governance.

   Analyze defined IT functions in the context of the firm's business drivers and assess where they best fit in the governance layers or around the complete cycle of an enterprise's operations from customer need to business requirement, IT project definition/delivery and support and maintenance. Once the functions are positioned, roles will evolve, to move from one function to another or to move from one stage in the cycle to the next; where roles do not have a natural fit, explore the possibility of a committee.

2. **ANALYSIS OF GOVERNANCE MECHANISMS**

   Analyze the contribution of IT projects to business strategy, the performance of standardized business processes and RoI for strategic initiatives. Analyze existing architecture standards in terms of definition, deployment and configuration controls. Analyze customer-satisfaction survey data; this provides insights on how effectively business needs are being met and the degree of alignment between business and IT. Analyze the arrangements and benchmark against MIT CISR industry-wise data of top performers. Debate on deviations, if any, and retain the arrangement if there is context-specific rationale. Alternatively, redefine the arrangement if there is a reward for change that outweighs the rationale for status-quo.

3. **ANALYSIS OF GOVERNANCE PROCESSES**

   Analyze the business perception on value realization from IT-driven initiatives; there should be awareness of new technology decisions. Analyze architecture standards and review for compliance; relaxation of rigor will lead to less flexible IT systems. Architecture teams must be involved early on for strategic projects. Analyze enterprise-process ownership, the absence of which will result in multiple solutions for similar business processes across various segments. Analyze policy standards and procedures since they enable improvement and management. Analyze responsibility and accountability and empower process owners to make decisions and take action. Analyze tools and automation; they enable end-to-end support of the governance process. Analyze skills and expertise; continuous improvement should be seen in personal, process and organizational goals. Analyze goal setting and measurement, establish integrated performance-measurement linking IT performance to business goals. Analyze awareness and communication protocols, leverage tools and alternative channels to reinforce the message.

4. **ANALYSIS OF GOVERNANCE MEASUREMENTS**

   Analyze financial measures like number of IT customers, cost per customer, cost efficiency of governance processes, delivery of IT value per employee. Analyze process measures like availability of systems and services, application development on schedule and budget, number of errors and amount of rework and cost of quality. Analyze customer measures like level of service delivery, customer satisfaction, number of new customers and number of new delivery channels. Analyze learning measures like staff productivity and morale, staff trained in new technologies/services and increased availability and adoption of knowledge systems. Analyze monitoring process and data-collection methods, process for reporting content and mechanisms to board and to executive management and pay attention to exception handling and remedial action identified and initiated.

The outcomes of this phase are findings from the gap analysis from a governance perspective to help articulate the right recommendations to achieve business objectives.

RECOMMENDATIONS AND REPORT

The objective of this phase is to recommend a governance roadmap addressing the governance focus areas in scope. The target audience is the engagement sponsor, the engagement coordinator, business leadership, IT leadership and chair of strategy, planning and governance committees.

KEY ACTIVITIES OF THIS PHASE:

1. **GOVERNANCE ROADMAP**

    Governance roadmap encompasses structures, mechanisms, processes and measurements, focusing on strategic alignment of business and IT, ensuring IT delivers promised benefits against strategy through well-defined and customer-focused systems. Governance guides proper management of critical IT resources: application, information, architecture, infrastructure and people. In essence, it builds a better IT for better business.

    The governance structure establishes organizational structures to ensure IT investments deliver on enterprise strategies and objectives. The structure covers the complete spread from strategy to management and operational roles with unambiguous responsibilities, accountabilities and practices for managing risk, resources, performance and avoiding internal breakdown or external oversight.

    At a minimum, the structure should include apex committees like the executive committee and the strategy and planning committee. The executive committee is chaired by the CEO and comprises his/her direct reports and the CIO. It meets once a quarter to ensure that an effective strategic planning process is in place, to ratify the aligned business and IT strategy, to ascertain that processes and practices are in place for IT to deliver value to business and to assess senior management's performance on IT strategies and operations. The strategy and planning committee is chaired by the CIO and comprises IT leadership and business relationship managers. It meets once a month to issue high level policy guidance on funding, sourcing and risk; to oversee delivery of value of IT; to assess competitive positioning and to monitor return on IT investments.

Governance mechanisms should spell out enabling alignment of IT with the business in strategy and operations, encouraging co-responsibility between business and IT for making strategic decisions and obtaining benefits from IT-enabled investments. The mechanisms should propagate standardized technology investments to the extent possible, thus avoiding increased cost and the complexity of multiple technical solutions. The enterprise's IT risk position should be transparent to all stakeholders.

The governance processes should be clear and consistent and must conform to architecture policies and standards. Assess IT infrastructure on a periodic basis to ensure that it is standardized wherever possible and interoperability continues to exist where required. Ensure management oversight for committed compliance to the process with full appreciation of its purpose.

Governance measures and performance metrics should be approved by key stakeholders. Reporting to executive levels should include the extent to which planned objectives have been achieved, deliverables obtained, performance targets met and risks mitigated. The board and executive should challenge these performance reports and IT management should be given an opportunity to explain deviations and performance problems. Upon review, appropriate management action should be initiated and controlled.

Governance is about accountability at the highest level; its responsibility cannot be delegated. It should play a bigger role beyond just IT scrutiny; it is certainly not another level of approval. IT governance must be explained and continuously reinforced if it is to ever gain traction. It requires executive buy-in and the attention of top management. Governance should not be for Governance's sake.

The outcome of this phase is the final deliverable, the Governance Consulting Report. This reflects on the IT organization in terms of IT domains, governance styles or archetypes, governance mechanisms, governance processes and governance measurements. It recommends a governance framework that is best suited to achieve enterprise goals. The report is prepared by the consultants and submitted to the executive sponsor for sign-off.

Key Learnings

IT has traditionally been treated as an entity separate from the business. IT is complex and requires more technical insight than other disciplines, to understand how it enables the enterprise, especially in the extended enterprise operating in a networked economy.

The role of IT Governance, therefore, is to establish a structure that can maximize value delivered by IT, through proven governance processes. The structure, in turn, is strengthened by well-defined roles and responsibilities. The roles mandate specific decision-making mechanisms pertinent to the specific IT domain. The mechanisms are supported by measurements that rightfully reflect their performance and are monitored by empowered committees. The beauty of this sequence is that it can withstand new business models, changing business practices and also balance IT costs.

Focus is on governance structures (the right arrangement of IT functions and governance mechanisms), linkages from projects to IT to business, governance processes (activities with responsibilities, accountabilities and key performance indicators and governance measurements), predefined measures encompassing lead and lag indicators and governance layers (IT functions spread across the strategic, tactical and operational layers of the enterprise).

Governance models are characterized by the envisaged span of control and sphere of influence. A utility model is process based and is defined by a high degree of structure and formality of interactions. IT resources usually reside in a central group focused on achieving efficiency. In a project-management model, business/IT interactions are centered on projects; control of certain key functions is shifted to the business units. A differentiated model is relationship-based; control of IT rests firmly with the business units. A transformational model is idea-based; IT plays a key role in driving business strategy, and business and IT work closely together to drive technology innovation.

MIT CISR has done pioneering work in the field of IT governance. Its Arrangement Matrix is a function of what decisions are to be made and who should make them. The former includes IT principles, IT infrastructure strategies, IT architecture, business-application needs and IT investment prioritization. The latter extends from business monarchy to IT monarchy, feudal, federal, duopoly and anarchy systems. The governance mechanisms here are decision-making structures, alignment processes and communication approaches.

Profit-oriented firms are centralized; growth-oriented firms are de-centralized. However, in today's economy, firms seek a blend of both, a hybrid IT organization that combines elements of a traditional, centralized organization with aspects of a distributed organization. The benefit of this construct is that it offers economies of scale because of the centralized role and improved business alignment and responsiveness by virtue of the decentralized role.

. Ω .

Chapter 7

IT Infrastructure Consulting

The term 'Infrastructure' implies a collection of physical assets assembled to provide a set of services that enable efficient operations for the enterprise. Extending this premise to the IT world, IT infrastructure would, therefore, be the entire computing platform, comprising hardware, software, networks, telecommunication and the facilities that host these physical assets.

IT infrastructure is the critical link that provides the capability to run business applications and business processes efficiently. IT infrastructure is not just about enabling business but also about running business operations smoothly and efficiently. For this, it needs to be responsive to business needs, resistant to changes in application and also cost effective. Key factors that impact the business from an IT infrastructure perspective are availability, performance, scalability, sustainability and security.

IT Infrastructure Consulting, the 'I' in SAPPGIO-T of the IT Consulting Spectrum, primarily deals with planning and design of required infrastructure components, budget distribution for capital and operational expenditure, right-selecting components and right-sizing configurations, operating level agreements and opportunities for consolidation or optimization.

In addition to a broad understanding of the IT Infrastructure Space, this chapter provides insights into Infrastructure Consulting Focus Areas, illustrates an Infrastructure Framework and an Approach to executing Infrastructure Consulting engagements.

Infrastructure Consulting Space

Infrastructure capability is a complex fusion of technology and human assets, shared throughout the business in the form of centrally coordinated, reliable services. Infrastructure links basic IT capabilities in the enterprise to business partners and external and public infrastructure.

Identifying infrastructure needs is not easy. While infrastructure components are commonly available commodities, the management processes used to implement the best mix of infrastructure capabilities to meet specific business strategy is always a challenge.

IT infrastructure can be deployed at different levels, enterprise-wide or at a business unit and are often shared across many applications and multiple business initiatives. This sharing requires negotiation about how much is needed, who pays for it, where it should be placed and who owns it.[27]

In 'Leveraging the New Infrastructure' Peter Weill and Marianne Broadbent, articulate the new infrastructure as: 'Utility View' a firm-wide IT infrastructure where clear cost savings are achieved; 'Dependent View' where infrastructure capability is driven by the current business strategy and finally 'Enabling View' where infrastructure is a core competence with extensive capability to increase strategic options.[28]

In IT Infrastructure services, the focus is first on cost: how to manage lean IT budgets. The associated levers are virtualization of servers and/or storage, network convergence, data-center consolidation, standardization of development and test environments. Secondly, the focus is on the future: how to plan for the future. The levers here are infrastructure capacity planning, simplified/standardized processes and process maturity. The next area of focus would be efficiency: how to improve operational efficiency. Applicable levers are batch-window reduction, storage optimization, automated asset management and optimized data life-cycle management. Lastly, the focus is on risk: how to manage and mitigate risks. The levers here are planning for disaster recovery and for system software upgrade.

INFRASTRUCTURE ECOSYSTEM

1. DATA CENTER

This refers to the host facility in which IT infrastructure assets are housed. It includes server infrastructure, storage infrastructure and network equipment. Server infrastructure consists of servers for application, collaboration, mail or exchange, storage, database and backup. Storage devices used to meet the data needs of business and IT make up the storage infrastructure. Network equipment incudes routers and switches to connect each workstation within the enterprise with the data center. Software components like the operating system, asset monitors and load balancers needed to run the physical assets are also considered part of the data center.

---

[27] Weill, P., Subramani, M. and Broadbent, M. (2002) IT infrastructure for strategic agility. *MIT CISR Research Article*

[28] Weill, P. and Broadbent, M. (1998). *Leveraging the new infrastructure*. Harvard Business School Press.

2. **End-User Computing**

   The user facility is a combination of end-user computing and IT service desk. End-user computing includes desktops, laptops, printers and scanners. IT service desk, also called the IT help desk, is the front-end of the IT infrastructure for the rest of the enterprise and is serviced by technology experts using a host of management and automation tools.

3. **Help Desk**

   This is a team of component-specific experts who help in planning, sizing and operating the infrastructure, in collaboration with Original Equipment Manufacturers (OEMs). Also referred to as Service Desk, the help desk provides a single point of contact for communication and technology needs of business and IT users, which can vary from a simple access request to critical incidents that can stall the business.

4. **Service Management**

   Basic IT infrastructure services are defined and administered in a process-oriented manner as per service-level agreements. IT service management refers to a series of workflows orchestrated through polices, governance mechanisms and organization structure to plan, deliver and operate IT services for the end users.

5. **Infrastructure Library**

   ITIL was originally developed by UK Government's Central Computing and Telecommunications Agency, currently owned by Axelos Ltd, a joint venture between HM Cabinet Office and Capita plc. ITIL offers a set of practices for IT Service Management and is the most widely adopted across the industry. ITIL provides guidance on defining infrastructure services and defines processes that enable these services.

Principles of IT Infrastructure

1. **Benchmark Frequently for a Fruitful Future**

   Benchmarking provides a clear insight into where the organization is spending more or less or even compared to the larger industry and select competitors. Benchmarking leads to corrective action to close the gaps and provides opportunities for optimizing IT infrastructure.

2. **REFRESH INFRASTRUCTURE PERIODICALLY TO AVOID COST OVERHEADS**

   The older the infrastructure, the costlier it is to maintain. Over the past decade, technology has changed dramatically, lowering the cost of computing. The latest releases offer sturdy computing capabilities and reduced infrastructure maintenance. With new releases, OEMs either decommission older ones or charge a premium for their maintenance. Therefore, keeping up with technology changes is in the best interest of the organization both from a cost and a support point of view.

3. **RESTRICT OEMS TO A SELECT FEW FOR ECONOMIES OF SCALE**

   The more diverse the OEM universe, the costlier the operations. Having too many OEMs in the IT mix limits the organization's ability to obtain volume discounts. In addition, the potential to scale is also low, since different OEMs have their own pace of maturity and technical advancements. Sourcing IT equipment from too many OEMs may impede radical changes in the IT infrastructure.

4. **OPTIMALLY UTILIZE INFRASTRUCTURE ASSETS FOR OPERATIONAL SUSTENANCE**

   Infrastructure assets should not be over- or under-utilized. Trying to enhance operational efficiency exerts pressure to increase utilization of infrastructure components, be it servers, storage or the network. An optimal bracket is believed to be 70–80% utilization. If utilization is below this, it could cause paid-for unused computing; utilization above the optimal bracket risks equipment breakdown and frequent maintenance. Even the data center must have free capacity, due to power and cooling limitations; it is impractical to target 100% utilization. Moreover, free capacity in the data center acts as a safety valve, to accommodate unplanned activities.

5. **MONITOR CONSUMPTION FOR POTENTIAL CHARGEBACK**

   Infrastructure cost must be accounted to business. Although IT infrastructure is considered a utility, it is prudent to note which business unit consumes how much infrastructure resources and how much this contributes to the total cost of operations. A formal chargeback may or may not be considered, but cost accounting of the data center helps understand consumption patterns.

INFRASTRUCTURE CONSULTING FOCUS AREAS

INFRASTRUCTURE UTILIZATION

Infrastructure utilization refers to the percentage of capacity in use by either servers or storage or network or the data center as a whole. In infrastructure operations, higher utilization is not always ideal. Infrastructure must have adequate free capacity at all times, to accommodate sudden peaks in business transactions or unplanned capacity expansion. Moreover, constant high utilization of IT assets may lead to frequent maintenance, thereby impacting IT performance. On the other hand, consistent low utilization clearly indicates scope for reduction of IT assets, thereby enabling cost savings.

Infrastructure utilization is measured for all infrastructure components, that is, servers, storage, network, end-user computing and data center. In case of servers, utilization is assessed by average central-processing unit utilization as a percentage. For storage, it is the percentage of storage capacity used against the total available storage. In networks, it is the ratio of current network traffic to maximum network traffic supported by each port, calculated for each deployed port to determine average network utilization. For data-center facilities, utilization is calculated as square footage occupied of the total available square footage.

Infrastructure Spend

Infrastructure investment or spend is the cost of infrastructure assets and infrastructure operations taken together. This is the single largest cost component in any firm's total IT spend. Infrastructure spend categories are hardware spend and software spend, each of which has a capital expenditure component and an operating expenditure component.

Hardware spend refers to the cost of physical equipment. Software spend is the cost of software required to run the hardware components. A third category is spending on external services, payments made to OEMs or local resellers who maintain the hardware and software on an annual maintenance contract. Equally important is the cost of internal personnel who operate or design the IT infrastructure.

Infrastructure Optimization

In infrastructure utilization and spend, the emphasis is on audit/benchmarking. Infrastructure optimization is an extension, leveraging insights from audit and results of benchmarking to explore ways to transition the good to better and the better to best.

Optimization can be in the form of standardizing infrastructure, restructuring maintenance, rationalizing external services, adjusting end-user computing, procuring licenses based on usage, readjusting test/production environments and future-proofing infrastructure configurations to reduce costs, increase productivity and extend the longevity of infrastructure investments.

INFRASTRUCTURE CONSULTING FRAMEWORK

An industry-recognized framework for infrastructure consulting is the ITIL developed by the Office of Government Commerce, UK. ITIL provides guidelines for the service management part of infrastructure consulting and asset management; most organizations have developed their own framework based on experience.

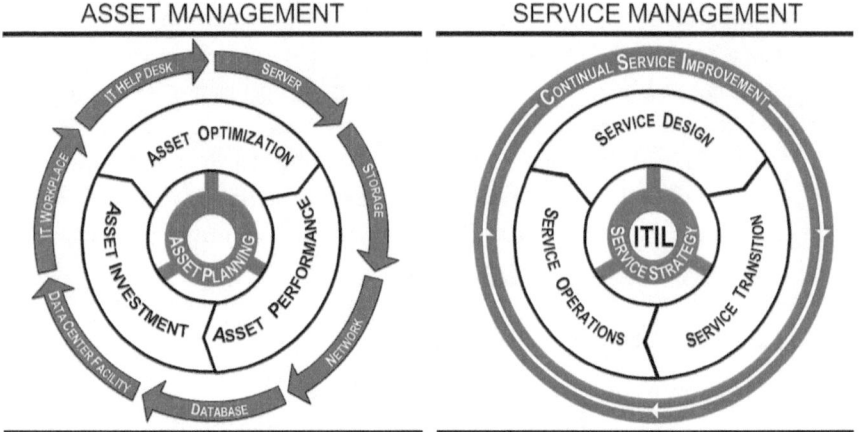

ASSET-MANAGEMENT FRAMEWORK

Asset management lacks a globally accepted framework, because it is highly contextual and complex. It focuses on acknowledging all possible assets in the IT department and proposing a common approach to optimize each category individually and collectively.

Infrastructure assets are categorized as 1) Data center: a collection of servers, storage, network, database and facility; 2) End-User Computing: a collection of desktops, laptops, printers and scanners and 3) IT Help Desk or Service Desk: considered an asset as it plays a crucial role in delivering infrastructure services to the larger enterprise.

ASSET PERFORMANCE

The focus here is on assessing the performance of existing IT infrastructure on a variety of parameters, ranging from infrastructure utilization to age of infrastructure, performance on service level agreements and maintenance history. Once individual asset performance is obtained, it is assessed along with other such assets within the location or for the function, to gauge overall performance and pinpoint areas where improvements are feasible. Asset performance provides a solid foundation for deriving infrastructure-optimization initiatives.

Asset Investment

Infrastructure assets are usually a firm's biggest cost item; even the slightest improvement in asset investments has the potential to deliver a considerable impact on the bottom line for the enterprise. The cost includes both the expense of physical assets and the essential software required to make them usable. A common practice is to examine a history of spend on each infrastructure component for three to five years and benchmark it against industry and competitor data. Investment variations are then studied in relation to the strategic business and IT decisions with the objective of rationalizing overinvestment or underinvestment without impacting business continuity.

Asset Optimization

Asset optimization is to be undertaken after achieving reasonable levels of maturity in asset performance and investment. The essence of optimization is to identify additional ways to utilize existing infrastructure and/or better ways to invest. It is important to phase out optimization initiatives and implement initiatives that have the potential to deliver short-term benefits first, so that savings can be re-invested for initiatives that deliver benefits in the longer term, thus creating a cyclic self-funding model.

Service-Management Framework

ITIL is built on a process-model view of controlling and managing operations, addressing the structure and skill requirements of an IT organization by presenting comprehensive management procedures. ITIL treats the IT department as a service provider and positions a service desk as the single point of contact to request services from IT and report incidents. ITIL suggests a service catalog containing details of IT services available to customers along with service-level agreements. ITIL is only a framework and not a standard against which assessments are made. The best practice for ITIL adoption is to develop a service management vision, technical architecture standards, tools and robust service-governance model that can facilitate the outcomes. In addition, change management plays a key role and must be adequately planned.

ITIL defines a life cycle for IT services consisting of five phases: Service strategy, Service design, Service transition, Service operations and Continual service improvement. While the first three phases are primarily concerned with bringing new or improved services to the service catalog, the remaining are concerned with service delivery and optimization of current services.

Service Strategy

This addresses strategic and governance processes like demand management, financial management, service-portfolio management, service-strategy principle generation, organization and sourcing. Service strategy is the strategic commitment for how IT services and service management will contribute to the achievement of business objectives. Service portfolio is the defined set of IT services that provide business value, including the full services life cycle, from proposed and in-development services to retired services. The focus is on funding, RoI and chargeback.

Service Design

This addresses operational processes like service-catalogue management, service-level management, catalogue management, capacity management, availability management, continuity management, information-security management and supplier management. Service catalog is a subset of the IT service portfolio. It lists the services currently available with associated service requests. The focus is on service catalog, policies and standards.

Service Transition

This addresses operational processes like transition planning and support, change management, service asset and configuration management, release and deployment management, validation and testing, evaluation, service-release acceptance, decommission and transfer and knowledge management. A roadmap with the approach required to implement and manage the IT service strategy. Focus is on release calendar and change schedule.

Services Operations

This supports operational processes like monitoring and event management, incident management, request fulfillment, problem management, access management and functions like technical management, operations management, application management, infrastructure management, facilities management and service desk. The focus is on service availability, causal analysis and incident statistics.

Continual Service Improvement

Applicable to all the above phases, this addresses processes related to measurement and control, service measurement, service assessment and analysis, process assessment and analysis, service-level management and improvement planning. The focus is on creating and maintaining value for customers, reducing operation cost, improving service quality and user satisfaction, ensuring compliance and exploring ways to enhance the service provision.

Infrastructure Consulting Approach

The execution model of an IT Infrastructure Consulting engagement would broadly traverse the following phases: Understand Context, Assess Current State, Define Target State, Analysis and Findings and Recommendations and Roadmap, touching upon the three focus areas of infrastructure consulting.

Understand Context

The objective of this phase is to understand the context in terms of the drivers, business, technology, stakeholders, scope and outcomes. The target audience is the engagement sponsor and/or the engagement coordinator.

Key Activities of this Phase:

1. **Understand Drivers**

   In infrastructure utilization, the driving force is reducing IT complexity, achieved by consolidating infrastructure, eliminating redundant infrastructure components and streamlining support and administration effort. The driver for infrastructure-spend analysis is achieving optimal cost-to-value by rationalizing infrastructure and consolidating OEMs.

   Infrastructure optimization is a combination of the drivers for utilization and spend in conjunction with right-sizing the infrastructure footprint towards establishing a target state operating model with a strong focus on service management.

2. **Understand Business**

   Understand the business of infrastructure along the following themes:
   - Service-Level Alignment: Validates the alignment of IT with the organization's service-level goals and the contribution of infrastructure to such an alignment.
   - Operational Efficiency: Analyzes the efficiency level at which the current Infrastructure is performing with the available resources and the cost to maximize outputs.
   - Risk Proofing: Determines how well the IT infrastructure is proofed/protected against threats and vulnerabilities.
   - Future Readiness: Forecasts the scalability and robustness of the current infrastructure to take up any future demands arising due to business growth and industry demands.
   - Industry Trends and Standards: Aids in analyzing the alignment of the current Infrastructure with Industry trends and standards.

- Innovation: Helps in understanding the innovation levels required to create differentiation.

3. **UNDERSTAND TECHNOLOGY**

    Understand infrastructure technology to assess impact of the following challenges:
    - Aging/Obsolete Technology: Infrastructure is taken granted for as long as the existing technology meets its stated purpose. Over time, these legacy technologies get heavily customized to meet user demands. Each change makes it more complex and rigid for future migration to a newer technology.
    - Out-of-Support Technology: As organizations continue to use dated technology, they are often stuck with out-of-support technology components. This happens due to the product vendor upgrading its technology stack and subsequently not supporting older versions in an effort to migrate all their customers to their supported stack.
    - Skill-Set Shortage: As technology evolves, the focus keeps shifting to the newer breed of technologies. Even academia focuses on newer technologies instead of legacy technologies. This slowly causes a skill-set shortage, as the number of people who know the legacy technology dwindles and getting skilled resources becomes an issue.
    - Compliance: Regulatory compliance is mandatory for all organizations. With physical boundaries diminishing and access to information becoming easy, the chances of security breaches are also increasing. This forces organizations to develop controls and procedures that will prevent any security leak and will ensure all established controls are in place to fulfil compliance. As the technology component enters a phase of obsolescence and existing vendors stop supporting it, these components become vulnerable to compliance requirements.
    - Standardization: In today's business environment, mergers, acquisitions and consolidation bring together diverse technology components. The new organization has to manage them and plan their future roadmap.
    - Vendor Stability: Organizations always want to use products from vendors who have good market standing and are stable. If vendor stability becomes an issue, it affects their ability to invest and expand the products they have, which, in turn, creates issues with competitiveness.

4. **UNDERSTAND STAKEHOLDERS**

    The stakeholder set is the widest in infrastructure consulting, ranging from engagement sponsor to engagement coordinator, financial analysts, business owners, application managers, enterprise architects, system engineers, database administrators and network managers. Every stakeholder plays a defined role in the infrastructure value chain and is privy to specific insights within his/her domain. Express caution while interpreting these inputs, filter out personal opinions and retain only professional advice.

5. **UNDERSTAND SCOPE AND OUTCOMES**

   The scope of an operational infrastructure consulting engagement typically is assessment of current-state IT Infrastructure landscape from a server and storage perspective to determine and document future-state infrastructure architecture, infrastructure roadmap, cost/benefit analysis and strategies to co-exist while transitioning from current state to target state. In transformational engagements, the scope extends to infrastructure life-cycle management, architecture rationalization, configuration optimization, server and storage consolidation or virtualization, business service-level management and next generation data center. Expected outcomes are opportunities for improvement classified as just-do-it, must-do-it and good-to-do-it, with a deployment cycle in manageable segments.

The outcome of this phase is a re-confirmed infrastructure scope, focus areas and a target operating model with expected service levels.

ASSESS CURRENT STATE

The objective of this phase is to baseline the entire infrastructure inventory, that is, details of infrastructure utilization, spend and potential optimization avenues. The engagement coordinator, financial analysts, business owners, application managers, enterprise architects, system engineers, database administrators, network managers and OEM representatives make up the target audience.

KEY ACTIVITIES OF THIS PHASE:

1. **CURRENT INFRASTRUCTURE UTILIZATION**

   Collect and baseline inventory details of servers, storage, middleware, network, help desk and data center. A variety of additional parameters for each infrastructure component needs to be captured for subsequent analysis. Utilization is assessed individually at a component level.

   For servers, utilization is measured as a percentage of CPU utilization over a period of time, usually a year. This metric is important to understand the potential peaks in the business cycle and how the server transaction volume is related to the same.

For storage, utilization is measured in terms of total available storage versus used storage. For other infrastructure components, utilization is broadly measured in terms of percentage of capacity used out of total available capacity.

Illustrative list of component-specific parameters:

SERVER	• PHYSICAL VS. VIRTUAL SERVERS • SERVERS BY OS	• SERVERS BY OEM • SERVERS BY FUNCTION • CPU UTILIZATION	• YEARS IN SERVICE • WARRANTY/AMC COVERAGE
STORAGE	• TOTAL USABLE STORAGE • TOTAL AVAILABLE VS. USED STORAGE	• DEGREE OF VIRTUALIZATION • ADOPTION OF LOW COST STORAGE	• STORAGE BY OEM • YEARS IN SERVICE • WARRANTY/AMC COVERAGE
NETWORK	• TOTAL NETWORK DEVICES • DEVICES BY OWNERSHIP • DEVICES BY FUNCTION	• DEVICES BY OEM • UTILIZATION OF DEVICES • YEARS IN SERVICE	• WARRANTY/AMC COVERAGE
DATABASE/ MIDDLEWARE	• TOTAL MIDDLEWARE INSTANCES • DATABASE BY TYPE • DATABASES BY FUNCTION	• TOTAL DATABASE SPACE AVAILABLE • TOTAL DATABASE SPACE USED	• YEARS IN SERVICE • WARRANTY/AMC COVERAGE
END-USER COMPUTING	• TOTAL DEVICES (DESKTOP, LAPTOP) • TOTAL PERIPHERALS (PRINTER, SCANNER)	• DEVICES BY OEM • DEVICES BY REGION	• DEVICES PER USER • YEARS IN SERVICE • WARRANTY/AMC COVERAGE
DATA CENTER	• TOTAL FLOOR SPACE AVAILABLE • TOTAL FLOOR SPACE USED • TOTAL POWER CONSUMPTION	• POWER USAGE EFFECTIVENESS • POWER DENSITY PER RACK • TOTAL COOLING CAPACITY	• RETURN AIR TEMPERATURE
SERVICE DESK	• TOTAL INCIDENTS PER DAY – MAJOR, MINOR • TICKETS LOGGED PER DAY	• CRITICAL SERVICES SLA • FIRST CALL RESOLUTION TIME • TOOLS USED	• ITIL COMPLIANCE • AVERAGE CUSTOMER SATISFACTION SCORE

Furthermore, the age and warranty coverage of infrastructure is also assessed. This helps in understanding which parts of infrastructure are outdated and could cause potential business risk. The primary focus at this stage is to audit the infrastructure in terms of performance and utilization and document any obvious risks or issues.

2. **Current Infrastructure Spend**

   Like utilization, spend on IT infrastructure is also calculated individually for all infrastructure components and accumulated to compute the Total Infrastructure Spend, a crucial metric. Infrastructure spend is broadly classified as Capital Expenditure (CAPEX) and Operational Expenditure (OPEX). CAPEX refers to the upfront cost incurred by the physical equipment including the essential software to make it usable. OPEX refers to incremental costs incurred to maintain and operate the physical equipment. OPEX includes maintenance fees, people expenses and external service costs.

   At a component level, Infrastructure spend (the total of CAPEX and OPEX for that particular component) as a percentage of the Total IT spend is computed and benchmarked by industry or by geography. This helps understand spend patterns and if there is over- or under-spending. In cases where there is a consistently high CAPEX - for example, on servers - current configurations would need to be examined to see if they are fit for purpose.

Benchmarking is mostly against industry standards/averages or against peers/competitors within the industry. Given the nature of confidentiality in such cases, most benchmark figures are defined in a range with minimum and maximum thresholds. Deviation from benchmark may be acceptable as long as there is a valid justification.

3. **POTENTIAL FOR INFRASTRUCTURE OPTIMIZATION**

    Utilization data, spend data and the component-specific parameters listed above provide meaningful insights into defining the potential for optimization.

    Consistently high utilization may cause faster wear and tear, increasing maintenance cost or early replacement. A very low utilization means unwanted capacity that has been paid for. Thus, optimization in the context of utilization is converging towards the prescribed range for that particular infrastructure component.

    Degree of virtualization is another parameter to assess potential for further virtualization or optimization. Similarly, age of infrastructure equipment provides a clear insight about which components are outdated and need to be decommissioned in the near future. Housing such equipment leads to high maintenance costs and significant business risk.

    Optimization may not always be driven by cost or utilization; in some cases, optimization might lead to initiatives for improving service quality. Therefore, identifying anomalies such as downtime of the equipment, outages and unavailability provide critical insights into how well infrastructure is deployed and managed and how it can be improved or optimized.

The outcome of this phase is baselined inventory of infrastructure and details of other component-specific parameters along with preliminary thoughts on potential for optimization.

DEFINE TARGET STATE

The objective of this phase is to conceptualize the future state of the infrastructure environment, aligned with the business and IT strategy and building upon the best practices and strengths of the current environment to further enhance the computing power of the enterprise. The target audience is the engagement sponsor, engagement coordinator, financial analysts, business owners, application managers, enterprise architects, system engineers, database administrator and network managers.

KEY ACTIVITIES OF THIS PHASE:

1. **INFRASTRUCTURE UTILIZATION IMPROVEMENT**

    Identify infrastructure components that have pockets of underutilization. Unless there is a business justification, utilization must be as close as possible to the optimal level, which is typically 70-80%.

    Goal categories to define the target infrastructure are:

    - Scalability: Infrastructure should be able to enforce security at the level of network access, function access and data access.
    - Manageability: Operational management of technology platforms and applications should be through a system-management framework that includes system operation, monitoring of resource utilization, performance and control. Infrastructure should be managed centrally and remotely.
    - Simplicity: All technology platforms should be consolidated across standard delivery architecture to avoid complexity.
    - Stability and Reliability: Technology platforms should be based on proven technologies and obsolete/out-of-support technologies should be eliminated.
    - Availability: Infrastructure should be able to support 24x7 processing windows. Fault-tolerant/high-available architecture for at least critical services is imperative.
    - Agility and Flexibility: Infrastructure should be able to seamlessly support business/application architecture and be flexible to change.

    A common practice is to partition underutilized equipment and use the partitions instead of purchasing new equipment. The size of the development and testing environment also impacts utilization. If development or testing infrastructure is consistently underutilized, their size should be reduced immediately.

    Virtualization of infrastructure is a proven technique to boost utilization at all levels. This has been a mainstream activity and has delivered positive benefits. Although there may be an upfront cost for virtualization, its benefits outperform the investment.

2. **INFRASTRUCTURE SPEND IMPROVEMENT**

    Study each deviation of spend with respect to benchmarks available and analyze any significant deviation either positive or negative. The cost of annual maintenance contracts of aged equipment is typically high. Undertake a cost-benefit analysis of such equipment and decommission it as appropriate. Fixing utilization may lower cost automatically; explore such opportunities.

Often spend on infrastructure relates closely to procurement efficiency. Bulk purchases can help leverage economies of scale and allow firms to negotiate significantly. While this is true of upfront capital costs, it is equally important to validate this in conjunction with the operational costs of annual maintenance. Also explore managed service models or hosted infrastructure that can take away CAPEX and incur only OPEX. On a smaller scale, an opportunity for improvement is investment in training of internal staff, which can deduct related cost from external services costs.

3. **Avenues for Infrastructure Optimization**

Infrastructure optimization takes the infrastructure spend, age, virtualization, benchmarking data as inputs and defines the target state of optimized infrastructure. At this stage, the role of infrastructure architecture is extremely important. The architecture should focus on standardization of infrastructure and reduction of complexity and provide scalability, timely delivery, reliability, and future-proofing of services offered. Establish guiding principles to maximize agility and minimize the business costs, while meeting business resiliency and regulatory requirements.

The outcome of this phase is an optimized target infrastructure environment with reduced complexity and cost of operations and an improved service quality.

Analysis and Findings

The objective of this phase is to analyze and benchmark findings from current-state assessment and gaps with regard to defined target state. A thorough assessment is required to fully understand the impact of any change in any of the infrastructure components on operations, technology and business. The target audience is the engagement sponsor, engagement coordinator, financial analysts, business owners, application managers, enterprise architects, system engineers, database administrator and network managers.

Key Activities of this Phase:

1. **Improving Utilization**

    Any initiative to improve utilization of infrastructure either results in reduction of physical equipment or redistribution of workload or a mix of both. Therefore, once underutilized infrastructure equipment is identified, analyze impacted workloads. This reveals which applications or functions or business units will benefit from the utilization-improvement exercise.

Although the changes are proposed at infrastructure component level, each impacted application owner and business unit owner should be made aware of the utilization-improvement exercise, its benefits and impact. A migration plan is then built and shared across the impacted stakeholder community to ensure business continuity and mitigate any potential risks. In case the plan involves changes to operating procedures, the infrastructure personnel need to be informed and trained.

2. **IMPROVING SPEND**

Spend-improvement initiatives usually involve rethinking infrastructure-sourcing strategy, pricing models, converting CAPEX to OPEX, restructuring annual maintenance contracts, redistributing suppliers and reallocating funding. Given the strategic nature of infrastructure spend, all improvement initiatives should be assessed for potential risks and be backed up with adequate cost-benefit analysis.

Even after meeting the above criteria, a wait might be necessary before some initiatives can be triggered, for example, maintenance contracts can be restructured only after pre-defined end dates of ongoing contracts expire. Furthermore, every effort must be made to ensure that none of the initiatives have an adverse impact on service levels or quality of services.

3. **OPTIMIZING INFRASTRUCTURE**

Generally, infrastructure is optimized by virtualization, standardization, consolidation, architectural changes or a mix of such initiatives. Infrastructure optimization may also involve revamping service desk, redefining infrastructure processes and workflows and deploying tools and solutions.

Infrastructure optimization may lead to a new technology landscape supported by a new category of service providers and other noticeable improvements in service delivery. Change management thus becomes critical for sustenance of optimization initiatives. Stakeholder set includes the infrastructure team, rest of IT and also the larger enterprise.

The outcome of this phase is an in-depth analysis of causes for deviation in utilization thresholds, variation in spending and leveraging findings to define strategies for optimization.

RECOMMENDATIONS AND REPORT

The objective of this phase is to recommend initiatives for infrastructure optimization and a roadmap for implementation. The engagement sponsor, engagement coordinator, business owners and application managers make up the target audience.

IT Infrastructure Consulting

KEY ACTIVITIES OF THIS PHASE:

1. **INFRASTRUCTURE-OPTIMIZATION INITIATIVES**

   The focus here is to identify infrastructure-optimization initiatives for improving utilization and spend and to provide necessary details to prioritize and make them actionable.

   Areas that require special focus are architectural changes, as they have an impact on how the organization operates, and risk assessment to ensure that business continuity is maintained. Risk and a comprehensive business case play a significant role in prioritizing optimization initiatives and obtaining management buy-in. The business case must justify RoI with a compelling payback period.

   All infrastructure-optimization initiatives are prioritized keeping in mind the client's business operations, financial constraints and risk appetite. Qualified initiatives are shared with all stakeholders.

2. **INFRASTRUCTURE-OPTIMIZATION ROADMAP**

   The optimization roadmap outlines the path to address the enterprise's business drivers, be it strategic alignment, business growth, operational efficiency, service agility or faster acquisition integration.

   The considered sets of parameters for this journey in the context of infrastructure optimization are scalability, manageability, simplicity, stability and reliability, availability, agility and flexibility. The roadmap sequences the initiatives such that the above parameters first optimize the infrastructure component individually and then, collectively.

   The roadmap should define time horizons, tools for automation or monitoring, resource requirements and associated skills and capabilities for the initiatives to be implemented and sustained.

The outcome of this phase is the final deliverable, the Infrastructure Consulting Report. The report reflects on initiatives for improving infrastructure utilization and infrastructure spend along with a roadmap leading to an optimized infrastructure environment. The report is prepared by the consultants and submitted to the executive sponsor for sign-off.

KEY LEARNINGS

Information technology is defined as the firm's total investment in computing and communications technology. It includes hardware, software, telecommunication and the myriad devices for collecting and representing data. The foundation for this IT portfolio is the firm's longer-term IT infrastructure, which, in turn, is linked to the external industry infrastructure.

Infrastructure ecosystem comprises data center or the host facility, end-user computing or the workplace, help desk or service desk, service catalog, service processes, service delivery, service management and service-level agreements. Infrastructure needs to be benchmarked and refreshed periodically, its consumption managed and utilized optimally. Restrict OEMs to a select few for economies of scale, without compromising on technological advancements.

Infrastructure consulting focuses on infrastructure utilization and infrastructure-spend analysis, with emphasis on audit and/or benchmarking. Once reasonable maturity is achieved, enterprises undertake optimization of infrastructure utilization and spend to better the benchmark.

The ITIL framework developed by the Office of Government Commerce, UK, provides guidelines for service life-cycle management of IT-enabled services, to improve the way different teams interact and manage IT infrastructure within their business. ITIL's life cycle for IT services goes through five phases: Service strategy, Service design, Service transition, Service operations and Continual service improvement. While the first three phases are primarily concerned with bringing new or improved services to the service catalog, the remaining are concerned with service delivery and optimization of current services.

Infrastructure systems should scale gracefully to support increasing volumes, if proportional processing, storage and communication resources are made available. Infrastructure should exhibit architectural features that enhance maintainability, enable easy configurability and support 24x7 operations. Systems should be standardized on platforms that can support diverse applications. Hardware, operating system, middleware and other platforms should be consolidated across a type of delivery architecture to avoid complexity of environment. Security access should be enforced at the data, function and network levels, ideally through single sign-on.

. Ω .

Chapter 8

IT Outsourcing Consulting

Outsourcing is the act of transferring some of the company's recurring internal activities and decision rights to outside providers, as set in a contract. Companies have strategically used outsourcing to improve time-to-market, reduce IT costs, access talent, adopt new technology and get flexibility of just-in-time resources.

Outsourcing has become a permanent fixture in twenty-first century organizational models. It offers strategic and economic benefits that are far too compelling to ignore. When it works, outsourcing decreases costs, increases flexibility, enhances expertise, increases discipline and provides the freedom to focus on core business. Outsourcing is really a mechanism for reconfiguring a firm's value chain, in ways that allow it not only to compete effectively today but also sustain market dominance in the future.

IT Outsourcing Consulting, the 'O' in SAPPGIO-T of the IT Consulting Spectrum, primarily deals with organizational readiness for outsourcing, outsourceability analysis of technology components, a resource model based on capability and capacity analysis, designing a sustainable outsourcing model, evaluation of suitable offshore locations and a service-level agreement.

In addition to a broad understanding of the IT Outsourcing Space, this chapter provides insights into Outsourcing Models, Outsourcing Consulting Dimensions, illustration of an Outsourcing Framework and an Approach to executing Outsourcing Consulting engagements.

Outsourcing Consulting Space

Outsourcing enables organizations to focus on their core business. It also reduces costs, provides access to skilled resources, improves process quality and takes advantage of difference in time zones. Organizations jumping on to the outsourcing bandwagon should have a realistic understanding of these benefits. They must objectively assess gains and risks associated with offshore outsourcing decisions. The effectiveness and success of outsourcing depends on how it is designed, implemented and managed.

Organizations should be willing to invest in time and talent to create long-term relationships. According to Michael F Corbett, author of *The Outsourcing Revolution*, for success in outsourcing, organizations must consider the long-term value of offshore outsourcing, building advantages that go beyond near-term cost-saving. Building long-term relationships and leveraging these becomes an integral part of organizations' strategic and tactical fabric.

In creating the outsourcing vision, it is best to begin with the end in mind. Organizations should have a clear vision of the end-result of outsourcing or offshoring efforts. If an organization does not know what results it wants to achieve, it risks being pulled in a certain direction for the wrong reasons - be it price, relationship or technology. In many cases, both the organization and the prospective outsourcer are only looking at cost as the primary decision criteria. Although this might seem like an obvious and mutually beneficial path, it is not necessarily the best, especially if the selected provider cannot deliver the needed service, or worse, goes out of business.

PLANNING FOR OUTSOURCING

Planning and preparation are critical to the overall success of an outsourcing journey. Organizations should undertake the following steps:

1. **ASCERTAIN READINESS TO OUTSOURCE**

    Assess the company's willingness to change and determine organizational gaps that need to be closed to ensure a successful transition to the new arrangement. Readiness assessment should evaluate 1) People: What skills exist and what are lacking? When will next-generation skills be required? How effective is project management? What is the company's culture on using third-parties for support? Does the company tend to build everything on its own or does it purchase everything it needs from vendors? 2) Process: How good are current processes? Are they ad hoc or repeatable? Does everyone adhere to the processes? Can they be replicated in an offshore environment? Do metrics exist? Are they comprehensive? Can they serve as the basis for SLAs? 3) Technology: Is the company a technology follower or leader? What specific technology skills are required? What new skills are needed?

2. **ASCERTAIN WHAT TO OUTSOURCE**

    Deciding what to outsource is the most important question when thinking about outsourcing. Get this right and you are on your way to creating a competitive advantage that will be hard to beat. Getting it wrong will have serious negative implications; hence, the need for comprehensive due-diligence.

3. **ASCERTAIN WHOM TO OUTSOURCE TO**

    Every outsourcing decision has two value chains that must be analyzed: the organization and the service provider. Ensure that all expected improvements in the organization's technologies, processes, skills, capabilities and resources are aptly complemented by the service provider to deliver the performance needed. Vendor selection criteria is shifting towards cultural alignment, contract flexibility, industry experience, financial engineering, vision for future IT, potential expansion and international skills.

4. **Ascertain How to Structure Outsourcing**

How to structure a deal is a function of how quickly the basis of competition in your industry will change. Long-term deals make more sense for non-core areas: what you are outsourcing is unlikely to figure in your ability to perform against competition in your industry now or in the future. A flexible approach to outsourcing is critical if a firm is to be able to reconfigure its value chain and deliver sustained performance that results in consistent shareholder value creation.

Models for Outsourcing

1. Staff Augmentation

In staff augmentation, resources are contracted based on demand and supply. The outsourcing partner is responsible for providing skilled resources that are governed directly by the client using their internal processes. This model is best suited for short-term and agile initiatives that require niche skills. Staff augmentation faces least internal resistance. Driven by client demand, screening and selection is controlled by the client. This offers considerable sourcing flexibility. Given the emphasis on resources, organizations cannot leverage the outsourcing partner's subject matter expertise and best practices; knowledge retention also becomes an issue. In terms of value, cost savings and economies of scale, the benefits are relatively low. The key challenge is obtaining resources with the right skills.

2. Co-Sourcing

In this model, organizations collaborate and work with the outsourcing partner's team to execute the task. The organization manages and governs the delivery of defined work packages; the outsourcing service providers could use their own processes for delivering their part of the work packet. The model enables faster response to business needs, better time-to-market, improved business/IT collaboration based on client control and increased productivity and quality and reduced development/support costs due to offshoring. The key challenge is the governance structure.

3. **MULTI-SOURCING**

    In the multi-sourcing model, organizations outsource to a pool of preferred suppliers ready to compete for various contract types. The organization can outsource to different suppliers for different business areas like knowledge management/customer relationship management or functional tasks like development/maintenance/testing or services like application and infrastructure support. Organizations create value by using the best-of-breed suppliers, stimulating price competition and testing relationships prior to scaling. The key challenge is vendor appraisal.

4. **MANAGED SERVICES**

    In managed services, organizations outsource management and operation of support systems to external service providers. The organization's involvement is minimal, restricted to strategic management, governance and monitoring of standards and processes. Yet, it has access to the service provider's experience, knowledge, tools and standardized delivery processes. Managed services offer greater control, flexibility, operational synergies and cost savings as the relative rise in cost for increase in scope of services is much smaller under managed services than staff augmentation or co-sourcing. The key challenge is data security and privacy.

5. **BUILD-OPERATE-TRANSFER**

    In the build-operate-transfer (BOT) model, service providers set up dedicated infrastructure to run outsourced operations for the organization. This is the build part, followed by the operate part for a contractually determined timeframe or milestone, at the end of which assets and operations are transferred back to the organization. BOT is a low-risk approach to moving a client's operational component to a dedicated IT establishment at offshore locations. The advantage lies in rapid and seamless scaling of operations, a facility that can become a potential profit center to the client after transfer. The key challenge is retention of intellectual property.

6. **JOINT VENTURE**

    In a joint venture, an outsourcing organization and a service provider set up a separate legal entity to provide IT services, typically operated from an offshore location. Joint ventures work best when there is a shared vision, alignment, commitment and an appetite for major growth in both parties. Organizations can outsource all their work to this entity, perception of reduced risk. Service providers need not compete any further as they become the sole partners.

Furthermore, both parties can take advantage of taxation benefits. The key challenge is managing higher overheads.

7. **SHARED SERVICES**

    In shared services, organizations have the unique opportunity to consolidate common functions, standardize them to reduce redundancies and leverage economies of scale to deliver consistent quality of service. Shared services usually start with low-risk functions and mature with time to become potential centers of excellence. Additionally, shared services can act as an epicenter for outsourcing, providing a single gateway to outsourcing service providers, thereby exercising better vendor governance. The key challenge is seamless integration of shared services with the rest of the organization.

8. **CAPTIVE CENTER**

    In this model, organizations set up their own operations to better secure their internal systems, typically in an offshore location. The entire spectrum of activities, that is, facilities, legal, government liaison, accounting, human resources, training, hardware, software and infrastructure become the client's sole responsibility. Organizations would seldom have all these skills on day zero; therefore, the best option is to partner with a top-tier service provider to create the entity and successfully launch day-one operations. The key challenge is recruitment and retention.

OUTSOURCING CONSULTING DIMENSIONS

OUTSOURCING CONSULTING

Outsourcing was first adopted in applications, predominantly application maintenance. This later extended to application development, followed by infrastructure outsourcing and business-process outsourcing. Irrespective of the type of outsourcing, the common starting point is organizational readiness to outsource, understanding what to outsource and whom to outsource to, bearing in mind the expected benefits. Clarity on these perspectives will help determine the best model for outsourcing, optimal timelines for a seamless transition and governance mechanisms for vendor management.

Application outsourcing consulting involves analysis of the organization's application portfolio to define a strategic roadmap based on outsource-ability analysis, cost-benefit analysis, target operating model analysis, knowledge-transition plans, resourcing models and structure of the retained organization to manage outsourcing. In business-process outsourcing, the emphasis is on business areas, functionalities and processes. In infrastructure outsourcing, the emphasis is on infrastructure facilities and services.

Shared Services Consulting

Shared services is an operational model that involves centralizing common functions in one or more physical location[s]. These functions would once have been performed in more or less similar fashion by different divisions or business units of the company. Consolidating common functions standardizes work and minimizes redundancies. Shared services boost efficiency and quality and reduce cost by leveraging economies of scale.

A good starting point is establishing a shared services center for IT, a dedicated unit that comprises people, process and technology (including physical assets) structured as a centralized point of service for a variety of participating entities. The center can subsequently be expanded to support business processes in functional areas like human resources, finance and accounting.

Shared services consulting involves feasibility assessment to ascertain viability of the business opportunity, its design/build to create a shared vision, its structure and its processes and to enable technologies and the operating model.

Captive Center Consulting

Companies dissatisfied with savings from conventional outsourcing and constrained by dependencies on service providers set up their own captive centers. This is particularly prevalent in the high-tech sector, where companies may already have offshore research and development centers, and in the financial services sector, where companies are looking to reduce costs and/or better secure their internal systems.

In some sense, captive centers are an extension of shared service centers. The difference is that a shared services center can be set up independently by the company or in partnership with a service provider in the company's host country or at a nearshore/offshore location. This duality disappears in captive centers since it is established by the company in an offshore location.

Captive center consulting involves feasibility assessment to gauge organizational readiness, maturity, capacity and bandwidth to set up a captive center and location analysis factoring in ease of doing business, availability of skilled manpower to support select services and ability to retain these resources.

Outsourcing Consulting Framework

In the absence of an industry body or standard, outsourcing advisory is based on in-house frameworks customized to determine what to outsource, whom to outsource to

IT Outsourcing Consulting

and where to outsource. The emphasis is on the breadth of coverage, from corporate strategy to complexity of systems and the culture of the enterprise.

The six most common dimensions are explained below as applicable to application outsourcing. They can also be adapted for infrastructure outsourcing or business-process outsourcing with minimal changes to the core parameters. The dimensions would still be valid for shared services or captive center consulting, but there would be a wide variation in weightages.

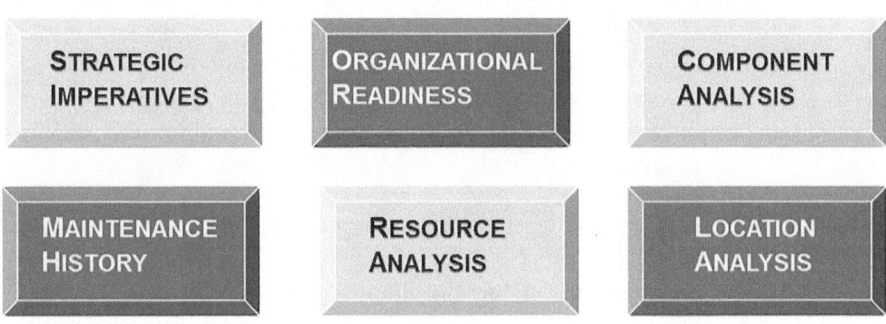

Framework Dimensions

Strategic Imperatives	Assess why the organization is outsourcing. Is it to refocus the organization on its core functions or reduce cost of operations or access world-class resources? Understanding the rationale for outsourcing will help select the right outsourcing model. Articulate the challenges/constraints of the chosen model and its impact on existing initiatives and indicate expected outcomes.
Organizational Readiness	This is a function of the organization's experience with external sourcing and the maturity of its internal processes. Sourcing experience is measured in terms of the nature of work outsourced, the number of vendors contracted and the geographical spread of offshore locations. Internal maturity is measured in terms of business/IT alignment, rigor of software development life cycle, maturity of demand management/release management processes, stability of application platform, portfolio, capacity and capabilities of resource pool.

Component Analysis	This helps arrive at the outsource-ability index derived from criticality of application, stability of the particular outsourcing component, that is, software application, business process or infrastructure service. Criticality is a function of number of users, acceptable downtime, business impact and application availability (lower the criticality, higher the potential to outsource). Stability is a function of the number of releases to production and number of defects fixed periodically (lesser the cost of maintenance, greater the return on outsourcing). Size is determined by business functionalities supported and technical parameters like number of screens, reports, batch jobs, online transactions and interfaces (smaller the size bigger the number to outsource).
Maintenance History	It needs to be studied to get a sense of the volume and nature of maintenance activities. Emphasis is on the resolution trends/results - percentage distribution of production support versus change requests or enhancement requests, average number of problems reported in a month, percentage of problems resolved within a day, percentage of incidents that turn out to be real problems, percentage distribution of errors in terms of problem type (related to user, data, environment or application) and percentage of SLA achievements.
Resource Analysis	This is a combination of capacity and capability analysis. Capacity analysis involves evaluation of demand and supply dynamics and scenarios for capacity augmentation. Size will help determine short-term specialized skill requirements, ability to ramp up/down as business needs change and ability to leverage onshore, nearshore or offshore staffing. Capability analysis involves identifying and prioritizing capacity-enhancement initiatives, developing capacity-enhancement quick wins. Profiles of in-house SME capability, based on roles being performed, job descriptions and area of expertise, will help in identifying and retaining critical capabilities and resource flexibility to source only commodity technical skills.
Location Analysis	Parameters are cost structure (to know average cost per associate), country-wide salary trend (to know rate of inflation and rate of increase), employee quality (based on education and experience), economic conditions (to know ease of doing business) and regulatory controls and political stability (to know the efficiency and reliability of government systems).

Outsourcing Consulting Approach

The execution model of an IT Outsourcing Consulting engagement would broadly traverse the following phases: Understanding Context, Current-State Assessment, Target-State Definition, Analysis and Findings and Recommendations and Roadmap, touching upon the three dimensions of outsourcing consulting.

Understand Context

The objective of this phase is to understand the context in terms of the drivers, business, technology, stakeholders, scope and outcomes. The target audience is the engagement sponsor and/or the engagement coordinator.

Key Activities of this Phase:

1. **Understand Drivers**

   The strategic drivers for outsourcing are improving customer focus, increasing shareholder value, exercising greater control, accessing global resources, time-to-market, focusing on core competencies or remaining competitive. Tactical drivers, on the other hand, are cost savings, operational efficiency, standardization of processes and quality of software development/application maintenance.

2. **Understand Business**

   The nature of business and the maturity of business, IT and governance processes play a key role in outsourcing decisions. It is equally important to understand how demand is managed, the degree of alignment between business and IT and how metrics are measured and monitored. The strength and sustainability of an outsourcing relationship depends on the cultural alignment of the two organizations. Emphasize on cross-cultural sensitization and communication from the beginning to empathize with each other's work practices.

3. **Understand Technology**

   Technology environment determines how diverse the hardware and software platforms are and how hardwired these systems are, as they have a direct influence on what can be outsourced and what needs to be retained in-house. Understand the IT organization structure, division of roles, distribution of responsibilities, contract- and vendor-management practices and ability to manage and monitor SLAs to ensure that the promised value is delivered.

4. **UNDERSTAND STAKEHOLDERS**

    The stakeholder set in outsourcing consulting spans the entire organization, beyond the conventional IT leaders and associated business owners to the functional heads of human resources, finance, facilities and even legal. The diversity of this stakeholder set mandates that the consulting team mobilize SMEs in every area, to negotiate meaningfully, to appreciate each stakeholder's challenges, apprehensions and expectations and to collaborate and conclude with a convincing business case.

5. **UNDERSTAND SCOPE AND OUTCOMES**

    In outsourcing, the outcome is not always cost arbitrage; there could be other business compulsions or regulatory compliance that drive organizations to outsource. Articulating the scope in relation to the drivers and co-relating these insights to the messages from the stakeholder will help determine the easiest path to achieve desired outcomes.

    The outcome of this phase is a re-confirmed outsourcing scope, understanding of organizational culture, work dynamics, preferred models/location, potential timelines for transition and indication on expected RoI.

ASSESS CURRENT STATE

The objective of this phase is to understand organizational imperatives/readiness for outsourcing, baseline outsourcing components and profile resources. The target audience includes the engagement coordinator, business owners, application managers, infrastructure architects and functional heads.

KEY ACTIVITIES OF THIS PHASE:

1. **CURRENT ORGANIZATIONAL ASSESSMENT**

    In outsourcing consulting, first, assess the current organizational structure, taking into account current roles, responsibilities and governance mechanisms. This will help understand the degree of centralization, articulate what parts of the organization are best suited for outsourcing and what governance mechanisms should be applied for the organization and the outsourcing service providers. Next, assess the demand-management process, taking into account the role of business in defining project scope, schedule and funding, the use of these functionalities and their geographical spread. This will help articulate the criticality of the supporting applications. Lastly, assess the organization's experience in outsourcing for help in defining and/or identifying the enhancements required for vendor-management processes.

In shared services consulting, first baseline the services provided by the business to its customers and the IT services provided by IT to the business, depending upon the scope for shared services. Next, assess each service in terms of cost, service levels, resources required, use of tools, degree of standardization and extent of automation, essentially to gauge the maturity of each process. Where available, benchmark these with best practices or with peers in the industry. Insights from these two assessments will help in streamlining services that can be good candidates for the shared entity.

Additionally, for shared services and captive center consulting, taking into account the organization's host country, region and geographical spread and identify potential locations for establishing the new operating unit, be it nearshore, offshore or in low-cost countries.

2. **CURRENT ENVIRONMENT ASSESSMENT**

In the context of outsourcing consulting, specifically for application outsourcing, the current state of the IT environment must be baselined on the following parameters:

- Business Related: This includes how well the scope is defined, how clearly business requirements/processes/interfaces are documented, how business is involved in project life cycle, how business measures IT value and most importantly, the business criticality of each application. Business-critical applications are those with no alternative processes available or those without which the business cannot continue to function. Non-critical applications may enhance productivity but their absence will not affect business functions significantly.

- Application Related: This includes description of application, size and stability, complexity and criticality, scope of services - development/maintenance, life-cycle phase, platform, programming languages, architecture standards, processes for maintenance/quality/testing, infrastructure requirements, storage needs, performance metrics, security and access controls, ongoing projects, SLAs, current challenges and future plans.

- Maintenance Related: This includes maintenance history, effort spent for production support vs minor enhancements, major bug fixes, average problems reported per month, levels of severity, percentage of problem fixes as per SLAs, amount of backlog, metrics collected and results from root-cause analysis.

In business-process outsourcing, the emphasis is on workflow of the process, points of manual intervention, automated steps, functions and resources touched upon by the processes and interfaces with other internal and external processes. In infrastructure outsourcing, the emphasis is on the services provided, infrastructure components and configuration, required uptime and permissible downtime and classification of services in terms of criticality.

In shared services consulting, business processes are reviewed to determine which part of the process must be performed by local business units and which part can be consolidated into shared services. Processes or part of processes that require direct contact with local operations or customers, that are unique to one site and do not occur in other sites, that require specific knowledge or are of strategic importance are usually retained locally. Processes that can be consolidated into shared services are those that are transactional in nature and display common traits across locations, unless there are legal or regulatory barriers.

Additionally, for shared services and captive center consulting, identify possible locations taking into account spread of business operations and proximity of external service providers, skill availability, supplier maturity, socio-economic stability, infrastructure availability and connectivity. Location search should include both primary site and secondary site for business continuity and disaster recovery. Captive center locations are typically in low-cost countries, which is not necessarily true for shared services.

3. **CURRENT MANPOWER ASSESSMENT**

   Manpower assessment is fairly common for all three dimensions of outsourcing consulting. Parameters to be assessed are number of associates, nature of employment (permanent, contract, full-time or part-time), role (domain specialist, IT analyst, application developer/tester), skill profile or capabilities, areas of specialization and training needs. Study open positions, reasons for the same and more importantly, understand the work culture.

The outcome of this phase is baselined inventory of software applications, business processes and infrastructure components in terms of their criticality, stability, size, interfaces and dependencies, resources profiled in terms of roles and responsibilities, documented challenges and apprehensions regarding outsourcing.

DEFINE TARGET STATE

The objective of this phase is to define the target state of the retained organization, operating model, preferred location, outsource-ability of business processes, software applications or infrastructure services, as the case may be, and resource distribution. The target audience is the engagement coordinator, business owners, application managers, infrastructure architects and functional heads.

Key Activities of this Phase:

1. **Target Operating Model**

   Defining the target operating model involves re-drawing the organization, the structure of the outsourced and retained organizations and the interfacing entities between the two. Guidelines for standard operating procedures are established to cover demand management, governance mechanisms, application development and maintenance, quality assurance, release management, change management, benefit management, risk management, performance and contract management. The entities in the retained organization reporting into the business on IT performance will now report on performance of both the retained and outsourced organizations, highlighting the returns on outsourcing.

2. **Target Outsourcing Model**

   For outsourcing consulting, the model should define the components (business processes, software applications or infrastructure services) that are ideal candidates for outsourcing, taking into account the organizational readiness, business criticality, profile of potential service providers and likelihood of adherence to SLAs and achieving set outsourcing objectives.

   In shared services consulting, the two main considerations in defining the target state are the extent of re-engineering required and the degree of standardization feasible. They not only determine the functioning of shared services but also the broader changes to business units' operations.

   Additionally, for captive center consulting, it is always advisable to seek the guidance of one of the preferred outsourcing service providers to help set up and operationalize the captive center. Target-state definition should, therefore, address who would qualify as guides, what capabilities and services they can anchor and their standing in the host country in business, social, political and economic terms.

3. **Target Resource Model**

   Target resource model involves definition of resource requirements both in capacity and capability terms - how much needs to be sourced based on how much is available in-house, how many need to be onsite, how many offshore and how the knowledge transfer and transition should take place. Earlier business/IT alignment was key; now, IT/service provider alignment is equally critical.

   Additionally, for shared services and captive center consulting, strategies for recruitment and retention and criteria for short-listing recruitment agencies and academic institutions should be defined.

The outcome of this phase is the structure of the retained organization, operating model, resource model and governance model to manage the outsourcing initiative and a defined set of components that are best suited for outsourcing.

ANALYSIS AND FINDINGS

The objective of this phase is to analyze insights from current-state assessment and gaps with regard to the defined target state, to evaluate impact of creating the retaining organizations and implementing the target operating model. The engagement coordinator, business owners, application managers, infrastructure architects and functional heads form the target audience.

KEY ACTIVITIES OF THIS PHASE:

1. **OPERATING MODEL ANALYSIS**

    In outsourcing consulting, the focus of analysis is on the integrity of interfacing units, that is, validation of the vendor-management processes, monitoring of metrics defined in the SLA and rigor of the knowledge transfer process.

    In shared services consulting, proof of concepts are designed for critical and complex IT services and piloted within the shared services center. Through this process, the shared service center gets an opportunity to build trust and demonstrate value, before it delivers directly to larger business units. Thereafter, services from the business units are gradually decommissioned and resources engaged locally are freed up or utilized for other core functions. To better manage pre- and post-launch shared IT services, a comprehensive plan is defined, elaborating on transition of process, people, technology and supplier.

    Additionally, for captive center consulting, the focus of analysis is on how much the local service provider, acting as guide/mentor, can help in setting up and operationalizing the unit and the transition strategy for a smooth handover.

2. **OUTSOURCING MODEL ANALYSIS**

    Outsourcing model analysis involves computing indices for readiness, suitability and outsource-ability, which individually and/or collectively can determine what to outsource and in what sequence.

    - Readiness Index: This is a function of organizational, technical, process and governance readiness. Organizational readiness is determined by sourcing experience, resource profile and breadth and depth of technical skills. Technical readiness is determined by architecture design and standards, environment stability, age of application portfolio and documentation. Governance readiness is determined by business/IT alignment, portfolio and project management maturity, risk management, vendor management and communication effectiveness.

- Suitability Index: This is a function of technical suitability and functional suitability factors. Technical suitability is determined by the architecture design complexity, hardware or operating system dependency, data sensitivity and confidentiality, integration ability, interface control, maintainability, reusability, scalability, security and performance. Functional suitability is determined by business user support, customer interaction, demand management, demand volatility, release management, time-to-market and vendor support.
- Outsource-ability Index: This is a function of business criticality, application stability and application size/complexity. Business criticality is determined by acceptable downtime. Application stability is determined by availability of application and frequency of changes. Application size and complexity is determined by diversity of programming languages, application environment, age of code and coding standards. These measures are rated individually and weighted to obtain individual parameter scores to determine the outsource-ability index, which is then analyzed collectively to determine the transition complexity band. This helps decide the transition schedule for that application.

3. **Resource Model Analysis**

In resource-model analysis, the criteria used to assess outsource-ability of resources/roles are frequency of interaction with internal customers, regulatory or company policy constraints, stability of business requirements, financial or operational risks, depth of domain-specific knowledge required, protection of intellectual property, clarity around deliverables and key performance indicators, connectivity and infrastructure-related issues.

Additionally, as the organization is restructured as an outsourced organization and a retained organization, quite a few roles change in position or responsibility or may even become redundant. With this, reporting lines also change. Proactively identify such changes and communicate the same in a timely manner.

The outcomes of this phase are options for the new organization structure and operating model, highlighting strengths and strategies to contain weaknesses and a high level business case of the outsourcing model.

Recommendations and Report

The objective of this phase is to recommend a strategy for outsourcing that includes what is to be outsourced, when, to whom and where, plus changes to the structure and resources in the organization in preparation for outsourcing. The target audience is the engagement sponsor, engagement coordinator, business owners and application managers.

KEY ACTIVITIES OF THIS PHASE:

1. **OUTSOURCING STRATEGY**

    Outsourcing strategy will cover the following topics:
    - Organizational Structure: Includes baseline information on current organizational structure/readiness and proposed structure for the outsourced organization and retained organization. The structure should illustrate key roles and delineate responsibilities between the organization and service provider. For structural gaps, if any, the strategy should spell out the job description and skill profile. For parts of the organization that are transient in nature, there should be a defined mechanism for transfer of responsibility from organization to service provider and back to organization.
    - Outsourcing Model: Elaborates upon the selected outsourcing model based on organizational readiness and experience with outsourcing. Assess business process, application portfolio or infrastructure services as per the scope of the engagement from a business, technology and maintenance point of view along the parameters listed to compute the outsource-ability index. Translate these findings into a phased model for transition. Additionally, in case of shared services consulting, provide directions for recruitment strategy and for captive center consulting, the service provider must furnish guidance to operationalize the unit.
    - Operating Model: Covers policies and procedures related to demand management, project management, application development, application maintenance, production support, assurance services, release management, vendor management, SLAs, metrics and measurement, monitoring and reporting in the current form within the organization and enhancements required for them to be equally effective in the outsourced scenario.

2. **OUTSOURCING ROADMAP**

    Outsourcing roadmap is essentially the transition strategy and covers the following topics:
    - Transition plan to define the scope and staffing requirements, resources to be mobilized, training needs and environment to be set up;
    - Transition readiness to outline the existing processes specific to a role, application or function and establishment of a process repository;

- Secondary support (shadow) to observe current team, get hands-on experience with the actual roles and document necessary procedures;
- Primary support (reverse shadow) to get primary ownership of transitioned areas and daily activities and establish credibility to perform the function without any external support/guidance; and
- Steady state to provide services independently, implement continuous improvement and close transition.

The outcome of this phase is the final deliverable, the Outsourcing Consulting Report. It reflects on the outsourcing strategy taking into account organizational readiness, IT environment, resource profile, supplier and location preference, and includes the roadmap from transition to steady state. The report is prepared by the consultants and submitted to the executive sponsor for sign-off.

Key Learnings

Outsourcing enables organizations to focus on their core business, leaving outsourcing service providers to provide non-core services. In planning for outsourcing, organizations need to ask themselves: What is our readiness to outsource? What do we want to outsource? Whom do we want to outsource to? Where do we want to outsource to? How do we structure our outsourcing model? And most importantly, what are our expected strategic and economic benefits?

Outsourcing models vary from simple staff augmentation where resources are contracted based on demand and supply to co-sourcing or working in collaboration with service provider resources. Multi-sourcing involves working with a pool of preferred suppliers, while managed services places the onus of management and operations on the service provider. Other models are BOT, joint ventures, shared services or captive centers.

Outsourcing consulting originated in application outsourcing with application maintenance and then application development and later extended into infrastructure services and business-process outsourcing. Organizations gained maturity in these forms of outsourcing and started to leverage this experience to set up their own shared services center or captive centers.

However, these initiatives also required the services of outsourcing partners, predominantly for expertise in business, economic and social know-how of the region and guidance to set up and operationalize the units, giving way to shared services consulting and captive center consulting.

In the absence of an industry body, there is no single framework for outsourcing. Consulting firms and service providers thus built their own frameworks based on experience and best practices. The most common dimensions are analysis of strategic imperatives, organizational readiness, component analysis, maintenance history, resource analysis and location analysis.

Post-outsourcing, in addition to cost savings, organizations end up developing capabilities for improved productivity, quality and accelerated time-to-market based on processes that focus on responsibility, accountability, measurement, reporting and continuous improvement. The real benefit is in the resulting self-funding model for strategic initiatives.

. Ω .

Chapter 9

IT Transformation Consulting

Transformation is turning vision into action, triple action to be precise - breaking from the past, managing the present and investing in the future, all in tandem. Transformation is making fundamental changes to the way business is conducted, significantly impacting people, processes and technology to gain a sustainable competitive advantage. Transformation is driven by the business, enabled by technology and measured by business outcomes. Transformation is a continuum; the journey is as important as the end.

IT Transformation Consulting, the 'T' in SAPPGIO-T of the IT Consulting Spectrum, primarily deals with IT-enabled business transformation. It starts with understanding transformation drivers, leading to the right selection of spectrum segments, relative positioning of the segments in terms of priority and prominence and holistic analysis of core and corollary segments, resulting in a series of cross-functional recommendations for transformation.

In addition to a broad understanding of the IT Transformation Space, this chapter provides insights into Transformation Imperatives, Transformation Method and an Approach to executing Transformation Consulting engagements. The focus is on change management, risk management and program management, components that are critical to transformation success.

Transformation Consulting Space

In literal terms, transformation is a thorough or dramatic change in form or appearance. On the transformation triad are demanding customers and their priorities, the changing business landscape and technology trends that impact the industry. Transformation triggers are launch of new business models, mergers and acquisitions, integration or consolidation of existing lines of business, improvement in time-to-market, control of CAPEX, reduction in OPEX or deployment of next-generation technologies. Transformation enables growth through market leadership, productivity through business process excellence and change through collaborative innovation.

IT Transformation is comprehensive change for an IT organization; the right strategic vision is critical, as execution is the hardest part of any transformation. IT Transformation, therefore, mandates executive commitment, a compelling business case, aligned business and technology, adequate risk management, structured governance, effective communication explained in a language everyone can understand and continuous focus on the challenges of change.

IT transformation involves at least two distinct phases: developing a new capability and then deploying it. The former can often be done separately from business as usual, but the latter inevitably competes with other operational priorities, which can seriously delay or even prevent its exploitation. The transformation manager should have expert knowledge in the area being changed and also in managing change in the organization.

Transformation Consulting Imperatives

In strategy or governance or outsourcing consulting, the emphasis is only on one segment of the spectrum. In transformation consulting, the emphasis shifts from a part to the sum-of-the-parts. However, the difficulty is identifying the right spectrum segments or more importantly which one is the core and what is its relation to other segments, the corollaries.

Does strategy drive governance? Does governance drive strategy? Does governance drive architecture? Does architecture drive governance? Does architecture drive infrastructure? Does infrastructure drive architecture? Does infrastructure drive process? Does process drive infrastructure? Or for that matter, does process drive strategy? Note of caution: address this challenge not from an advisory or academic standpoint but from the perspective of the customer's context or need and their definition of transformation. The reality is that each segment can be the core or corollary depending upon the timing and nature of transformation.

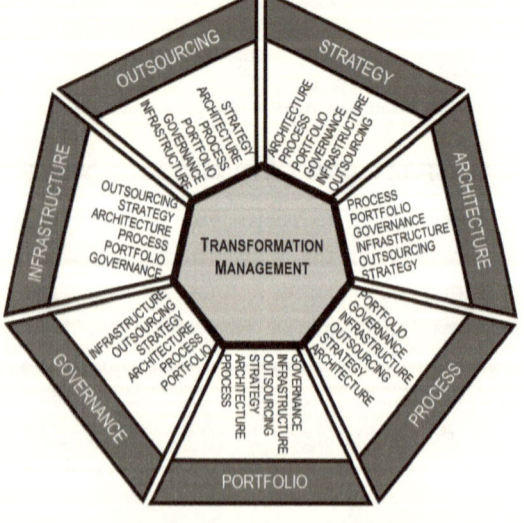

Consider a couple of illustrations to understand this concept:

Organizations transforming their operating model to improve time-to-market would position strategy at the core and governance, architecture and infrastructure as corollary segments. Organizations leveraging technology to enable business transformation would position architecture at the core and strategy, process and infrastructure as corollaries.

Organizations aiming for standardization as a transformation theme would positon process at the core and governance as corollary to ensure sustainability. Organizations post-merger or acquisition would position portfolio at the core, to rationalize the application portfolio, and process and infrastructure as corollaries. Organizations redesigning their structure to cater to new markets would position governance at the core and process as corollary. Organizations optimizing their environment to support 24x7 operations would position infrastructure at the core and architecture and outsourcing as corollaries. Organizations expanding their global footprint would position outsourcing at the core and strategy and governance as corollaries. The position of a segment as core or corollary does not undermine its importance; on the contrary, correctly positioning each segment enhances the success of transformation.

Transformation Management

Irrespective of what segment of the spectrum is at the core or what segments are corollaries, the common capability required is transformation management. Transformation programs are high-investment initiatives, run over long time horizons and successful only if the organization as a whole is ready to embrace the change, thus giving rise to the need for additional consulting capabilities in change management, risk management and program management.

1. Change Management

Managing change is a critical component of any major transformation and plays a key role in helping organizations successfully implement new strategies. Change management by definition is a structured process and set of tools for leading the people side of change.

Change management at an organizational level involves engaging sponsors, creating ownership for the change process and addressing cultural dynamics. At the individual level, it involves people understanding what the change is and internalizing why it is important, believing that it is the right thing to do, being willing to step out of their comfort zone and believing they can bring about the change. Members of the organization are nominated as change agents and made responsible for facilitating change in their area.

Change management comprises six work streams: organizational change, stakeholder management, communication strategy, learning and development, organizational readiness and benefits management.

Organizational change work stream identifies business change both at an organizational and an individual level and then defines the change strategy and plan to move employees from old ways of working to new. Negative change impacts will be minimized and mitigated and positive influencers identified and utilized to create a shared vision and buy-in for the change. Key activities are change-impact assessment, change-agent engagement and maintenance of the change strategy and plan.

Stakeholder engagement is a means of capturing information about the people involved in or affected by a change and then using it to plan change interventions to move them effectively along their change journey to a point where they are positively helping to influence transformation outcomes. Stakeholders can be individuals or organizations, internal or external to the business. The focus is on how and when each stakeholder group is involved in the program, to minimize resistance or increase receptiveness by increasing ownership of and commitment to the overall program. Key activities are executive alignment, devising stakeholder-engagement strategy and establishing interventions to address stakeholder issues and concerns.

Communication is at the heart of transformation management and is essential for any successful transformation. Communication strategy provides an overall framework for management to coordinate and deliver communication across the organization to all staff affected by change implementation. The key principles of the communication strategy are development of a communication plan identifying key audience groups, standard messages to be used, appropriate individuals responsible for delivering the messages, timing of delivery and feedback mechanisms and development of branding for the change program for all affected employees. Communication is cyclical and will continue throughout the transformation.

Learning and development includes identifying training needs, developing a training strategy/plan, creating training materials and delivering the training content. People who are trained well will be able to work with speed and accuracy, resulting in high levels of customer satisfaction.

Organization readiness involves assessing willingness to go live with the business change. Readiness assessments are performed through the course of transformation - initial, intermediary and pre go-live. Objectively analyze the results at each stage and empower change agents to act on required course correction. Readiness assessment itself is reviewed to ensure that criteria are appropriate and accurate. The process continues until the employees are ready to accept the new system.

Benefit is the measurable improvement resulting from an outcome which is perceived as an advantage by the stakeholder. Benefits are anticipated when change is conceived. Benefits management is a work stream dedicated to definition, planning, structuring and actual realization of the benefits of the transformation program. The key input is the business case, an aggregation of specific information about the transformation program that can be used to judge whether the program is and remains desirable, viable and achievable. The business case should include planned benefits with a logical link between business drivers, transformation vision and business outcomes.

Organizational culture refers to the unwritten, unspoken but powerful 'rules of the game' that determine appropriate ways to 'think, act and feel', viewed as a shared perception of the organization in terms of practices, policies, procedures, routines, aligned behaviors and expected rewards. Cultural assessment is enabled by stakeholder interviews/surveys and analysis of information using assessment tools. Recognized behavioral indicators include: leadership approach (hierarchical or consensus), communication style (formal or within the network), work orientation (people or task), etc.

All work streams must be performed in parallel and iteratively for optimal results.

2. Risk Management

Enterprises are exposed to a variety of internal and external factors that can potentially damage the business or deviate it from its preset objectives. These uncertain events or conditions are called risks.

Risk management is identifying, assessing, prioritizing and mitigating such events proactively. While all risks cannot be mitigated because of lack of control or limitation of resources, risk management needs to factor a judicious allocation of enterprise resources to high-impact risks. Key components of risk management are a risk-management framework and function comprising a dedicated risk-management team, risk register and risk-management processes within the enterprise.

In the context of transformation, risks primarily belong to two broad categories: 'Initiative Risks' and 'Enterprise Risks'. Initiatives risks are typically contained within the scope of the transformation program and can be mitigated by adjusting the variables, which is fairly within the control of the transformation sponsor. Enterprise risks originate within the purview of the transformation but can potentially impact parallel initiatives and the larger enterprise. Mitigation of such risks needs broader management decisions/involvement. Enterprise risks are sometimes also referred to as strategic or business risks.

A risk-management framework is a comprehensive set of rules and norms that link the risk-management function with the enterprise strategy and goals. The framework provides a detailed approach for risk classification, prioritization, management and reporting and guidelines for maintaining a cost-effective risk function, ensuring compliance with regulatory mandates.

The analysis and evaluation of risks helps assess the criticality of risks and assign the right priority to them. Based on risk priority, resources are allocated to manage or treat them. Once a risk is treated, it is tracked for a reasonable duration to assess the effectiveness and efficiency of the entire process and come up with improvements.

Risk controls refer to certain pre-defined measures or methods or techniques to contain risks. These controls can either completely eliminate the risk or substitute high risk with low risk or isolate a risk. Risk controls evolve over time as the enterprise accumulates experience with risk management. They provide invaluable insights into what has or has not worked successfully within the enterprise.

Risk rating is a mathematical approach to quantify the potential impact of a risk, calculated both pre- and post-application of risk controls. Risk tolerance is the risk rating with 'acceptable' impact and probability of a risk; it varies from business to business and function to function. Risk register is a central repository for all identified risks. It includes information such as risk probability, impact, countermeasures and risk owner. Risk register is a mandatory document, specifically for audit and compliance.

Key activities of risk management are risk identification, risk-register creation, risk analysis and evaluation, risk-mitigation control and monitoring.

3. **PROGRAMME MANAGEMENT**

    Programme is a group of related projects managed in a coordinated way to obtain benefits and control not available when managing them individually. Key components of programme management are governance, management method, project management and Programme Management Office (PMO). Together, they underpin a key critical success factor of delivery process excellence.

    Transformational changes impact the entire enterprise. Programme governance is the framework that enables the organization to realize program vision and objectives of the transformation initiative by providing a controlled environment for relevant stakeholders to take the right decisions at the right time, backed by appropriate processes. Key activities include strategically aligning transformation objectives with business strategy; adapting program objectives to environmental changes; establishing a structure aligned with the organization structure with clearly defined, documented roles and responsibilities communicated to all stakeholders; executing program activities consistent with transformation methodology; making provision for phase gate/periodic reviews and controlling costs and risk limits.

    Establish committees as appropriate. At a strategic level, the program steering board provides executive sponsorship and direction to the transformation program in terms of business case approval and accountability for program performance. At the operational level, the program leadership group monitors progress and performance on a weekly basis as per the program charter, through the PMO.

PMO is an organizational structure that has standardized program-related governance processes, facilitating the sharing of resources and adopting standardized methodologies, tools and templates. PMO core processes are program governance, programme planning and tracking, scope management, quality management, risk and issue management, programme - performance management, resource management, integration management, contract and financial management, vendor management, release management and knowledge management. Standard templates designed and maintained by the PMO are program status report, risk register, issue log, budget tracker, minutes-of-meeting templates and benefit-profile template.

Transformation Consulting Method

Business Transformation Management (BTM) Method[29] was developed by the Business Transformation Academy.

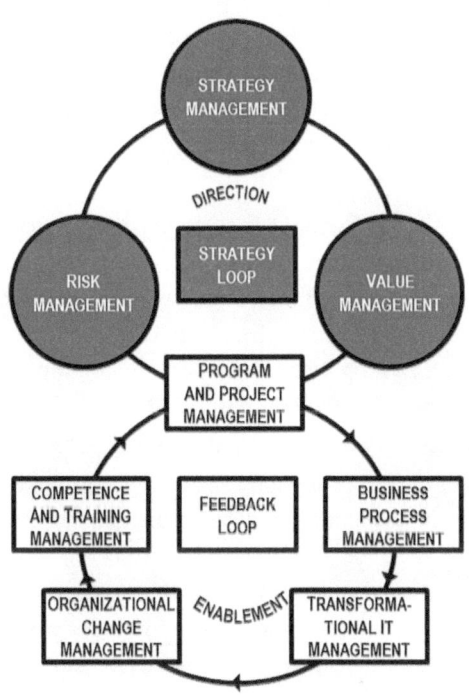

---

29 BTM Method is adapted from pages 156 to 159 of Uhl, A. and Gollenia, L. A. (2013). *Business transformation management methodology.* Gower.

It provides an iterative life-cycle model (envision, engage, transform and optimize) that helps understand business transformation as a holistic process and offers an overall business transformation structure, including management layers and formal and informal management roles. The focus is on the dimensions of the BSc for planning and controlling measures. It delivers decision criteria for choosing the right leaders and promoters for key positions and facilitates transformational leadership. It creates culture and values on the basis of transformational principles and guidelines to internalize and institutionalize transformation goals. It provides communication and engagement principles and supports feedback loops.

The BTM Method includes management disciplines like Strategy Management, Value Management, Risk Management, Business Process Management, Program and Project Management, Transformational IT Management, Organizational Change Management and Competence and Training Management.

The first three disciplines are referred to as the 'Strategy Loop'. Here, the transformation strategy is defined, considering time and budget restrictions and associated risks. BTM's directional disciplines make the case for action and vision of the future and set the direction for the transformation effort. The remaining disciplines enable management and synchronization of changes in IT, processes and organizational structure in addition to creating new competencies through training, orchestrated through an organizational program-management capability. Together, they form the 'Feedback Loop' that helps adjust changes to transformation strategy.

1. **STRATEGY MANAGEMENT**

    The strategy definition phase links the transformation program to fundamental changes in the business environment and corporate direction. These changes represent triggers for transformation and may relate to sustainability changes or new technologies. Strategy definition aims to understand transformation drivers, how they affect the existing business model, the vision of the future enterprise, strategic partners and management motivation.

    Steps for strategy definition in the envision phase are project start-up, as-is data collection, analysis of transformation needs and causes, design of business vision, design of business model and developing an integrated transformation plan.

2. **VALUE MANAGEMENT**

    Value management is an essential activity at all stages of the transformation life cycle. Value does not mean just financial benefits; it includes all the improvements perceived as beneficial by the organization's internal and external stakeholders.

    In the envision phase, the emphasis is on determining what new or additional value business transformation could create for the organization in relation to its business strategy. During the engage phase, that strategic value is translated into specific benefits that should accrue to the organization and all its stakeholders. In the transform phase, each of these benefits is owned by specific stakeholders and is tracked and reviewed to ensure that it is still achievable. In the optimize phase, potential for further improvements are established.

3. **Risk Management**

Risk management provides fundamental guidance to the planning, development and effective execution of business transformation. Organizations need to go beyond simply addressing risks that are inherent to an individual business transformation, since such aggregation in isolation provides only limited guidance to those seeking to understand and manage the complex interdependencies that surround strategic risks.

In the envision phase, identify strategic risks using tools like scenario planning and create a strategic risk map. In the engage phase, analyze risk and its impact based on cost, schedule and deliverables. In the transform phase, execute the risk-response plan and monitor emergence of risk events. In the optimize phase, review and evaluate risks for improvements.

4. **Business Process Management**

Processes are essentially what organizations do; therefore, transforming organizations essentially means changing an organization's processes, that is, designing new processes to implement new business practices.

In the envision phase, create the big picture of process management. In the engage phase, analyze as-is processes, innovate to-be processes and put in place a governance structure to frame the implementation of new processes. In the transform phase, implement the new processes. In the optimize phase, find ideas for continuous improvement of the processes.

5. **Transformational IT Management**

Transformational IT Management evaluates the impact of current IT processes, competencies and systems on business transformation and enables operations, maintenance and support of transformational deliverables.

In the envision phase, assess and enable the organization's solution readiness. In the engage phase, define to-be analysis and assess gap to as-is. In the transform phase, deploy IT services and implement IT governance. In the optimize phase, manage IT life cycle and improve IT operations.

6. **ORGANIZATIONAL CHANGE MANAGEMENT**

    Organizational change management deals with the people who have to change their method of working because of business transformation. It deals with their expectations, their needs, their abilities, their motivations, their concerns and their resistance.

    In the envision phase, set up a foundation for effective organizational change management with regard to governance and assess readiness. In the engage phase, define a comprehensive communication strategy and performance management, for the particular transformation and also for the organization at large. In the transform phase, apply and adopt stakeholder management. In the optimize phase, collect feedback about the level of success of implemented interventions.

7. **COMPETENCE AND TRAINING MANAGEMENT**

    Competence and training management provides qualifications and enables selection of key groups with the competence required for business transformation and the strategic core competencies vital for future success.

    In the envision and engage phases, training needs and objectives are specified and compared with the results of the as-is analysis. In the engage, transform and optimize phases, develop training measures for identified gaps, foster learning and eventually analyze success of the measures.

8. **PROGRAM AND PROJECT MANAGEMENT**

    Program management serves as an overall vehicle for the transformation effort and supports the implementation of the decided strategy to achieve the expected benefits of business transformation. A program is a group of related projects managed in a coordinated way to create value. A project, on the other hand, is a temporary endeavor that has defined start and finish points, with the aim of delivering a predetermined output.

    In the engage phase, programs are set up, quality requirements are identified and the need for additional capacity and skills are evaluated. In the transform phase, budgets and efforts are monitored to ensure that they are not exceeded throughout the business transformation.

TRANSFORMATION CONSULTING APPROACH

The execution model of an IT Transformation Consulting engagement would broadly traverse the following phases: Understand Context, Assess Current State, Define Target State, Analysis and Findings and Recommendations and Roadmap, touching upon all segments of the spectrum that can address the transformation imperatives.

Understand Context

The objective of this phase is to understand the transformation imperatives in terms of the drivers, business, technology, stakeholders, scope and outcomes. The target audience is the engagement sponsor and executive management.

Key Activities of this Phase:

1. **Understand Drivers**

    Large-scale transformations are primarily driven by a required change to the business model, triggered by external impetuses like a merger, acquisition, divestiture, changes in customer buying behavior, enhanced product mix or advent of new technologies or internal motivations like simplifying the business and operations, improving stakeholder experience or improving operational efficiency.

    A successful start to transformation would mean rightfully pegging the trigger and deriving the transformation imperatives that the transformation journey should address to achieve the transformation objectives and successfully reach the end. In other words, identifying the core and establishing required corollaries that collectively change the business model.

    The net result at this stage is a lens to view the business, technology and human aspects of change, to effect transformation of the enterprise.

2. **Understand Business**

    Changes to the business model are expected to consolidate the organization's strength and position in the market and against competition. The new business models are expected to bring in flexibility for future organic and inorganic growth. Understand business in terms of how it can drive the transformation imperatives: would it be through growth in current markets, expansion to global markets, leadership in products or improved agility.

    Pay special attention to the partner ecosystem on the supply and demand fronts, as transformation imperatives may necessitate fundamental redefinition of their roles and responsibilities.

3. **Understand Technology**

    The options prioritized by the business to address transformation imperatives will determine the role of technology in the transformation. Understand technology in terms of how it can best enable business to transform: would it be achieved by reducing complexity of technology stack, rationalizing applications, streamlining current operations, simplifying governance processes, standardizing processes or virtualizing infrastructure?

Pay special attention to the feasibility of technology transition as transformation may affect a number of business-critical applications that may force a reverse think on the business direction.

4. **UNDERSTAND STAKEHOLDERS**

   The stakeholder set in transformation consulting spans the organization, beyond the conventional business-unit leaders and associated business partners to CxO-level executives and probably even board-level directors. Understand the stakeholder dynamics: the executive driving the transformation, the impact of the transformation program on the executive at a personal level, other ongoing transformation programs and any known conflicts or dependencies between them, including timelines for implementation and realization.

   Pay special attention to the leadership style and the standing of the c-level executive sponsoring the transformation program; the biggest challenge in transformation may be a leader wedded to past or current successes. Transformation sponsors are expected to provide thought leadership, demonstrate commitment and be hands-on, all with equal ease.

5. **UNDERSTAND SCOPE AND OUTCOMES**

   In transformation, the scope is a function of the defined transformation imperatives, the selection of a spectrum segment as core and the supporting spectrum segments that would be corollaries. The outcome of the transformation would be the changed business model.

   Pay special attention to the scope and outcomes, as they are likely to be revisited and reprioritized as the transformation journey progresses.

The outcome of this phase is re-confirmed transformation imperatives, positioning of a spectrum segment at the core, possibilities of corollary segments, understanding of business impact, required technology enablement and insights into leadership style of sponsor and alignment of stakeholders.

ASSESS CURRENT STATE

The objective of this phase is to baseline the segments of the spectrum that address the transformation imperatives. The target audience is made up of the engagement sponsor, engagement coordinator, business owners, business partners, functional heads, application managers and enterprise architects.

IT Transformation Consulting

KEY ACTIVITIES OF THIS PHASE:

1. **TRANSFORMATION IMPERATIVES RELATED**

   Refer to the current-state assessment section in the related chapter for spectrum-specific activities.

2. **TRANSFORMATION MANAGEMENT RELATED**

   An illustrative set-up of activities related to transformation management performed around this stage are:

   Organizational impact assessment is conducted at a high level to understand structure, roles, responsibilities, skills, capabilities, culture and behavior. Leverage the above results to create change-management strategy, highlighting change interventions and impact on transformation imperatives.

   Identify risks based on transformation imperatives and business objectives. Document the same in a risk register, to be maintained and monitored through the transformation journey.

   Create a charter for the transformation program that demonstrates alignment with organization vision and a comprehensive plan to achieve the transformation imperatives.

   The outcome of this phase is a baselined profile of the select segments in relation to the transformation imperatives.

DEFINE TARGET STATE

The objective of this phase is to define the target state of the transformation program based on target considerations for each segment of the spectrum. The target audience is the engagement sponsor, engagement coordinator, business owners, business partners, functional heads, application managers and enterprise architects.

KEY ACTIVITIES OF THIS PHASE:

1. **TRANSFORMATION IMPERATIVES RELATED**

   Refer to the target-state definition section in the related chapter for spectrum-specific activities.

2. **TRANSFORMATION MANAGEMENT RELATED**

   Illustrative setup and execution activities related to transformation management performed around this stage are:

Identifying change agents who can help deliver the business change by promoting it among peers and colleagues, enabling people to work effectively as they plan, implement and experience change and increasing people's ability to manage future change.

Analyze and evaluate risks to determine potential impact and probability of occurrence in the transformation program. Results are leveraged to prioritize risks and define mitigation strategies.

Establish and operationalize the transformation-management office with responsibilities for developing the master plan for transformation, stakeholder management, financial management and communications management.

The outcome of this phase is a defined target of the select segments that can collectively help in realizing transformation outcomes.

ANALYSIS AND FINDINGS

The objective of this phase is to analyze insights from current-state assessment and gaps with regard to the defined target state, in order to define and prioritize transformation initiatives. The target audience comprises the engagement coordinator, business owners, business partners, functional heads, application managers and enterprise architects.

KEY ACTIVITIES OF THIS PHASE:

1. **TRANSFORMATION IMPERATIVES RELATED**

    Refer to the analysis and findings section in the related chapter for spectrum-specific activities.

2. **TRANSFORMATION MANAGEMENT RELATED**

    Illustrative execution activities related to transformation management performed around this stage are:

    Detailed impact assessment to understand business changes at a role or even individual level, so that change activities can be focused to be more effective. Leverage the above results to identify change actions, communication concerns, training requirements, risks and issues.

    Determine controls to bring risks to acceptable levels, formulate strategies for risk mitigation and mechanisms for monitoring risk and design a risk dashboard to record frequency of occurrence/impact and options to overcome recurrence.

    Establish effective program-management practices that drive clarity and consensus related to transformation initiatives and appropriate tools and techniques, feedback mechanisms and benefit-realization metrics and ensure executive commitment and participation in leading the cause for business transformation.

The outcome of this phase is a set of prioritized transformation initiatives across segments of the spectrum supported by business cases.

RECOMMENDATIONS AND REPORT

The objective of this phase is to recommend a transformation roadmap, addressing all the transformation imperatives. The target audience is the engagement sponsor and executive management.

KEY ACTIVITIES OF THIS PHASE:

1. **TRANSFORMATION ROADMAP**

    Transformation roadmap is a series of prioritized transformation initiatives across the segments of the spectrum and includes quick-wins and transformation-management related elements. Equally critical are the governance structure and controls, envisioned with executive commitment and oversight. The roadmap is typically spread over three time horizons, short-term (Year I), medium-term (Year II) and long-term (Year III).

    The report is developed in two parts, strategy and implementation.

    Transformation strategy outlines the transformation vision, strategic improvements, conceptual EA, technology enablement, business case for transformation initiatives and implementation master plan.

    Transformation implementation elaborates on the governance structure, mechanisms and process; transformation-management office setup, structure and reporting; change-impact analysis, readiness assessment, stakeholder management and communication management; risk management, risk logs and risk mitigation; performance management and benefit management.

    The outcome of this phase is the final deliverable, the Transformation Consulting Report. The report reflects on transformation imperatives, the segments of the spectrum that need to be addressed to achieve the transformation outcome. The report is prepared by the consultants and submitted to the executive sponsor for sign-off.

KEY LEARNINGS

Transformation is embarking on a fundamental change to the way business is conducted. It must have a clear strategic rationale, explained in a language everyone can understand. The outcome of a transformation program depends on how clearly and comprehensively the transformation strategy, value and risks have been articulated and communicated to all stakeholders. Successful transformations address the organizational, people and capability aspects first, then the process and IT components.

Transformation is usually a combination of two or more of the segments of the consulting spectrum. What is important is not the number of segments selected, but pegging the right segment at the core and populating relationships with the other segments, the corollaries. Equal attention has to be paid to transformation management, which includes change management, risk management and program management.

The BTM Method defines direction and enablement as the two pillars of transformation. The former consists of strategy management, value management and risk management - the 'Strategy Loop'. The latter is a combination of program and project management, business-process management, transformational IT management, organizational change management and competence and training management - the 'Feedback Loop'.

Transformation is a continuum; the journey is as important as the end.

. Ω .

Part Three

Consulting Competencies

Chapter 10

Consulting Competencies

Consulting is much more than content, which can be sourced externally through industry forums/analyst firms or internally through the organization's solutions, methodologies or knowledge-management systems. All these elements individually or collectively are, at best, door-openers, beyond which they become excess baggage. What really matters, when one stands in front of a CEO, CFO, COO, Chief Marketing Officer (CMO) or a CIO is the consultant's 'Individual Equity' measured in terms of experience in the customer context, ability to think beyond the obvious and provide thought leadership, strength to empathize with and empower the customer and expertise in creating business value.

In Part II we have addressed the 'Content' aspect, that is, the hard facts applicable to the consulting dimensions. Now, in Part III, we will address the 'Context' aspect, that is, the soft skills required to build a consultant's own equity.

In addition to the basic skills required for consulting, this chapter covers skills/competencies required for Consulting Sales, Consulting Proposals, Consulting Teams, Consulting Delivery, Consulting Presentations and Consulting Reports, concluding with some thoughts on Consulting Measures, Career and Maturity.

Consulting Skills

A majority of the entrants into the IT consulting space are from the technology world and one of the very first things they require is a mindset change. A lot of traits, habits or skills that work in the IT services world are actually counterproductive in the consulting space, thereby necessitating some unlearning before the learning starts.

Guiding Principles to Develop Basic Consulting Skills

1. **Withhold Tendency to Dive-in and Debug; Speed of Solution is Not Necessarily a Strength**

   In the IT services world, speed to solve is definitely a strength. Therefore, every time a problem is posed, the tendency is to dive-in and debug in the shortest time possible. However, in the consulting space one always needs to think before acting. It is extremely important to understand the context and expectation before attempting solutions.

2. **CULTIVATE THE HABIT OF STEPPING BACK; STRATEGIZING AND PROVIDING THOUGHT LEADERSHIP**

   In line with the previous skill, a good consultant needs to step back and strategize, asking the right questions. Remember, if you have all the answers you are bound to be suspected, but if you pose the right questions you will be respected. Moreover, only the right questions provide meaningful insights to create the right hypothesis, the starting point for consultative solutions.

3. **DEVELOP A BROADER PERSPECTIVE OF THE SITUATION; VIEW THE FOREST AND NOT JUST THE TREES**

   Once the right hypothesis has been formulated, the consultant needs to view the situation from a broader perspective. The problems may be many, the answers even more, but they may not necessarily be the real answers. Therefore, one must challenge not just the questions but also the top-of-mind answers. Logically, the cause can be equated to the trees, which may not always be responsible for the problem; one needs to explore the symptoms which could be the cause. Understanding the symptoms is thus equally critical in consulting; this is viewing the forest, the broader perspective.

4. **SHARE TO SUCCEED; VARIED VIEWPOINTS ARE BETTER THAN INDIVIDUAL IDEAS**

   Contrary to conventional belief, the more you share, the more you and your intellect will be known, resulting in increased credibility as a consultant. If you do not believe in this, think of the converse and you will find it alarming: why would anyone come to you if they do not know who you are, what you are worth or what value you bring to the table? Cultivate this habit; you will have varied viewpoints to build the right hypothesis and to analyze causes as well as symptoms.

5. **TEAMWORK TRIUMPHS; THE TEAM HERE REFERS TO BOTH CLIENT AND CONSULTANT**

   The ability to be a team player is the greatest asset and an enduring skill for a consultant. In the consulting world, engagements succeed not because of any one individual, but because of the collective expertise and varied viewpoints of the individuals in the team. It is important to note here that the team includes individuals from both the client and the consulting firm. While the consultants bring in subject-matter expertise and experiences of similar situations, clients have a better understanding of the ground realities of the current state and underlying political dynamics. Together these are force-multipliers for the team to triumph.

6. **HARVEST HOUR-GLASS ANALYTIC SKILLS, PRACTICE COMMUNICATION SKILLS**

    Consulting engagements require convergent analysis, when the hypothesis is broad and the expected outcome is a singular strategic direction, and divergent analysis wherein the hypothesis is a simple statement but the expectation is to have a view of all possible options. Taken together, we call it 'Hour-Glass Analytics'. Communication skills, on the other hand, is basic and assumed to be inherent; hence, the need is only to practice. However, for maximum benefit, complement hour-glass analytics with sound communication skills, oral or written, for a convergent outcome or for divergent options.

7. **UP-SKILL AND CROSS-SKILL; KEEP ABREAST OF INDUSTRY TRENDS AND DEVELOPMENTS IN THE CONSULTING SPACE**

    Learning is a lifelong experience; much like the ability to be a team-player, the aptitude to learn should be in your armor of consulting skills. Constantly enhance your skills within your domain, not being complacent but aiming for the next level of competency. An added advantage is if you can acquire skills in related functions or related industries. Clients frequently ask "What is happening in my industry? What are my competitors doing?" Trivial as this may sound, the intent could be to subtly find out what others are doing that can be emulated or to secretly evaluate if any competitor is anywhere close to their next plan of action. Hence, it helps to keep abreast of industry trends. For additional mindshare, present your knowhow, leveraging new developments in the consulting space.

8. **INCULCATE THE FINE ART OF LISTENING; INTENSE LISTENING AND INSIGHTFUL QUESTIONING IS KEY**

    We have one mouth and two ears and we often use them in the opposite proportion. All of us talk more, knowing very well that we should focus on listening. Listen carefully to what is being said; more importantly, listen intensely to what is not being said, as these conversations are continuous and their context/content are building blocks to your hypothesis, analysis and even recommendations. The trick to master this advantage is simple - talk less. When you talk less, you listen more, and you can then ask insightful questions, which is another tool to increase your credibility.

9. **OBSERVE AND ABSORB; RECAPTURE THE CURIOSITY OF A CHILD**

    Endless possibilities of new thinking pass us by, because we are pre-occupied with... the less said, the better. For starters, make it a habit to observe everything in your environment: the taglines of an advertisement on a billboard, the language of an editorial in a magazine and the caricatures in a cartoon strip. As you observe, you involuntarily absorb, and you never know what would come in handy and when. Analogies from daily life are your best bet to express a new idea, to analyze a new finding, to seed innovation in thinking. If you find this difficult, observe a child's curiosity about anything and everything and try to emulate it.

10. **PROGRESSIVE APPROXIMATION: RUN WITH THE BEST POSSIBLE AND IMPROVISE, RATHER THAN STRETCHING TO CREATE THE COMPLETE SOLUTION**

In consulting engagements, timelines are short yet expectations are high. Given such high stakes, creating the complete solution utilizing the complete timeline is a risky proposition. A more rational approach is to interactively work with the client in incrementally building the solution through progressive approximation, gaining customer buy-in at every stage. The result of this approach would be a win-win proposition.

11. **READ, RESEARCH, REFLECT AND REPRODUCE**

Read more to know more, to learn more. And when you come across an interesting idea of relevance, research more; this will help sharpen your analytical skills. Reflect on your conclusions and reproduce as appropriate. Do not forget to reference back to your original readings. This will demonstrate how well-versed you are and how varied your interests are and how skillful you are in stringing them together, which is yet another tool to increase your individual equity.

12. **ATTIRE, ACCESSORIES AND ATTITUDE**

Last, but not the least: physical appearance also matters. As much as your work reflects your penchant for perfection, so should you present your personal self. The idea is not to become brand conscious, but to be presentable within one's means. Simple things to consider: a well-fitted suit, polished shoes, a good writing instrument and a nice folio to hold your notepad. Once these material elements are taken care of, carry yourself with a positive attitude that exudes confidence.

CONSULTING SALES

In the technology world, IT services are sought through a formal 'Request for Information' (RFI) or 'Request for Proposal' (RFP), which defines requirements, scope of services, service-level agreements, evaluation criteria, timelines, etc. However, in the consulting space, formal RFPs are a rarity; often, it is a brief written note or an e-mail or an action point triggered by CxO-level discussions. Given this limited information, mostly abstract in nature, the way we respond must transcend from a form of science to an art.

Guiding Principles to Win a Consulting Sale

1. **Understanding the Sales Trigger**

   In a consulting sale, the first and foremost task is to understand the sales trigger. Why does the client want to engage external consultants? What is the real motive? What are the timelines and expected outcomes? Ask yourself these questions, challenge the answers, pose additional probing questions and then evaluate the responses. Note of caution: do not settle on the first closest response, explore further as other responses could also be relevant to zero down on the real sales trigger.

2. **Customer Touchpoints and their Domain of Influence**

   With a reasonable understanding of the sales trigger, the next step is to know who in the Client's organization is involved in this particular request for advisory services. It could be one or many; it is important to understand the role of each. Who is front-ending the request? Who is the sponsor? Who could be the beneficiaries? What is their domain of influence? Together, they form the stakeholders to address in this sale. Having a sense of their profile, influence and expectation will help shape a winning sales proposition.

3. **Synchronizing with Stakeholders, Aligning with Influencers**

   Knowing stakeholders and their profiles is a great starting point. The competitive advantage, however, lies in how well you are able to synchronize with their problems and expectations and convince them of empowerment. Get to know the influencers, executives who are decision makers, who are sponsoring the program, etc. A tip from experience: the real influencers are not necessarily the senior-most executives in the stakeholder set. You can consider yourself successful if they become your evangelists in the organization.

4. **Insights into Organizational Growth Plans**

   Now, shift focus from a stakeholder's point of view to an organizational perspective and study growth plans, not just for the immediate future but also of the recent past, to know more about what has worked and what has not. Hopefully, some patterns will emerge, relating to the organization's strategic directions, risk appetite and maybe even the real reason/rationale for the current requirement. Even if there is no connection, by leveraging organizational insights, you can co-relate how the benefits of your solution can directly or indirectly aid growth plans; either way, you gain.

5. **Never Under-estimate Client or Competition**

   Consultant might have an illusion of having a halo, of having acquired sage-like wisdom, and thereby assuming that others are of lesser intellect. A basic principle of sales in general is to be wary of competition. In consulting sales, the principle extends to being cautious of both competition and client. On a lighter note, most CxOs are ex-consultants themselves and are probably aware of all the tricks of the trade. On a serious note, bear in mind that what the client is buying here is not a product or service, but value. Often, they know the answer but are still going through the process to validate or confirm their thinking or maybe for better buy-in with management.

6. **Positioning Consulting - Practical Advice from Practitioners**

   Having understood the buy side of consulting, start looking at the sell side. Firstly, positioning; the success mantra here is to take a practitioner's and not a preacher's approach, so do not stop with advice. As a practitioner, you have to impress upon your client that you are capable of stretching beyond advisory services into assisting in implementation. This reflects conviction that you stand by your recommendations and that they are realizable.

7. **Demonstrating Individual Equity**

   After positioning your approach, you would need to position yourself. Nine times out of ten, deals turn in your favor depending on the way you demonstrate your individual equity. Quoting from your experiences is key, irrespective of whether you are involved directly or indirectly or what results are achieved. One is not expected to know all the answers, but one definitely needs to articulate a logical approach at a minimum and the resources that can be accessed for details. Remember to cover the extremes, the rewards of action as well as the risk of inaction.

8. **Technology Marketing versus Selling Consulting**

   In marketing technology, we could rely on capability brochures, product demos, past proposals, etc. In consulting, every deal is so unique that conventional collateral does not sell. A successful sale is dependent purely on the brand value of the consulting firm, experience of the consulting practice and expertise of the consultant assigned to the engagement. Make sure that these three dimensions are covered, not in general but customized to the context. Of the three, consultants are on top, so assemble your top team, even if they are not full-time and make sure you bring in the experts as required.

9. Technology Experts versus Business Managers

With respect to clients, you should also be aware that you would now be dealing with business managers and not technology experts. So, you need to be well-versed with the client's industry/business and be able to express even technology aspects in business terms. Domain knowledge is a mandatory skill in the consulting space. It is the first filter that clients apply when short-listing consultants for an engagement and also within the consulting organization.

10. Problem Statement versus Problem Hypothesis

The problem statement is always defined in RFIs/RFPs in IT services, but in the consulting world, as mentioned earlier, the requirement is often abstract. What is known is, at best, a hypothesis. Therefore, understanding the hypothesis and the underlying requirement from a client's perspective is a pre-requisite for consulting sales. The next task is to translate the hypothesis into a problem statement, through iterative interactions with the client. Once again, your ability to listen will stand you in good stead.

11. Fixing Problems versus Future Positioning

A problem fixed is a measure of success in IT services. However, in consulting, if you think an abstract demand is difficult, think again; the expectation is not definitive either. The measure of success is future positioning which is not absolute, but relative to the context, time and client. So, how do you target success? Through active stakeholder involvement, interim presentations on analysis and findings, predicting potential recommendations and gaining upfront buy-in, although the timeframes in consulting are short.

12. Project Teams versus Consulting Communities

Technology teams are static, comprising a project manager, analysts, testers, programmers, etc., each allocated for a specified period of time, until the completion of the phase for which their specialty is required. Consulting teams, on the other hand, are dynamic, assembled as per the need/phase of the engagement, typically for a limited time and able to be rotated, as the need for their subject matter expertise arises. Consultants are not allocated on full-time basis for a fixed duration; instead, they have the flexibility to work on multiple engagements simultaneously. Consulting teams comprise an engagement manager, to co-ordinate and collaborate, an engagement director, for executive connect and commitment, and a pool of SMEs and business analysts. The role of the engagement manager is thus critical for an engagement's smooth execution; key skills would be negotiation with client and network to tap into the best SMEs.

13. **Pricing Solution versus Pricing Services**

    The difference between technology projects and consulting engagements extend beyond expectation and execution into pricing; the variation is in what we price for and how we price. In technology projects, the end solution is priced, calculated on the resources and effort spent, a quantitative formula. In consulting, services are priced, calculated on the basis of the expertise brought in and the value they deliver, a qualitative derivation. The selling skill required, therefore, is the ability to demonstrate the value that the consulting team can deliver and the potential benefits of the same to the client's business.

14. **Technology Innovation versus Thought Leadership**

    Sustenance of technology projects is a function of the innovation introduced in the project, whereas sustenance of consultants in the engagement or beyond lies in the value of the thought leadership they articulate. Demonstrating this ability early in the sales cycle is critical to clinching the deal. Practice thinking beyond the obvious, outside the box. This is easier said than done, which is why the need to practice. A good starting point is to deviate from the conventional path, to be bold in thought, yet sound confident about delivering what is needed.

15. **Market Share versus Mind Share**

    Every sale is aimed at increasing market share for the organization, but in consulting it is mindshare that matters most; market share will follow. Increasing mindshare requires the consultant to capture the attention of the client from day one, be it in understanding the requirement, in empathizing with the clients' context or in assembling the best resources; the most important trait is the honest aspiration to empower the customer.

Consulting Proposals

Consulting proposals have to be crisp. The table of contents per se do not change; it is the response that needs to be concise. The proposal needs to clearly articulate our understanding, approach to engagement and execution, consulting expertise, experience in delivering required outcomes and, most importantly, ability to deliver business value. The pre-requisite to winning proposals, therefore, is to accurately 'Sense' and precisely 'Respond'.

Guiding Principles to Write a Consulting Proposal

1. **Understand the Requirement**

    The team that creates the proposal should be the one that interacts with or has direct access to the client. In case this task is delegated to SMEs, a briefing session should be scheduled with all stakeholders. In consulting proposals, it is prudent to hear the requirement directly from the horse's mouth or the buyer of advisory services and use this opportunity to lay the foundation for a strong relationship.

2. **CREATE A SCOPING PHASE**

   To articulate the requirement, as visualized by the client, it is a good idea to create a scoping phase to come to a common understanding. Imagine pre-fixing a phase zero to your consulting approach, even at the cost of being an investment. Typical activities of this phase are stakeholder alignment, requirement validation, confirmation on expectations/outcomes and agreement on timelines, all leading to a jointly developed statement of work.

3. **PRESENTATION FORMAT PREFERABLE**

   Given the short timeframes of consulting proposal submission and evaluation, the presentation format is preferable for both consultants and clients. In this format, it is easier to present the big picture and anchor the same to walk through all the details, dynamically clarifying all queries or concerns. Also, consulting proposals are seldom evaluated offline; there is always a presentation that precedes the selection. Having the proposal in presentation format upfront, can help you gain a time-advantage, since you are creating re-usable components.

4. **BRAINSTORM ON SOLUTION OPTIONS**

   An innovative solution framework is feasible even for canned requirements. The idea is to always explore alternative ways to address the problem, even if it is a standard requirement for which you already have readymade solutions. Through such brainstorming sessions, you challenge the context and would be able to dig deeper to extract the real cause and ask the right questions. The effort you put in here demonstrates empathy towards your customer's situation and will win their appreciation. In the process, you also add another solution option to your consulting repository.

5. **STRUCTURED ENGAGEMENT APPROACH**

   The engagement approach should be structured and logical, a process-oriented method for problem solving. Each phase should be distinct with a defined purpose and objective, indicating the resources required from the client and the SMEs required from the consultants. Each phase should list the various activities to be performed, explain the analytical tools or techniques that would be used and the outcomes that are to be generated. There should be seamless switchover from one phase to another, incrementally building upon the solution that would empower the customer.

6. **CREATE A BIG PICTURE**

   In building the solution framework, always start with the big picture, a high-level view of the solution components and their interactions. In one slide, you should be able to present your entire proposition from the people, process and technology perspectives. The big picture also serves as an anchor in all the detailed slides to indicate current status, what has been covered and what needs to be done, visually represented as a condensed image in a corner with the current phase highlighted. The big picture can also be your elevator pitch to the sponsor.

7. **HANDCRAFT EVERY SLIDE**

   Every slide should be handcrafted, with attention to every detail - be it consistency of font, readability of font size, correctness of grammar, accuracy of spelling or visibility of image. Equal attention is required for the slide layout - create a common frame with consistent placeholders for image and text so that viewers are not distracted. The transition from one slide to another should ensure continuity, picking up the thought that concluded in the previous slide.

8. **CONSULTING PROPOSAL OUTLINE**

   Typical outline for a consulting proposal:

1. Executive Summary (In 1 slide)	Summary of the consulting proposition.
2. Engagement Context (In 1 slide)	Client's corporate profile, business drivers, scope of engagement and expected deliverables.
3. Our Understanding (In 1–2 slides)	Our interpretation of the client's context, articulating what is in-scope and out-of-scope and what will be delivered and when.
4. Engagement Model (In 1–2 slides)	Outline of the big picture, depicting all the solution components at a phase level, their interactions/dependencies, high-level timelines and resources required from client and consultant.

5. Execution Model (In 12–15 slides)	Details of each phase, showing the inputs or pre-requisites to initiate it, the activities to be performed, the tools/techniques to be used, the intermediary outputs that will be delivered, detailed work breakdown with timelines and the resources that will participate. Adopt a similar structure for each phase. Factor in interim presentations to report on status, highlight risks and table draft findings from analysis. This will help a great deal in getting the client's buy-in and making course corrections as required.
6. Relevant Experience (In 1–3 slides)	Case studies relevant to the client's industry and context, presented as a summary in a single slide or as separate slides (one for each case study).
7. Consultant Profiles (In 1–3 slides)	Key consultant profiles, with relevant experience and the role they would be playing in the engagement, presented as a summary in a single slide or as separate slides (one for each profile).
8. Commercials (In 1–2 slides)	Commercial proposition with terms and conditions.
9. Value Proposition (In 1 slide)	Value that the firm and the consultants bring to the engagement.
10. Additional Information	Optional: may include details of methods/frameworks used in the engagement, sample outputs from previous engagements, etc.

In all the above content, two slides that can make or break a consulting proposal are the ones on executive summary and value proposition. They are the alpha and omega of your proposal and both need to be presented in exactly one slide. Therefore, crafting these slides is an art. Do not rush over them in the end, after devoting most of your time to the remaining sections. For best results, dedicate time to these slides when your mind and thoughts are fresh, working from first principles.

9. **Executive Summary**

The executive summary slide should contain everything about your proposition in one slide, crisp statements conveying the essence of all the table of contents, from context to commercials. Since this is the first slide, it should be compelling enough for the client to explore further or, even better, to make a case for you to the decision makers. Concise in form, yet complete in content is what will get you the attention of busy C-level executives.

10. **Value Proposition**

Similar to the executive summary, the value proposition slide is also extremely important although it comes at the end. (One school of thought believes that it should be covered upfront.) This slide should be client-focused and context-related; everything else is peripheral and not primary for evaluation. Like humans, organizations will also ponder: what is in it for me? Every statement should go beyond the conventional content of what we do, how we do, why we are better, etc. The central point should be the value we can bring to the client's business.

Consulting Teams

Consulting teams are dynamic, varying in type of roles, number of resources and duration of requirement. A one-member advisory or a large team of consultants could work on multiple work streams. At a minimum, there is a consulting partner and an engagement manager and depending on the size of the engagement, a team of SMEs reporting directly to the manager or lead consultants who own individual work streams. A reasonable expectation is to have mirrored structure at the client's end, as represented in the below graphic.

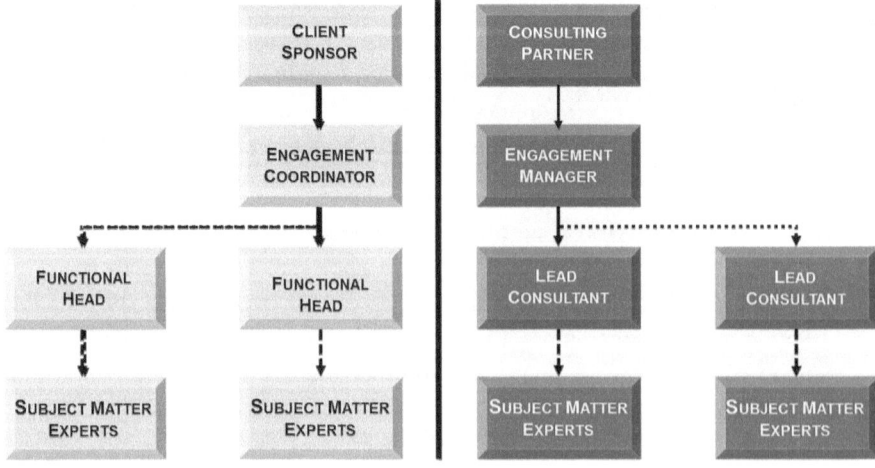

Illustrative Roles and Responsibilities

1. **Client Sponsor**

   The client sponsor is a CxO-level executive or one of their direct reports designated to spearhead the initiative and will have direct responsibility for partner selection, budget control, executive oversight and benefit realization. The role is more active in pre-engagement during partner selection, negotiation and post-engagement for ensuring that value is delivered from the current engagement as well as synergies with other ongoing initiatives.

2. **Consulting Partner**

   The consulting firm will assign a partner-level executive with direct responsibility to liaise with the client sponsor, deliver business value and build relationships. Responsibilities include executive oversight, cross-industry experience leverage, availability of best-suited SMEs and networking in the client organization.

   In large consulting engagements, the client sponsor and the consulting partner are part of a steering committee along with other C-Level executives. The committee monitors the program on a quarterly basis for progress against plan, value of potential recommendations and reports to the board.

3. **Engagement Coordinator**

   The engagement coordinator ensures smooth functioning of the engagement execution, plans and schedules client meetings and facilitates information required by consultants. An equally important task is to monitor the progress of the engagement, deployment of right SMEs by the consulting firm and confirm deliverables as contracted. Essentially the coordinator is the operational in-charge of the engagement.

4. **Engagement Manager**

   The role of the engagement manager, at the consultant's end, can take dual forms. One is similar to the engagement coordinator, where the tasks to be performed are the same. The other form, as envisaged by some consulting firms, requires the engagement manager to play the role of a principal consultant, with ownership of both operational and directional aspects of the engagement. In addition to monitoring, the manager would need to mentor the team.

   In large consulting engagements, the engagement coordinator and the engagement manager form part of a management committee or program committee along with the client sponsor and consulting partner. The committee monitors the program on a monthly basis for progress against plan and reports to the steering committee. In smaller engagements, the engagement coordinator and the engagement manager meet on a weekly basis and review the progress of the engagement.

5. **Functional Heads**

   The functional heads provide deep insights into their domain. Key responsibilities include defining the current state, its challenges, concerns, validating the analysis/findings of the consultants and shaping the target state that is best suited for their environment.

6. **Lead Consultants**

   The lead consultants drive the interview, information-gathering and analysis efforts required to deliver desired outcomes. They play an active role in articulating recommendations and presenting the rationale and potential impact of the same to the management/steering committee.

7. **Subject Matter Experts**

   SMEs, as the name implies, are experts in their field or domain. This role is fairly similar on both sides. SMEs form the team that undertakes data gathering, data crunching and data analytics to arrive at fact-based findings that are the foundations to realizable recommendations.

Consulting Delivery

Consulting engagements typically follow a four-phase approach: Initiation, Information Gathering, Analysis and Recommendations. In this section, the first three phases are covered in terms of critical success factors. The fourth phase, which typically includes presenting recommendations and report writing, are covered subsequently in separate sections.

Initiation Phase

1. **Making the Right Impact**

   Meet the client sponsor first on a one-on-one basis for context setting. Re-confirm the scope, expectations on deliverables and understand organization dynamics. Review the draft engagement plan and identify stakeholders to interview, request a designated engagement coordinator, preferably full-time.

   Meet all identified stakeholders in workshop mode, have the client sponsor introduce you and the engagement, emphasizing the business need and expectations from them and the organization's view of the end goal. Present the engagement objectives, execution plan and expected outcomes, making sure these are clearly understood by all stakeholders.

Jointly refine the engagement plan and fine-tune activities, taking into account the stakeholder's perspective of ground realities, their ongoing professional commitments and personal plans.

The end game is to create a sense of belonging and ownership among the stakeholders and be accepted as a genuine partner. The pitfall to avoid is being seen as another consultant out to give some more '*gyan*'!

Information Gathering Phase

2. Asking the Right Questions

All information-gathering tools must be customized with the interviewees in mind, taking into account their current span of control. Prioritize your questions to fit the duration of the interview.

For every question, be prepared with a rationale, reason for asking and expected responses. Also, have a set of related questions that you can pose, time permitting. Ensure that there is no repetition of questions.

Be prepared for hostility, negative or no responses. Never challenge; you have to be patient and go through the rest of the interview, hoping to get at least some responses even if they seem vague.

If you draw an absolute blank from the interview, ensure that you have backup plans or alternative avenues to get the desired information. Only as an exception, discuss this with the engagement coordinator and escalate to the client sponsor if the information you seek is extremely critical to your analysis.

Prepare minutes of every interview session and have them accepted within the agreed timeframe. This process requires absolute rigor and discipline as data-points from the minutes are the foundation for analysis.

Analysis Phase

3. Finding the Right Answers

Analysis should be fact-based, interpreted from the information gathered and not inferences from any other analyst reports, industry reports or consulting reports.

Findings should have backward traceability to the information source, be it client-shared document or minutes of your meetings. Every finding should also indicate the forward benefit or risk as the case maybe; this will help in shaping the right recommendation.

Frameworks used for analysis should be consistent and limited, preferably one umbrella framework rather than an amalgamation of frameworks that can help only in point analysis. Moreover, by using multiple frameworks, you run the risk of being unsure of your technique.

Care should be taken in articulating findings, to avoid hurting any organizational sensitivities. None of this should be made public, in any form of media. However, you must share the same in private with the engagement coordinator and/or client sponsor.

Findings should be previewed with the client sponsor to gain upfront acceptance, buy-in and the right way to present the finding. Use this opportunity to discuss potential recommendations.

Consulting Presentations

The purpose of consulting presentations is three-fold: 1) To Tell or explain the results of your analysis and findings, 2) To Sell or explain to your client the value of your recommendations and 3) To Impel or explain to your client why action or change is necessary. To get your message across effectively, pay attention to the audience, your behavior, content and delivery. Clients are likely to be impressed by your ability to respond exactly to their needs and to deliver from a well-written script. A good presentation is often an invaluable vehicle for explaining and gaining support for your recommendations.

Guiding Principles to Make a Compelling Presentation

1. **Present All in No Time**

    Post analysis, you would invariably have much to present, yet the time you would get with your target audience - the steering committee or the board - would be very limited. Hence, the question: how do you present all in no time? The key is making the content crisp, every finding backed by facts and every recommendation with rationale and potential value.

2. **Remember Every Minute Counts; Target Audience has a Limited Attention Span**

    Once you crystalize your content, you would need to rehearse for a time check, as every minute counts. Bear in mind the extremely packed schedules of your target audience, the multiple initiatives they spearhead and ask yourself, how you can keep their attention. The answer lies in making the content relevant to every stakeholder, presenting the problem, articulating your analysis and demonstrating the value of your recommendations in a seamless manner.

3. **BE PREPARED EVEN FOR EXTREME ALTERATIONS TO THE AGENDA**

   Now, factor in additional complexities such as a last-minute alterations to the agenda, a change in the target audience or chair, a challenge to the validity of your assumptions, a gap in your understanding of scope of study or even a judgmental question from some stakeholders. Visualize such scenarios and push your thinking beyond content and timing to be fully prepared.

4. **USE ACTION-ORIENTED HEADLINES WITH CLEAR MESSAGE IN CONCLUSION**

   On individual charts, the headline should be a complete statement, setting out a direction supported by a reason. The way to develop these statements is by creating a storyboard first. Then, list the top 10 themes you want to present and string them into meaningful sentences that are complete by themselves and connect from one to another seamlessly. Each of these statements would be on a separate slide to detail the inference, interpretation or insight. Every slide should have a distinct takeaway.

5. **BE PERSUASIVE AND INSPIRE ACTION**

   With respect to presenting style, it goes without saying that your tone/tenor and body language should demonstrate passion for your craft, belief in your analysis and conviction in your recommendations. The direction you provide should empower your client and inspire action. To do that, you need to be persuasive, for which you need to be thoroughly prepared.

6. **CONNECT WITH THE ENTIRE AUDIENCE**

   This is a standard presentation tip that cannot be emphasized enough in a consulting presentation. Your target audience is made up of high-powered executives, some of whom you may never have met before, yet need to connect with and inspire with the same level of confidence in your work as you would have done so far with the rest of the stakeholders. Always bear in mind that not all are on your side, despite the quality of your work.

7. **TARGET INFLUENCERS AND DECISION MAKERS**

   Connect with the entire audience, but pay additional attention to the influencers and decision-makers. You should have strong supporters in the audience who are in favor of the direction you define and can influence decision-makers on your behalf. The need of the hour, therefore, is a clear case for change that is backed by data and has a promise for future value.

8. **Learn to Think on your Feet**

    Even with the best of preparations you could be caught off-guard, so develop this trait. To emerge from such situations, firstly, be calm and maintain your composure. You must sound convincing and respond positively. You can afford to be diplomatic, but not at the cost of hiding facts. Lastly, if you do not have an answer, be courageous enough to say, 'I do not know'.

9. **Substantiate Findings with Data, Present Recommendations with Rationale**

    Fact-based analysis is the cornerstone of good consulting work. The source of such facts can be client-provided documents, minutes of meetings or even external analyst/research reports. Only if you can justify every finding will your recommendations sound credible. While presenting recommendations, you should provide a strong rationale both in terms of how it will benefit the organization and how it is aligned with market/industry trends and customer needs. Recommendations must be worded carefully, as they are often proposals for the future.

10. **Always Remember, Consultants Advice and Clients Decide**

    This is an old but important adage. Post a successful presentation, most consultants jump to decide on the future course of action. A good practice is to express restraint, table your advice and empower the client to decide. This will earn you respect and enhance your credibility.

Consulting Report

The consulting report is the end product of your engagement, the only artifact left behind that represents your work and the reputation of your firm. Utmost care should be taken to ensure that your final deliverables are best in class. These reports would be copied, circulated and critiqued. Remember that although there may be executives in your favor, there will also be executives working against you. Therefore, any half-baked report would only ruin all your hard work.

Guiding Principles for Writing a Consulting Report

1. **Practice Clarity in Thought and Coherence in Output**

    The report should be well-structured and easy to read without being verbose or overrun with jargon; it is not a literary piece to showcase your language skills. The primary skill required is clarity in thought to cover the engagement end-to-end. The paradox is that it needs to be complete in coverage but concise in form; therefore, the secondary skill needed is coherence in output.

Consulting Competencies

2. **ADDRESS STRATEGIC OBJECTIVES, BUSINESS AND TECHNOLOGY DRIVERS**

   The first thoughts of any reader of the consulting report are: Have strategic objectives been met? Have business and technology drivers been addressed? Ensuring that these concerns are addressed is a pre-requisite for further reading; make sure your report highlights these factors upfront. First, state your understanding, then, reference your analysis to the drivers and the impact on business, concluding with how the outcomes accomplish the stated objectives.

3. **SPEAK THE CLIENT LANGUAGE**

   Like individuals, organizations also have a certain characteristic, ingrained in their culture, in their communications, etc. When browsing any internal communications, try and get a sense of this, understand the form and format. Mastering this will allow your report to connect better and thereby gain faster acceptability.

4. **READ AND RE-READ, WORD-BY-WORD, BOTH SOFTCOPY AND HARDCOPY**

   Having lived through the engagement, documented dozens of minutes from day one and prepared endless presentations, do not be surprised if some lethargy sets in or some overconfidence causes you to overlook obvious errors. The remedy is to read and re-read the report with the eye of a proofreader; read the report line-by-line, word-by-word, first the softcopy and then the hardcopy. You will be surprised at how many revisions you mark on the margins.

5. **ENSURE PROTECTION OF BOTH CONSULTANT ASSETS AND CLIENT DATA**

   Compliance to confidentiality is not a skill to be developed, but a discipline to demonstrate. There are no other choices, no excuses; it is as simple as that. Clients share so much data and insights in good faith that irrespective of a non-disclosure agreement or not, you should honor your commitment. You would also be sharing your firm's assets, methods, etc., which are meant to be used only for the current engagement for the current client. Mark them for protection.

CONSULTING MEASURES

Consulting engagements come to a logical end at the time of submitting the consulting report, which is not necessarily the right time to measure the success of the engagement. The right time to evaluate it is when the recommendations are realized and value is delivered, but for this to materialize there is a time lag, which incidentally is not in the hands of the consultants. The client has to decide the timelines to roll-out the recommendations.

Parameters for a Balanced Evaluation

1. **Satisfaction of Stakeholders**

    The first parameter to measure the success of a consulting engagement is your stakeholders' satisfaction with you work. The experience of the firm and expertise of the consultants is taken for granted or you would not have been awarded the contract. Satisfaction is measured in terms of your attitude during the course of the engagement, openness to hear other's opinions and commitment to the engagement.

2. **Quantum of Business Impact**

    The depth of your analysis is reflected in the quantum of benefit, within the organization and in the marketplace. The benefit could be operational or strategic; what matters is the insights your findings reveal and their impact on the client's environment. This is measured in terms of operational efficiencies, optimal utilization of resources, increased end-user satisfaction, etc.

3. **Implementation of Recommendations**

    The number of engagements implemented and the timeframes by which they are implemented is also a measure of your success. It is even better if you are invited to be part of the implementation phase, since this indicates belief in your report and trust in your capability. A double bonus is repeat business, also a key performance indicator in consulting firms.

4. **Tangible and Intangible Benefits**

    Tangible benefits are quantifiable like productivity gains and RoI as per your business case and could be planned or realized. Intangible benefits, on the other hand, are qualitative and could be result of a changed organizational structure, business process or work ethic.

5. **Learnings from the Engagement**

    A key internal measure is the learnings from engagements. It is measured in terms of the assets used, assets created, automation achieved, industry know-how, innovation seeded, etc. Equally important is the network created, the relationships built and the client's willingness to stand up as a witness for your workmanship.

Consulting Career

Consulting firms invariably have a matrix structure: your level in the organization vis-à-vis the role you play in an engagement. The role is a function of the size and complexity of the engagement, in which the client also has a say. The level at which you are pegged in the organization is a function of your competence and experience. The career path in a consulting organization starts at analyst/consultant, moving onto managing consultant, principal, partner and eventually managing partner. In large firms, there could be additional roles like senior managing consultant, before becoming a principal, and associate partner and then, a partner.

Consulting Levels and Associated Competencies

1. **Consultant**

    The entry level in a consulting firm or practice, this requires about three years of work experience. The role performed is either that of an analyst responsible for data gathering and analysis or of a researcher mining data sources and extracting relevant information. In the early stages of your career, you are unlikely to have a client-facing role. Often, you are part of back-office teams, supporting one or more engagement teams. This is your learning ground; make the best use of this time and reach out to as many engagement leads as possible, volunteer to participate and contribute. You must demonstrate aptitude to learn and the ability to be a team player right from the beginning. From a skill standpoint, all you need is sound analytical skills.

2. **Managing Consultant**

    Some organizations have a senior consultant level before you can become a management consultant. You need to gain experience as a consultant or senior consultant, being part of client-facing engagement teams to become a managing consultant. At a managing-consultant level, you will start to experience a leadership role, either for a work stream or for a phase of the engagement. You would get visibility of all the consulting phases and exposure to stakeholder management. Primary skills required are subject-matter expertise, communication skills and people management.

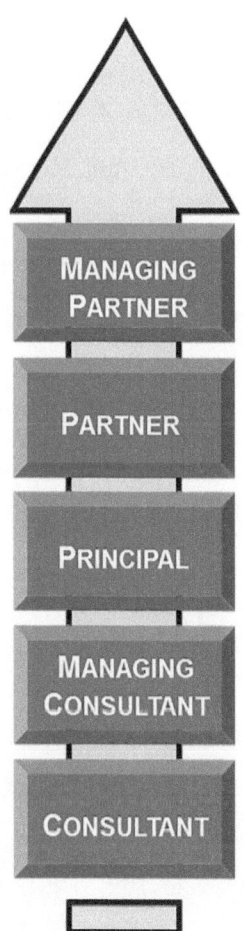

3. **PRINCIPAL**

   A principal in a consulting firm is responsible for a particular domain or practice, leads engagements and begins to be involved in consulting sales. He/she would be responsible for mentoring practitioners and building the practice and its offerings/solutions and frameworks/methods. Primary skills required are deep subject-matter expertise, cross-industry exposure, sales and negotiation, presentation, people management and client relationship.

4. **PARTNER**

   Partners have responsibility for profit and loss responsibility, a particular vertical and all its operations or for marquee clients, servicing all their consulting needs as their trusted advisor. Partners need to be extensively networked and recognized as thought leaders in their space.

5. **MANAGING PARTNER**

   Managing partners are equivalent to CEOs, heading a particular domain or business unit globally or heading all functions in a particular geography.

CONSULTING MATURITY

Maturity in consulting evolves as you gain experience and the breadth of your engagements widens; from being an analyst crunching data, you emerge as a trusted advisor, setting agenda. The bad news is that the industry mandates patience and perseverance, testing your tenacity to survive in demanding circumstances. The good news is that all the consulting skills and competencies captured in this chapter remain current, even at the peak of your consulting career. Never let your enthusiasm to explore falter or eagerness to learn dwindle.

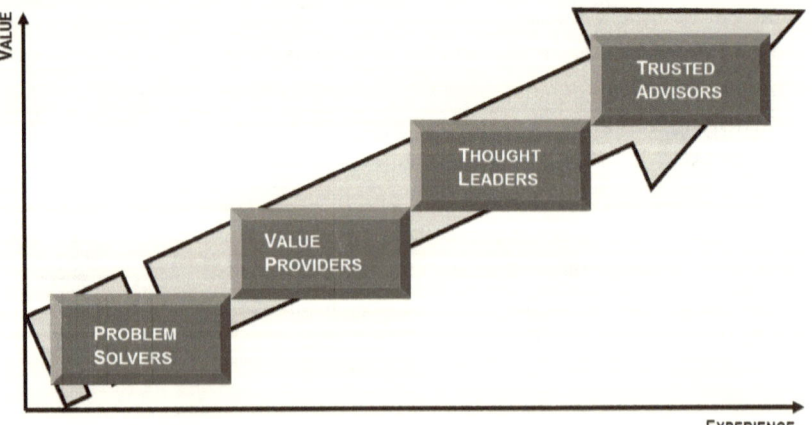

Maturity Levels and Associated Characteristics

1. **Problem Solvers**

   In the first stage, you are a problem solver, taking orders on tasks with a defined input/output and a defined process to adopt. There is not much of a window for creativity or imagination. Maturity would come, not from speed in solving or capacity to be compliant, but from the ability to grasp underlying concepts, bringing in relative learning and application across tasks.

2. **Value Providers**

   In the second stage, you would be equipped with reasonable experience, having seen a couple of consulting engagements in entirety. The maturity trait here is to go beyond problem solving, to demonstrate how results deliver value to the client's business and how that value can be enhanced. Start thinking long term; seed relationships.

3. **Thought Leaders**

   In the third stage, you would mature from a seasoned consultant to a recognized thought leader. Your advice is no longer restricted to addressing standard business drivers targeting standard business outcomes, but running with new ideas, leveraging cross-industry best practices. You start creating your brand value through coaching and mentoring, publications and speeches.

4. **Trusted Advisors**

   In the fourth stage, you set the agenda, you seed innovation and you would have mentored a pool of prodigies who can be your idea implementers. You become the trusted advisor that CEOs will reach out to; you do not have to sell or market yourself. Your digital eminence is spread far and wide, you become the cynosure of the conference circuit and your publications are eagerly awaited.

Key Learnings

Consulting soft skills are as important as subject-matter expertise. Cultivate them with an open mind; they are simple and easy to learn. This is a learning that would be valid life-long.

In consulting sales, the key is to understand the sales trigger and connect with the right stakeholders to develop the right hypothesis. Position yourself as a practitioner who brings in innovation and implementation capabilities. Consulting proposals must have a structured approach with a solution framework driven by the big picture.

Start with a single all-encompassing view, the executive summary, and end with a client-focused value proposition.

Consulting delivery requires a four-phased approach: Initiation, Information gathering, Analysis and Recommendations. Minutes should be kept for all meetings, all analysis should be fact-based and all recommendations should have a rationale. Consulting reports should speak the client language, addressing all strategic objectives and deliver on promised outcomes.

Consulting teams are dynamic, mandatory roles being that of an engagement manager to co-ordinate/facilitate and of SMEs to deliver. Consulting careers start with an analyst role and grow to the level of partners, evolving from being problem solvers to trusted advisors.

Consulting measures must present a balanced viewpoint. Externally it is the satisfaction of stakeholders and internally the learnings from the engagement.

In conclusion, the list of consulting soft skills presented in this chapter are neither exhaustive nor are the guiding principles prescriptive. Remember: Consulting is still an 'Art' and not a 'Science'.

. Ω .

Epilogue

Concepts learnt, competencies built, it is now time to apply and experience the same. The consulting space is a battle of minds. Those who move with vision and create value, win time and again. In the consulting battlefield, strategies come alive as thought leadership reigns supreme.

Time to lay down the book and reflect on the end product, this may not be a bestseller but if it has, in any way, molded anyone to be a true-blue consultant, then I would consider my mission accomplished. I would also have an answer to my father's longstanding question, "What do you create at work?". He was a civil engineer and had several solid standing structures as proof of his workmanship. I can now tell him, "I have created Consultants".

And finally, to end with some words from Winston Churchill, "This is NOT the END. It is NOT even the BEGINNING of the END. It is perhaps the END of the BEGINNING."

Go Ahead! Make your Move...

Bibliography

Cope, M. (2000). *The seven 'C's of consulting*. FT Prentice Hall.

Czerniawska, F. (2007). *The trusted firm: How consulting firms build successful client relationships*. Wiley India Pvt. Ltd.

Kancharla, M. (2007). *Software Engineering Approaches for Offshore & Outsourced Development*: Turn on lean governance for return on outsourcing. Springer

Kaplan, R.S. and Norton, D. P. (2004). *Strategy maps: converting intangible assets into tangible outcomes*. Harvard Business School Press.

Kaplan, R.S. and Norton, D. P (2001). *The strategy-focused organization: How balanced scorecard companies thrive in the new business environment*. Harvard Business School Press.

Lientz, B. P. and Larssen, L. (2004). *Manage IT as a business: How to achieve alignment and add value to the company*. Elsevier.

Maister, D. H. (2003). *Managing the professional service firm*. Simon & Schuster UK Ltd.

Maister, D. H., Green, C. H. and Galford, R. M. (2002). *The trusted advisor*. Simon & Schuster UK Ltd.

Maizlish, B. and Handler, R. (2005). *IT portfolio management step by step*. John Wiley & Sons.

Mintzberg, H., Ahlstrand, B. and Lampel, J. (1998). *Strategy safari*. The Free Press.

Rasiel, E. M. (1999). *The McKinsey way: Using the techniques of the world's top strategic consultants to help you and your business*. McGraw-Hill.

Rasiel, E. M. and Friga, P. N. (2003). *The McKinsey mind*. Tata McGraw Hill.

Ross, J. W., Weill, P. and Robertson, D.C. (2006). *Enterprise architecture as strategy: Creating a foundation for business execution*. Harvard Business School Press.

Sadler, P. (2003). *The handbook of management consultancy*. Kogan Page India Pvt. Ltd.

Stanford, N. (2007). *Guide to organisation design: Creating high-performing and adaptable enterprises*. The Economist.

Stern, C. W. and Deimler, M. S. (2006). *Boston Consulting Group on strategy: Classic concepts and new perspectives.* John Wiley & Sons.

ten Have, S. ten Have, W. and Stevens, F. (2003). *Key management models: The management tools and practices that will improve your business.* FT Prentice Hall.

Thomas, M. (2004). *High performance consulting skills - the internal consultant's guide to value added performance.* Thorogood.

Toppin, G. and Czerniawska, F. (2007) Business consulting: A guide to how it works and how to make it work. *The Economist.*

Uhl, A. and Gollenia, L. A. (2013). *Business transformation management methodology.* Gower.

Weill, P. and Broadbent, M. (1998). *Leveraging the new infrastructure: How market leaders capitalize on information technology.* Harvard Business School Press.

Weill, P. and Ross, J. W. (2004). *IT governance: How top performers manage IT decision rights for superior results.* Harvard Business School Press.

INDEX

A

Accenture, 7
Alexander Ostenwalder, 24
Application architecture, 42, 55, 56, 63, 64, 65, 66, 67, 69, 70, 72, 150
Application rationalization, 78, 83, 91
Asset-Management Framework, 142
Architecture blueprint, 67, 70, 72
Architecture Development Method, 57, 58, 73
Architecture governance, 63, 64, 71, 72, 73
Architecture review board, 64, 71, 72

B

Balanced Scorecard, 23, 34
BCG Matrix, 23
Big-picture envisioning, 19
Boston Consulting Group, 7, 33
Brainstorming, 19, 24, 43, 44, 45, 199
Bruce Henderson, 33
Bryan Maizlish, 76
Business analysis, 46
Business architecture, 42, 55, 56, 58, 59, 60, 61, 63, 64, 65, 66, 67, 68, 69, 70, 72, 73
Business case, 6, 21, 36, 47, 48, 49, 54, 96, 153, 164, 169, 174, 177, 179, 187, 210
Business consulting, 4, 6, 8, 9, 10, 13, 29, 30
Business Model Canvas, 24, 40
Business Motivation Model, 37
Business process simplification, 77
Business Transformation Management Method, 179

C

CapGemini, 8
Capability Maturity Model, 97
Captive center consulting, 160, 161, 165, 166, 167, 168, 170, 171
Change management, 7, 8, 10, 62, 73, 94, 129, 143, 144, 152, 167, 173, 175, 180, 182, 185, 188
CMMI Framework, 98
CMMI Maturity levels, 101
CMMI Process areas, 99, 100
COBIT, 125, 126, 127
Cognizant Technology Solutions, 8
Consulting artifacts, 17
Consulting career, 210, 212, 214
Consulting cycle, 3, 13, 30
Consulting defined, 3
Consulting delivery, 191, 204, 214
Consulting frameworks, 3, 22, 30, 93, 97, 117, 122
Consulting market, 12
Consulting maturity, 212
Consulting measures, 191, 209, 214
Consulting presentations, 191, 206
Consulting proposals, 191, 198, 199, 213

Consulting report, 6, 21, 22, 30, 114, 135, 153, 171, 187, 191, 205, 208, 209, 214
Consulting sales, 191, 194, 196, 197, 212, 213
Consulting skills, 4, 191, 193, 212
Consulting space, 3, 4, 7, 29, 30, 93, 117, 137, 155, 173, 191, 193, 194, 197
Consulting spectrum, 3, 29, 30, 33, 51, 75, 93, 117, 137, 155, 173, 188
Consulting teams, 191, 197, 202, 214

D

David Norton, 23, 34, 35
Data center, 68, 70, 138, 140, 141, 142, 147, 154
Deloitte, 8, 9

E

Edward de Bono, 27
Elements of IT strategy, 35
End-user computing, 139, 141, 142, 154
Enterprise architecture domain, 51
Enterprise architecture components, 54
Enterprise architecture principles, 52
Ernst & Young, 9

F

Fiona Czerniawska, 4
Functional consulting, 6, 29, 30

G

Gilbert Toppin, 4
Governance consulting space, 117
Governance layers, 122, 130, 132, 136
Governance measurements, 121, 130, 132, 133, 135, 136

Governance mechanisms, 36, 42, 43, 64, 118, 121, 128, 130, 131, 132, 135, 136, 139, 159, 164, 167
Governance models, 136
Governance processes, 43, 117, 120, 121, 130, 132, 133, 135, 136, 144, 163, 179, 184
Governance roadmap, 134

H

Heat Maps, 18, 22, 43, 101
Help desk, 139, 142, 147, 154
Henry Mintzberg, 33, 34

I

IBM, 9
Information architecture, 55, 56, 57, 58, 60, 61, 63, 64, 65, 67, 69, 70, 72, 73
Infosys, 9
Infrastructure consolidation, 78, 83
Infrastructure consulting space, 137
Infrastructure optimization, 141, 142, 145, 149, 151, 152, 153
Infrastructure spend, 141, 145, 148, 150, 151, 152, 153
Infrastructure utilization, 66, 140, 141, 142, 145, 147, 150, 153, 154
Investment Analysis Framework, 81
Investment management, 78, 81, 83, 90, 122
IT Consulting, 6, 12, 29, 30, 33, 51, 75, 93, 117, 137, 155, 173, 191
IT Strategy, 8, 29, 30, 33, 35, 36, 37, 39, 40, 41, 47, 48, 49, 51, 59, 79, 84, 134, 149
IT Transformation, 9, 29, 30, 173, 174, 182
ITIL, 46, 139, 142, 143, 154

Index

J
Jeanne Ross, 52, 118, 120, 122, 123

K
KPMG, 10

L
Lean Principles, 97, 102, 107, 109, 111, 113

M
Management consulting, 3, 4, 7, 10, 11, 12
Marianne Broadbent, 138
Mark Thomas, 4
McKinsey, 10, 24
McKinsey 7S Framework, 24
Michael Porter, 26, 34
Mike Cope, 4
Mike Rollings, 51
Mississippi Chart, 108
MIT CISR, 46, 52, 81, 82, 85, 91, 118, 120, 122, 123, 133, 136, 138
MIT CISR Asset Class Framework, 81, 91
Multi-variate analysis, 87, 88, 91

O
Object Management Group, 37
Operational consulting, 6, 7
Optimizing infrastructure, 152
Organization analysis, 47
Organizational collateral, 17
Outsourcing consulting, 29, 30, 155, 159, 160, 163, 164, 165, 166, 167, 168, 171, 174
Outsourcing Consulting Framework, 160
Outsourcing consulting space, 155

Outsourcing models, 155, 171
Outsourcing roadmap, 170
Outsourcing strategy, 170, 171

P
PESTLE, 25
Peter Weill, 52, 81, 82, 118, 120, 122, 123, 138
Policy Objective Matrix, 26
Porter's Five Forces, 26
Portfolio Analysis Framework, 79
Portfolio management, 6, 29, 30, 75, 76, 77, 79, 81, 82, 83, 84, 89, 90, 91
Portfolio management space, 75
Portfolio management tenets, 76, 91
Portfolio optimization, 79, 90, 102
PricewaterhouseCoopers, 10
Principles of IT governance, 118
Principles of IT infrastructure, 139
Process consulting, 29, 30, 93, 96, 97, 104, 105, 106, 114, 115
Process consulting dimensions, 93, 96
Process consulting space, 93
Process improvement, 10, 93, 94, 95, 96, 97, 98, 101, 104, 105, 106, 109, 110, 111, 112, 114, 115
Process improvement commandments, 94
Process optimization, 7, 96, 97, 104, 107, 108, 109, 111, 112, 113, 114, 115
Programme management, 178

R
Research material, 17

Risk management, 65, 96, 99, 112, 113, 114, 122, 167, 169, 173, 174, 175, 177, 178, 180, 181, 187, 188
Robert Handler, 76
Robert Kaplan, 23, 34, 35

S

SAPPGIO-T, 29, 30, 33, 51, 75, 93, 117, 137, 155, 173
Scenario Planning, 19, 27, 181
Service management, 46, 97, 100, 105, 122, 139, 142, 143, 144, 145, 154
Service-Management Framework, 143
Shared services consulting, 160, 165, 166, 167, 168, 170, 171
SIPOC, 108
Six Thinking Hats, 27
Strategy consulting, 5, 29, 30, 33, 36
SWOT Analysis, 18, 22, 28

T

Target operating model, 128, 147, 159, 167, 168
Target outsourcing model, 167
Target resource model, 167
Tata Consultancy Services, 11
Technical architecture, 51, 54, 55, 57, 61, 63, 66, 68, 70, 72, 143
Technology analysis, 46, 47, 87
TIMWOOD, 103, 111, 115
TOGAF, 46, 57, 58, 59, 72, 73
Transformation consulting imperatives, 174
Transformation consulting space, 173
Transformation roadmap, 187

V

Value stream, 97, 103, 107, 108, 109, 115
VoC, 108

W

Workshop Methods, 28

Y

Yves Pigneur, 24

www.ingramcontent.com/pod-product-compliance
Lightning Source LLC
Chambersburg PA
CBHW020640220526
45464CB00001B/222